A Reader on International Media Piracy

MediaMatters is a series published by Amsterdam University Press on current debates about media technology and practices. International scholars critically analyze and theorize the materiality and performativity, as well as spatial practices of screen media in contributions that engage with today's (digital) media culture.

For more information about the series, please visit www.aup.nl

A Reader on International Media Piracy

Pirate Essays

Edited by
Tilman Baumgärtel

Amsterdam University Press

Cover design: Suzan Beijer
Lay-out: Crius Group, Hulshout

Amsterdam University Press English-language titles are distributed in the US and Canada by the University of Chicago Press.

ISBN   978 90 8964 868 6
e-ISBN   978 90 4852727 4 (pdf)
DOI   10.5117/9789089648686
NUR   670

© T. Baumgärtel / Amsterdam University Press B.V., Amsterdam 2015

All rights reserved. Without limiting the rights under copyright reserved above, no part of this book may be reproduced, stored in or introduced into a retrieval system, or transmitted, in any form or by any means (electronic, mechanical, photocopying, recording or otherwise) without the written permission of both the copyright owner and the author of the book.

Every effort has been made to obtain permission to use all copyrighted illustrations reproduced in this book. Nonetheless, whosoever believes to have rights to this material is advised to contact the publisher.

Printed and bound by CPI Group (UK) Ltd, Croydon, CR0 4YY

Table of Contents

The Aesthetics of Piracy

Conclusion

Acknowledgements

Brian Larkin's essay "Degraded Images, Distorted Sounds: Nigerian Video and the Infrastructure of Piracy" was published in *Public Culture* 16.2 (2004).

Tessa Dwyer's essay "Slashings and Subtitles: Romanian Media Piracy, Censorship and Translation" was published in *The Velvet Light Trap* 63 (2009).

Jens Schroeter's essay "Reproducibility, Copy, Simulation: Key Concepts of Media Theory and Their Limits" and Stefan Meretz's essay "On the Political Economy of Copy Protection" were originally published in German in *Navigationen* 1 (2010).

All the other essays here were written for this volume.

I would like to thank all the contributors to this book for their participation and their patience, specifically Jens Schröter for facilitating the translations of the essays by himself and by Stefan Meretz from the German original.

1. Media Piracy

An Introduction

The Democracy of the Pirate Market

The MRT train arrives at the above-ground Carriedo station and the doors open, a rush of hot air blows into a cabin packed with people that the creaking air con barely cools. I push my way through the crowd to the door, bumping into an elbow here, shoving a backpack aside there, mumbling *"Pinagsisisihan."* Tagalog for "Sorry." The doors slam shut behind me, just when I have finally made it to the platform. A mass of people pushes me down the concrete stairs, two stories to the street, past vendors with baskets full of candy, coconuts, soft drinks, and cigarettes. Once I enter the Avenida Rizal, I have to shelter my eyes against the glaring tropical midday sunlight. An old man sells small towels from a makeshift table – just what I need. I buy one and wipe the sweat from my face.

The Avenida Rizal once was the fanciest shopping street of Manila with its modern department stores, restaurants, and cinemas. It was the main thoroughfare of Quiapo, one of the first suburbs outside of the walls of the historic city center Intramuros, an affluent neighborhood, where the emerging upper class of Manila built their villas and mansions from 1900 onward. Twenty cinemas lined the Avenue in the 1950s: the Avenue Theater, designed by National Artist Juan Nakpil in the 1930s, seated over a thousand patrons; the Scala Theater, with its tea rose marble floors and its curved wall made out of glass blocks, was designed by Pablo Antonio, another National Artist for Architecture; and the modernist Ever Theater, which was supposedly praised by German Bauhaus architect Walter Gropius, when he visited Manila in the 1950s. Most of these cinemas have been closed, or – like Nakpil's Art Deco-style Avenue – torn down and replaced by a parking lot. The ones that remain, the Jennets and the Lords, show scratched prints of sleazy, violent Filipino soft porn flicks from the 1980s and 1990s and serve as cruising areas for adventurous gay men.

The middle and upper class have long moved on to gated communities in boroughs further and further away from the historic city center, leaving Quiapo to the urban poor. One reason for the decline of the Avenida and the whole neighborhood of Quiapo was the very LRT train that just spit me out onto the simmering pavement of the boulevard. The tracks of the elevated train cover the street for its entire length, making the Avenida dark and murky. When it opened in 1984 – it was the first metropolitan rail system in Southeast Asia – it scared away the shoppers and amblers that once animated the streets. Most shops moved into the shopping malls that started to mushroom all around Metro Manila. Today, one of the most historic neighborhoods of the capital of the Philippines has turned into a gigantic slum, and its remarkable wooden townhouses, proud villas, and once grand boulevards have been taken over by those who are too poor to live anywhere else.

There are many such dilapidated neighborhoods in Manila, but Quiapo's name still has a special ring to it – not just because of the historic churches like the Quiapo church or the iron San Sebastian church, the private homes that national hero Jose Rizal used to frequent and that he immortalized in his novel *Noli Me Tangere*, or the amazing market on Evangelista Street, where you can find Betel nuts, herbal folk medicine, uncanny statues of the Infant Jesus, magical talismans, and green jade crucifixes in street stalls next to the desks of fortune tellers. When Manileros hear the name Quiapo, they think of one thing in particular: pirated movies.

I turn into busy Carrideo Street and walk toward Plaza Miranda, passing the boarded-up building that still has the remnants of a rotating restaurant on its top floor. Down the stairs I go to what was once the first underpass in Manila under Quezon Boulevard and is now a noisy flea market, and then up to Hidalgo Street, once one of the most elegant addresses in town.

As soon as I surface from the underpass, I am in pirate land. It is not as obvious as it used to be, when pirated DVDs and CDs were sold from ramshackle carts right on the street. But if you know what door to open, you end up in a veritable video warehouse. Loud music is blasting, so one almost does not hear the "DVD DVD Sir" calls from the vendors. They stand in small stalls, with piles and piles of DVDs stacked up to the ceiling. The latest Hollywood blockbusters, some of which have not even opened in the US. European art house classics. US cult series like *Mad Men* and *Breaking Bad* in neat boxed sets. Korean telenovalas, Chinese martial arts films and, under the table, pornography galore – a whole audiovisual cosmos opens up in front of me. Forty pesos – less than a dollar – per disk is the asking price, but the more you buy, the more generous the discounts.

Children in torn T-shirts run through the dark aisles, an old woman sits on the floor of her stall, putting DVDs from a large stack into jewel cases from another large stack, then passes them on to another old woman, who puts covers into the jackets. Every stall has a TV set, and they seem to be in a competition to discover which one can drown out the others with the thundering sounds of Dolby Surround-enhanced fisticuffs and gun battles from American action movies. Some vendors slouch in their plastic deck chairs and watch their films and others sleep, while the most motivated greet potential customers with their mantra of "DVDs DVDs."

Apart from music and movies, there are also heaps of pirate software disks: operating systems, installers, anti-virus programs, browsers, text editors, spread sheets, audio- and video-editing programs, which often cost thousands of dollars in their original versions. They have all become subjects to the democracy of the pirated market, where every disk, regardless of their content, costs a dollar. That also goes for the computer games, from PC games to console games to game cartridges for handheld consoles like the Nintendo DS, that are piling up at specialized stalls.

Enterprising pirates have put together enticing collections of their own design: a CD with cracked versions of all major DVD-burning programs, for instance, or a garden variety mixture of many small utilities that the average Windows user might find useful. On pirated DVDs, you might find other examples of pirate curating: all the films with Bruce Lee or a collection of super hero movies, the most popular blockbusters of the last year or a condensed retrospective of the films by Jim Jarmusch, all squeezed on one Dual Layer DVD in blurred, highly compressed versions. If you do not want all these disks, there are obliging entrepreneurs who will load MP3 tracks of your choice directly onto your cell phone or iPod, or copy a whole music library onto a flash drive in seconds. If you have more time, they will even search for the file you want on the Internet and download it for you to their antique desktop computer.

In a country where broadband Internet is still the privilege of the rich, Quiapo is not the only market for pirated media in Manila, but it is the most notorious one. Pirated disks are also openly on sale on the sidewalks, in the markets, and even in upscale shopping malls in the business districts of Makati and Ortigas. But Quiapo has become almost synonymous with the sale of pirated goods. While the streets around Hidalgo are the place to look for pirated DVDs and CDs, other neighborhoods are famous for other illicit goods: on G. Puyat Street you can find pirated versions of consumer electronics, and Carriedo Street and the Divisoria area are famous for knockoffs of designer clothes, shoes, and perfumes.

The "Pirates of the Avenida," as Manileros jokingly call the vendors in the streets of Quiapo in allusion to the popular pirate movies starring Johnny Depp, have taken over the quarter where in the past glamorous movie houses showed big screen feature films. And therefore, even bourgeois and upper-class film buffs, who do not leave their air-conditioned homes and offices as long as it is not absolutely necessary, will on a regular basis squeeze themselves into a Jeepney (the popular mini-buses of the Philippines) and spend a sweat-drenched afternoon in the sweltering streets of Quiapo on the look out for rare cinematic gems. The pirated movies from Quiapo are not just for the slum dwellers who live in the neighborhood. An anonymous blogger from the Philippines puts it like this:

> All sectors of Filipino society patronize the pirate's lair. From students from MLQU, to priests from San Sebastian Church, to nurses and doctors, to SM employees, to rich SOBs riding their FORD F150, to *barong*-clad personnel from Malacañang, to DVD resellers coming from the provinces, to Caucasian and Korean tourists in shorts and *puka*-shell necklaces. No one is exempted. (Idiotboard 2006)[1]

For years, I was one of those who religiously and regularly traveled to Quiapo. Soon after I moved to the Philippines in 2004, I discovered this seemingly boundless source of cinematic pleasures. I found Chinese silent films from the Shanghai of the 1930s, that I had never heard of, and that have since become part of my pantheon of favorite silent movies next to those by Papst, Murnau, Dovzhenko, Sjöström, and Von Stroheim. When I got hired the following year to teach film at the University of the Philippines, I celebrated by availing myself with a neatly packaged, faux leather boxed set that supposedly contained all the Oscar-winning movies since 1929, but was really a collection of a hundred classic movies, including *Battleship Potemkin* and *The Bicycle Thieves*, but not *Gone with the Wind*.

The multiplex cinemas of the Philippines show almost exclusively US blockbusters and local mainstream movies. There are no art house cinemas in Manila and you cannot buy off-beat or classic films on DVDs. (Imagine: A country where neither *Citizen Kane* nor *Sunset Boulevard* were ever officially available!) Hence, it was a relief that I could still partake in the development of world cinema via pirated DVD. The Japanese horror films post-*Ringu* that were all the rage then, the works of Apichatpong Weerasethakul, Wong Kar-Wei, Lars von Trier, or Park Chan-wook, the strangely entertaining films of the Pang Brothers and the new Asian martial art movies starring Jet Lee, Donnie Yen, or Tony Jaa, and many of the latest award-winning films from the festivals in Berlin, Cannes, or Venice, came to Manila on pirated disks.

Then there were film classics from Eisenstein's *October* to Godard's *Contempt* to the collected works of Fassbinder to the shorts of Maya Deren and the ethnographic films of Jean Rouch. And cult films like Seijun Suzuki's *Branded to Kill*, Monte Hellman's *Two Lane Black Top*, or the complete works of Alejandro Jodorowsky or Jean Rollins. The films that Western film aficionados rediscovered, lovingly restored, and rereleased in opulent editions with many special features on DVD labels such as Criterion Collection, Rialto, Kino, or Masters of Cinema for a lot of money inevitably appeared sooner or later in Quiapo for a dollar.

And it wasn't just me. When I joined the Film Institute of the College of Mass Communication at the University of the Philippines in 2005, all of my colleagues were avid collectors of pirated DVDs and swapped tips and success stories over lunch or during coffee breaks. Every other week a somewhat shady character named Ronnie showed up at our department with a plastic bag full of classic and cult films that he had procured in Quiapo and resold them at a slightly higher price, saving us the trouble of going there ourselves.

When I arrived at the Film Institute, its film collection consisted mostly of VHS copies of the canonic classics, from *Workers Leaving the Factory* to *The Matrix*. But in the following years the film collection grew uncontrollably as everybody brought their latest finds into the Film Institute to have them copied for the use and benefit of our students. The workshop of our technician Ric turned into a pirate's den in its own right, where the disk drive of his ageing computers was always noisily copying newly purchased DVDs brought in by the professors. When the department moved in 2010 to a new building, one would have been forgiven for thinking that this was because we needed more space for all those DVDs.

We all knew that buying those discs was technically illegal, but nobody cared. First of all, the chance of actually getting caught in the act of buying them was close to zero, as the raids were infrequent and the more good-natured of the always well-informed DVD vendors would warn their customers when one was in the offing. And everybody was doing it: as my former University of the Philippines colleague Rolando Tolentino has argued, pirated media allow the Filipinos – somewhat awkwardly – to access the globalized consumer and media culture that they desire so badly (Tolentino 2008/2009).

The Manila Police and the Optical Media Board of the Philippines regularly conduct raids in Quiapo. These raids are often spectacular affairs where whole buildings are padlocked and containers full of disks are confiscated and destroyed with bulldozers and steamrollers. These activities are typically performed in front of television cameras and the media dutifully report on them. None of them, however, has actually stopped Quiapo from serving as the unofficial media superstore of Manila. The frequent raids might have forced the pirate vendors from the sidewalks into less easily visible shops and the mayor, Alfredo Lim, has taken credit for having "erased" piracy in the downtown of Manila. But if you know where to look, the stalls are all still there, and they are doing brisk business.

The ominous raids, however, have enabled the Philippines to remove itself from the permanent "watch list" of countries that are infamous for disregarding the intellectual property rights that is maintained by the Office of the United States Trade Representative. The content industry of the United States has – in close cooperation with government institutions – established a wide-ranging and relatively effective regime to coerce Third World countries into (at least feigned) recognition of the Western notion of intellectual property rights that often has no equivalent in local traditions or current cultural practice: "Some respondents in our... survey did not understand the concept of piracy, obliging the researcher to explain the term," observed Primo and Lloyd (2011, 121) when they were conducting a study of DVD piracy in a township in South Africa.

However, industry trade groups such as the Business Software Alliance (BSA) or the Motion Picture Association of America (MPAA) have – through insistent lobbying, by exerting downright pressure, or by providing "logistical support" for policy raids and other law enforcement activities – managed to get many countries in Asia and Africa to cooperate in their attempts to "stamp out" piracy. The BSA, for instance, claims on its website that it has anti-piracy enforcement programs in over 60 countries worldwide and that in 2012 alone it investigated over 15,000 reports of software piracy across the globe (BSA 2015). The raids and operations that these organizations conduct frequently are organized with the participation of the press, which is able to take spectacular footage of raided stalls or steamrollers driving over piles of pirated disks.

This kind of piracy has often been associated with large-scale organized crime or even terrorism.[2] While these publications are typically based on newspaper accounts or the reports of nameless law enforcement agents, the on-the-ground reports compiled in the global study *Media Piracy in Emerging Economies* (Karaganis 2011) paint a picture that is far less grim. A conclusion of the researchers that looked at piracy in Mexico states:

> Piracy is not organized to a significant degree by gangs, drug cartels, or other large organizations, even in notorious markets such as Tepito, but instead is carried out primarily by networks of smaller family-based producers and vendors. There are consequently few "ringleaders" whose arrest could have a significant impact on the pirate economy. This is what makes targeted investigations of piracy ineffective and larger, sweeping enforcement actions relatively high risks for social unrest. (Cross 2011, 306)

The Underbelly of Globalization

To me, digital media piracy is the outcome of the very properties of the digital technology with which they are produced: The proliferation of relatively cheap computers, scanners, and DVD burners has turned the pirating of digital media into a cottage industry in the Third World, whether it is the production of pirated DVDs or the printing of covers. In the West, where the kind of street-level piracy that I encountered in the Philippines never existed to the same extent, a similar process could be observed on the Internet. Here, enterprising pirates created websites for the online distribution of pirated material via torrents or by streaming that also had the characteristics of small-scale companies: The German website kino. to, which was accessed four million times a day during 2010 before it was closed down by the police, was run by a group of four people. One of the members of the group admitted to having uploaded 120,000 film files in one year (Patalong 2012).

I have argued elsewhere that piracy is a kind of "globalization from below" (Baumgärtel 2006). The type of media piracy that has developed from the second half of the 1990s onward is a result of the technological development – but also of the economic and political globalization – of the last two decades. The deregulation of national markets after the neoliberal reforms that began under Thatcher in the United Kingdom and Reagan in the United States and that has had a significant impact on the economic policies in many other countries in the West, in the postcommunist countries of Eastern Europe, and in countries such as China, Vietnam, Laos, and Cambodia, was partly responsible for the globalized media piracy of today.

Many countries have cut back on law enforcement and reduced border patrols. At the same time, the spread of access to the Internet and the proliferation of comparatively cheap and powerful technologies enabling digital reproduction on a large scale also supported the raise of networks that aided media piracy. The creative, do-it-yourself aspects of digital media, which have been hailed by many educators and thinkers (see Lessig 2004; Benkler 2006), also allow for the mass production of illegal media products. The flexibility provided by these new technologies grant creators of pirated material a crucial advantage over governments. In many respects, piracy is the illicit underbelly of globalization. In this type of globalization, the participants are not multinational corporations anymore, but smugglers, small-time crooks, and criminal gangs. Their organization is flexible, fast, and efficient, and it crosses national boundaries.

Such organizations have a ready market for their product: In many countries of the Third World piracy is the only way for access to much-needed material (be it school books or business software) that often is not available on the local market at all or only at prohibitively high prices. Countries like China – and to a lesser degree India – have used piracy to level the playing field in international commerce and to compensate for the relative underdevelopment of their economies.

Creating Knowledge

Piracy also plays an important part in the cultural education in many countries (Story et al. 2006). As I have shown elsewhere (Baumgärtel 2012), the boom of independent films in some of the countries of Southeast Asia was partly triggered by the film literacy that many young directors gained from watching pirated versions of art films that were not available in any other way in their countries. The young Filipino director John Torres even went so far as to offer one of his films to the DVD pirates in Manila, since he felt their organization would allow for a much better distribution of his film than any legitimate company (Torres 2012).

The home-grown film industry of Nigeria, that has become known under the moniker "Nollywood", also made use of the distribution structures that emerged to facilitate the sale of pirated VHS tapes (see Brian Larkin's essay in this volume). In Russia, piracy provides for many intellectuals "access to the world of non-blockbuster media goods – independent music, art-house films, and much Western media. Such access is not a luxury for members of this group, but in many cases the basis of their professional activities as musicians, writers, editors, and producers. Piracy – not the licit market – enables them to participate in the international cultural arena. Consequently, it is also the condition of their survival and renewal as a professional class." (Sezneva/Karaganis 2011)

When China opened up to Western capitalism in the 1980s and 1990s, pirated movies were instrumental in creating a whole generation of film critics, who shaped the perception of cinema for the whole country, writes Angela Xiao Wu: "The first generation of Chinese film critics emerged as the Internet fuelled the piracy market. Typically born in the 1970s, these new critics were either working in an unrelated profession – for example, Weixidi was a structural engineer – or were college students majoring in film-related areas during the movie forums' heyday (1998-2004). Five to ten years later, these people became influential critics and editors of domestic mass media, or graduate students in film (usually at overseas institutions), while still maintaining active online presences. Besides the most renowned figures, the Internet also gave birth to numerous amateur film critics and everyday-life film reviews." (Wu 2012) She mentions a remark from film director Jia Zhangke, who frequently refers to his own dealings with pirated movies and how he mingled with cinephiles, who worked as airplane repairmen and bill stickers in their day jobs.

For a whole generation of film makers in Third World countries, the pirate market seemed to serve a function similar to the French or the German film clubs of the 1950s and 1960s. These amateur organisations screened classical films that had disappeared (or were erased) from the collective memory during the Second World War. They started their own publication and began the research on film makers out of which much of Western film studies developed. At the same time, these film clubs were the breeding ground of a new generation of film makers who were knowledgeable cinéastes. Film movements such as the *Nouvelle Vague* in France or the *Neuer Deutscher Film* in Germany developed directly out of this cinematographic grass roots movements. Today, pirated films are to a great extent responsible for creating a knowledge of world cinema in countries where there are no legitimate channels for the distribution of this kind of material. To a large extent, this goes for music or literature as well.

Some writers have even attributed a certain degree of originality to the work of the media pirates. A number of studies have looked at subtitling as a way of how movie pirates add value to the materal they are bootlegging (Hu 2004, Dwyer/Uricaru 2009, Hu 2010) or can be read as cultural assimilation of foreign media (Pang 2007, 63-79). According to Monique Vandresen, Brazilian subtitling groups have become so efficient that they can release a subtitled version of the American show "Lost" on the same day that the show has been aired in the United States (Vandresen 2012).

This example is just one of the instances that show how piracy has the potential to change the expectation that an international audience has in terms of media consumption. Internet piracy has created an environment where a breathtakingly wide selection of movies, music, books, and other artistic productions can be found. This has forced the media industry into a situation where their consumers expect to find the material they want on the net – immediately and without artificially high restrictions. Piracy is very much ahead of what the legitimate media industry is offering in terms of the speed and ease of use that the audience has come to expect – including being able to see their favorite US shows outside of the United States on the very same day it was aired.

Previously, movie studios and television stations had often employed meticulous strategies of "windowing" the release films and television shows. The internet has put an end to this strategy: a good number of the most highly anticipated Hollywood movies are available on the internet and on the streets of many countries with lax law enforcement even before they have been released theatrically in the US, as the example of the American movie *Slumdog Millionaire* shows. Even though the film was shot in India and was highly anticipated there, it did not fare very well upon its release: A Indian distributor explained: "By the time (Slumdog Millionaire) came to India, it was already out in the market on pirated discs and the majority of people had downloaded and seen the English movie." (Liang/Sudaram 2011) In other instances, material that was not ready for release appeared on the internet via P2P-services – famous examples include a demo of the song "I Disappear" by Metallica in 2000 to a unfinished rough cut of "X-Men Origins: Wolverine" in 2009 without the digital special effects.

Politicizing Piracy

The first reaction of the media industry against this type of piracy has been using the legal system to punish internet music and film pirates. In the late 90s, the American media industry filed spectacular cases against individual file sharers and later against companies like Napster, Pirate Bay or Megaupload that facilitated the downloading of copyrighted material. At the same time, industry groups lobbied national governments to pass stricter anti-piracy laws, and a good number of countries have introduced new legislation or have made existing laws more severe: Recent examples include the HADOPI law in France,[3] that makes a three strikes policy against file-sharers possible.

The case against the Pirate Bay was of particular significance here, as it was the beginning of the politicisation of a segment of its users that resulted in the foundation of the first Pirate Party in Sweden. This website came out of a debate on the merits of copyright that had been initiated by a group called "Piratbyrån" (Pirate Bureau). The group advocated the unrestricted sharing of information and intellectual property, that lead to the setting up of Pirate Bay.

Similar Pirate Parties were founded in more than 40 countries, and some – such as Swedish Piratpartiet and the German Piratenpartei – were able to win significant numbers of votes in local or even national elections. While it remains to be seen whether this political movement will have staying power, it should be noted that issues related to piracy or copyright – until recently a rather insignificant issue in politics – have mobilized significant numbers of activists and protesters on a global level in the last decade. The international protests against the Stop Online Piracy Act (SOPA) in 2011 or the Anti-Counterfeiting Trade Agreement (ACTA) in 2012 were the most visible examples of international resistance against the tightening of intellectual property regulations. In Germany, protests against the German performance rights organisation GEMA[4] were also examples of the mobilizing force of copyright regimes that were considered stifling by music fans. These demonstrations were joined by thousands in the major German cities, and an anti-GEMA-online-petition was signed by more than 285 000 people.

Piracy has been an important force in the massive changes in the distribution of media that has taken place over the last two decades. Arguably, piracy has forced book publishing houses as well as music and film companies to offer consumers new ways of accessing their products that the media industry was previously reluctant to explore – often precisely because of the fear of having their product pirated. While the actual impact of piracy on the sales of DVDs, CDs and legitimate MP3s has never been conclusively proven, it is safe to say that piracy had a significant impact on the way that media are consumed and distributed today.

Writers such as Lawrence Lessig (Lessig 2004) and Yochai Benkler (Benkler 2006) have even argued that piracy has even facilitated certain forms of creative expressions. Art forms such as Remixes, Mash-Ups or Bastard Pop have indeed often been initially based on the appropriation of copyrighted material. Lessig has not only criticized the often excessive restrictions that copy-right owners impose on their intellectual property via Digital Right Managements schemes and other measures, but established an alternative scheme to licenses content that provides a flexible range of protections and freedoms for authors, artists, and educators. The Creative Commons license system has been an important foundation of the "Copyleft" movement that has started to re-think of the role of the "commons" and of the Public Domain in the information age.

This book, however, is not a book in defence or versus piracy. It takes piracy as a phenomenon that is a given in current net culture, and looks at some of the peculiarities that other recent studies of piracy (such as Johns 2009 or Karaganis 2011) have not paid attention to. Tony Tran and Yonatan Reinberg look at the specific cultures of piracy in Vietnam, and Brazil respectively. Mirko Tobias Schaefer looks at another pirate culture, the scene of Mod Chip hackers, while Jonas Andersson addresses the specific ethics of internet media pirates. Three last essays of the book address the subject of piracy from a more theoretical point of views: Stefan Meretz discusses the issue of copy protection from the point of view of a political scientist, while Jonathan Marshall and Francesca da Rimini place the issue of piracy in a historical discussion of concepts of property, ownership and theft. The book concludes with Jens Schröter's discussion of some of the basic concepts of media theory in relation to piracy: Reproducibility, Copy, Simulation.

All these essays were written specifically for this book. I have included two essays that have been published previously elsewhere, because they I feel that they add greatly to the understanding of the history and the cultural significance of piracy: Brian Larkin's study about the VHS piracy in Nigeria that has lead to the emergence of the "Nollywood" film industry in Nigeria and an essay on the subtitling practise of Romanian movie pirates by Tessa Dwyer and Ioana Uricaru. The book concludes with an essay by myself that summarizes the most recent development of media piracy on the internet.

Conclusion

The battle over piracy is far from over: While the media industry was in some countries of the West to some extent successful in curbing peer-to-peer piracy, new sites that screen pirated movies and television shows have taken their place. A growing number of downloads happen via Virtual Private Networks, encrypted with the Tor software or in "Darknets" that are only accessible to a small number of users, making it difficult to detect for law enforcement agencies.

At the same time, some industry representatives have expressed their dissatisfaction with the way piracy has been handled in the past that might anticipate a radical change in the industry tactics against piracy. Adobe's Anti-Piracy chief Richard Atkinson has publicly said: "Everyone is tired of the entire concept and term 'Anti-Piracy', even the term 'Content Protection' too." (Ernesto 2013 a) And David Kaplan, the Anti Piracy Chief of Warner Brothers, has even argued: "We view piracy as a proxy of consumer demand." (Ernesto 2013 b) And David Petrarca, director of the successful *Games of Thrones* television series, has recently downplayed the damage that piracy has done to the financing of the show (Sottek 2013). So far, these are only individual opinions, not a shared point of view of the media and software industry as such. But it might be a sign that a growing numbers of companies are reconsidering their heavy-handed approach towards piracy.

In the meanwhile, the industry that makes a living out of fighting piracy, already has its eyes on the next battleground: The American company OpSec has identified 3D printing as "the new challenge in anti-counterfeiting". "What should stop consumers from printing branded shoes, spare parts, action figures, or jewelry?", asks the company on its website. "Much like what the digital industry had to face over past years as software, music and film was shared and downloaded for free over the internet, online libraries are springing up where people can share object files for 3D printing. One can only imagine how these libraries will grow once more consumers own 3D printing devices." (Imkamp 2013)

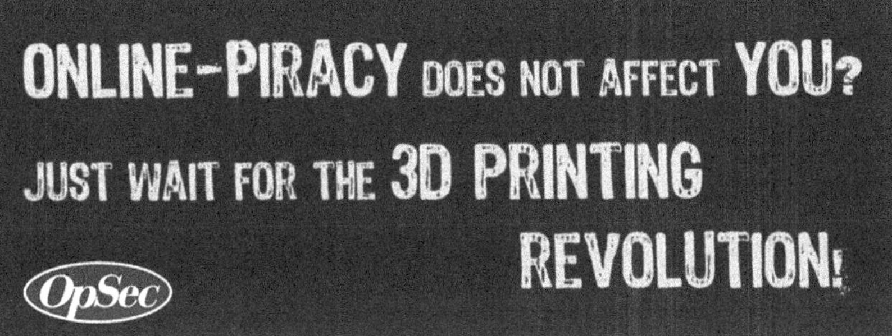

Notes

1. MLQU is the Manuel L. Quezon University, SM is the biggest chain of shopping malls in the Philippines, Malacañang is the palace of the Philippine president, and the *barong* is the traditional Philippine shirt for men.
2. See, for instance, Naím 2005, Phillips 2005, or, most notoriously, a report from the RAND Corporation (Treverton et al. 2009).
3. Haute Autorité pour la diffusion des œuvres et la protection des droits d'auteur sur internet (Law promoting the distribution and protection of creative works on the Internet).
4. Gesellschaft für musikalische Aufführungs- und mechanische Vervielfältigungsrechte.

Bibliography

Alford, William. 1995. *To Steal a Book is an Elegant Offense*, Stanford: Stanford University Press.
Baumgärtel, Tilman. 2006. "The Culture of Piracy in the Philippines." In Kim Shin Dong and Joel David, eds., *Cinema in / on Asia*, Gwanju 2006 (Asian Culture Forum). Available online at: http://www.asian-edition.org/piracyinthephilippines.pdf.

Baumgärtel, Tilman. 2012. "The Piracy Generation: Media Piracy and Independent Film in Southeast Asia." In Ingawanji/McKay, 195-208

Benkler, Yochai. 2006. *The Wealth of Networks: How Social Production Transforms Markets and Freedom*. New Haven, CT: Yale University Press.

BSA. 2015. "Enforcement" BSA, The Business Software Alliance website. http://www.bsa.org/anti-piracy/enforcement.

Cross, John C. 2011. "Mexico." In Joe Karaganis, ed., *Media Piracy in Emerging Economies*. New York: Social Science Research Council.

Danaher, Brett, and Joel Waldfogel. 2012. "Reel Piracy: The Effect of Online Film Piracy on International Box Office Sales." *Social Science Research Network*, 16 January. http://ssrn.com/abstract=1986299.

Dwyer, Tessa, and Ioana Uricaru. 2009. "Slashings and Subtitles: Romanian Media Piracy, Censorship, and Translation." *The Velvet Light Trap* 63: 45-57.

Ernesto. 2013a. "Tired of the 'War on Piracy,' Adobe Hopes to Turn Pirates into Customers." *TorrentFreak*, 25 June. http://torrentfreak.com/tired-of-the-war-on-piracy-adobe-hopes-to-turn-pirates-into-customers-130625/.

Ernesto. 2013b. "Warner Bros: Pirates Show Us What Consumers Want." *TorrentFreak*, 24 June. http://torrentfreak.com/warner-bros-pirates-show-us-what-consumers-want-130624/.

Ertuna, Irmak. 2009. "Digital Pirates and the Enclosure of the Intellect." *darkmatter* 5: 16-22. http://www.darkmatter101.org/site/2009/12/20/digital-pirates-and-the-enclosure-of-the-intellect/.

Hu, Brian. 2010. "Korean TV Serials in the English-Language Diaspora: Translating Difference Online and Making It Racial." *The Velvet Light Trap* 66: 36-49.

Hu, Kelly. 2004. "Chinese Re-makings of Pirated VCDs of Japanese TV Dramas." In Koichi Iwabuchi, ed., *Feeling Asian Modernities: Transnational Consumption of Japanese TV Dramas*. Hong Kong: Hong Kong University Press, 205-226.

Idiotboard. 2006. "Pirate's Lair." The Idiot Board blog, 2 September. idiotboard.blogspot.com/2006/09/pirates-lair-2006.html.

Imkamp, Mecky. 2013. "3D Printing – The New Challenge In Anti-Counterfeiting." Opsecurity.com, 24 June. http://blog.opsecsecurity.com/3d-printing--the-new-challenge-in-anti-counterfeiting.

Ingawanij, May Adadol, and Benjamin McKay, eds. 2012. *Glimpses of Freedom: Independent Cinema in Southeast Asia*. Ithaca, NY: Cornell Southeast Asia Program Publications.

Johns, Adrian. 2009. *Piracy: The Intellectual Property Wars from Gutenberg to Gates*. Chicago: University of Chicago Press.

Karaganis, Joe, ed. 2011. *Media Piracy in Emerging Economies*. New York: Social Science Research Council.

Larkin, Brian. 2008. "Pirate Infrastructures." In Joe Karaganis, ed., *Structures of Participation in Digital Culture*. New York: Social Science Research Council, 74-87.

Lessig, Lawrence. 2004. *Free Culture: How Big Media Uses Technology and the Law to Lock Down Culture and Control Creativity*. New York: Penguin.

Liang, Lawrence, and Ravi Sundaram. 2011. "India." In Joe Karaganis, ed., *Media Piracy in Emerging Economies*. New York: Social Science Research Council, 339-398.

Mattelart, Tristan, 2009. "Audio-visual Piracy: Towards a Study of the Underground Networks of Cultural Globalization." *Global Media and Communication* 5 (2009): 308-326

Naím, Moisés. 2005. *Illicit: How Smugglers, Traffickers and Copycats are Hijacking the Global Economy*. London: William Heinemann.

Pang, Laikwan. 2007. *Cultural Control and Globalization in Asia: Copyright, Piracy and Cinema*. London: Routledge.

Patalong, Frank. 2012. "Razzien in fünf Bundesländern: Werbevermarkter von kino.to verhaftet." *Der Spiegel*, 13 April. http://www.spiegel.de/netzwelt/netzpolitik/razzien-in-fuenf-bundeslaendern-werbevermarkter-von-kino-to-verhaftet-a-827344.html.

Phillips, Tim. 2005. *Knockoff: The Deadly Trade in Counterfeit Goods*. London: Kodan Page.

Primo, Natasha, and Libby Lloyd. 2011. "South Africa." In Joe Karaganis, ed., *Media Piracy in Emerging Economies*. New York: Social Science Research Council, 99-148

Sarai Media Lab. 2006. *Contested Commons/Trespassing Publics: A Public Record*. Delhi: Sarai Media Lab. http://archive.sarai.net/files/original/b6fe93e8dbe6d3cc655aa00f11d743f8.pdf.

Sezneva, Olga, and Joe Karaganis. 2011. "Russia." In Joe Karaganis, ed., *Media Piracy in Emerging Economies*. New York: Social Science Research Council.

Sottek, T. C. 2013. "'Game of Thrones' Director David Petrarca Shrugs Off Piracy, Says It Doesn't Hurt the Show." *The Verge*, 27 February 27. http://www.theverge.com/2013/2/27/4035390/game-of-thrones-director-piracy

Story, Alan, Colin Darch, and Debora Halbert, eds. 2006. *The Copy/South Dossier: Issues in the Economics, Politics, and Ideology of Copyright in the Global South*. The Copy/South Research Group, May 2006. http://www.opensocietyfoundations.org/sites/default/files/csdossier_20060613.pdf

Rolando B. Tolentino. 2008/2009. "Piracy Regulation and the Filipino's Historical Response to Globalization." Social Science Diliman 5, Nos. 1-2 (2008-2009): 1-25

Torres, John. 2012. "Piracy Boom Boom." In May Adadol Ingawanij and Benjamin McKay, eds., *Glimpses of Freedom: Independent Cinema in Southeast Asia*. Ithaca, NY: Cornell Southeast Asia Program Publications, 63-73

Treverton, Gregory F., et al. 2009. *Film Piracy, Organized Crime, and Terrorism*. Santa Monica, CA: RAND Corporation.

Vandresen, Monique, 2012. "'Free Culture' Lost in Translation." *International Journal of Communication* 6: 626-642.

Verzola, Roberto. 2004. *Towards a Political Economy of Information: Studies on the Information Economy*. Quezon City, Philippines: Foundation for Nationalist Studies.

Walton, Zach. 2013. "Music Piracy Rates Down As More Turn to Streaming Services." *WebProNews*, 26 February 26. http://www.webpronews.com/music-piracy-rates-down-as-more-turn-to-streaming-services-2013-02.

Wu, Angela Xiao. 2012. "Broadening the Scope of Cultural Preferences: Movie Talk and Chinese Pirate Film Consumption from the Mid-1980s to 2005." *International Journal of Communication* 6: 501-529.

Case Studies

2.   Evasionary Publics

Materiality and Piracy in Rio de Janeiro, Brazil

Yonatan Reinberg

On Tuesday, 26 January 2011, Rio de Janeiro initiated the largest anti-piracy operation in its history, and among the largest in the history of Brazil, with the shutdown of the Uruguaiana Camelódromo (street vendors' market) in the busy city center, or Centro. More than 150 members of the civil police arrived at the market at 5 a.m. that morning, entered it, and ensured nobody was inside. Afterward, they encircled the entire structure with chains, all before any of the vendors opened their stalls at regular business hours.

By 9 a.m. I was there to witness a more bustling scene than normal at this high traffic urban market. Uruguaiana was cordoned off, with many of the stall owners milling about just outside the building, watching in panic as a panoply of vaguely official looking people rifled through their stalls. City workers in bright red shirts prevented access to anybody on the outside, while the various arms of Rio de Janeiro's police milled around indolently.[1] Among the regular gallery of police, two organizations stood out. The first, the Delegacia de Repressão aos Crimes de Propriedade Imaterial (DRCPIM) or the intellectual property crimes division of the Rio police, had set up trucks in the center of market, alongside the second curious visitor, the Receita Federal, the federal institution in charge of collecting taxes and other revenues, including customs duties.

The events of 26 January at Uruguaiana represented a dramatic change in the relationship between property and "being Brazilian" that accompanied the shift from the Lula regime to that of his successor, Dilma Rousseff, under the same political party. These shifts, painted in larger strokes, show a country straining under its growth and reacting to international pressure in new configurations. Below I examine how these shifts have changed public space and piracy in Rio de Janeiro. I suggest that piracy stands in as a continuous process and discourse – not merely an act – that creates a cultural space involving specific actors, limits, times, and places. It does this against the assumptions of a meritocratic and flatly interconnected world, sans boundaries, that typically accompanies a state's entry inclusion into the respectable world order, such as Brazil's recent anointment into the BRIC group. As the Brazilian public forays into a new world of capital, clashing public spheres come into play.

Evasionary Publics

This essay initiates a conversation framing pirate publics – or the public spheres brought together by pirating acts – as *evasionary publics*. These are publics that do not derive from earlier spheres or "commons" as if on an evolutionary scale (Fraser 2005; Kambouri and Hatzopoulos 2011). Rather, these are publics stitched by the materials that they pirate. They are publics on the new frontiers of rentier capitalism, that emerge from the lives of objects disembedded from the labor of their creators or owners. Here I follow recent scholars of materiality regarding the power of objects to create their world (Sansi 2010; Naro, Sansi-Roca, and Treece 2007; Latour 1993; Morley 1995) to argue that pirated objects, and the pirating practices themselves accrue value to their circulators. As a discourse, piracy fundamentally argues: property is control, technologically and spatially. Pirates play with the architecture of state capitalist distribution to create counterstate narratives through material circulation and value disembedding.

In the transmission of media and other pirated goods and in the usage, conscious and not, of transnational legal and value discourses in the markets, these evasionary public spheres are constructed and taken apart rapidly. They are not infinitely networked connections. I suggest the opposite, in fact. I am inspired in this research by Marilyn Strathern's (1996) rejection of the academic tendency to see networks in everything; she suggests our time would be better spent attending to "stops" in these networks, sudden combinations of technology and humanness that challenge the interpretive possibility of limitlessness: the kinds of interests, social or personal, that invite extension also truncate it, and hybrids that appear able to mix anything can serve as boundaries to claims.

Although Strathern does not draw a direct line in her essay, her challenges to limitlessness are precisely the challenges piracy poses to the limitlessness of peer-to-peer. In opposition to conventional market methods of distribution that rely on a tripartite model of creator-vendor-consumer, music and other media pirated from capital's convenient networks of circulation obtain a temporary potential for subaltern critique, value and archival power that allow, in Elizabeth Povinelli's (2001, 320) words, "radical worlds in the shadow of the liberal diaspora" to remain engaged with the tense poverty and other forms of disparity neoliberal approaches ignore. Piracy also mirrors recent concerns with freedom of information as the principal marker of democratizing forces.[2]

I do not suggest that piracy as an evasionary public is the decentralized sharing haven of equality many proponents make it out to be, but it does perform valuable work in disrupting the naturalized capital divisions of producer and consumer, expert and nonexpert, owner and robber, or what Pierre Bourdieu (1977, 168) calls "what is essential [that] goes without saying because it comes without saying." By valuing not the labor of the creator, but the myriad other ways value can emerge from an object – be they reputation, demand, cultural symbolism, or another property – piracy disturbs the reigning registers of capitalism. Like the pirates of the Atlantic Ocean, themselves value escaped from the bloody colonial system of circulation, contemporary pirates bring anxiety to the normal "order of things" by suggesting that humans interact with objects and consequently their value in more than the capitalist way. Piracy – the removal of an item from predictable circulation – can be managed, criminalized, persecuted, but it cannot be restrained and protocolized.

Background

I had arrived in Rio a few months earlier to research piracy and Brazilian opposition to US/European domination of the discourses – and legal regimes – of intellectual property, copyright and technology. So far, my experience with anti-piracy enforcement had been minimal. In a cable released by WikiLeaks and written in November of 2006, for example, a US State Department official had lamented that "much remains to be done to educate a highly accepting [Brazilian] public that is still unaware of or unconcerned about the real damage done by piracy to the economy and the labor market" and "the urgent need to continue efforts to educate the public, and the necessity for stronger governmental and legal intervention" in present-day Brazil (WikiLeaks 2006). Not just North Atlantic allies were annoyed by the Brazil's apparently lackadaisical capitalistic ethic. Even Mexico, on a separate but related subject, stressed its "willingness to join the Anti-Counterfeiting Trade Agreement (ACTA) negotiations and their push back against Brazilian efforts to undermine IPR [intellectual property rights] in international health organizations" (WikiLeaks 2007).

In this same era of Brazilian pushback, Internet use in Brazil rose dramatically from 9% of the total population (17.5 million) in 2005 to an anticipated 22% of the population (43.7 million) in 2011, making it the third most Internet-adapted country in the Americas after the United States and Canada. Brazil's TIM and Claro phone networks had unleashed high-speed Internet connections to all its customers at comparably low rates and the Internet cafes, or "LAN houses," of urban Brazilian cities proved to be immense social centers and Internet providers.[3] As reports showed that almost 50% of poor urban dwellers engage the Internet through these avenues (Barbosa 2010), one observer noted that in 2010 there were over 130 LAN houses in the famous Rocinha *favela* (slum) alone, with many others spreading across other enormous *favelas* like the Complexo Alemão (which I discuss below).

Alongside this uniquely Brazilian hybrid of alternative stances toward intellectual property and rapidly increasing digital inclusion, Brazil's Ministry of Culture had launched the Ponto de Cultura initiatives, broadly defined as figurative and spatial/physical "cultural points" where alternative engagements with property and history were encouraged for impoverished Brazilian populations. Under the guidance of Gilberto Gil, outspoken Afro-Brazilian activist and Minister of Culture under the regime of Luiz Ignacio da Lula's Partido dos Trabalhadores (2003-2010), the Pontos de Cultura played on historical divergence from European models of cultural heritage, pushing nonmainstream ideas of cultural participation and ownership often emanating from Brazil's sizeable population of Afro-Brazilians, or African-descended Brazilians. By 2001, 1,122 cities in Brazil had over 2,000 total Pontos de Cultura where residents could burn CDs, access digital cameras, and connect to the Internet for free, all techniques animated by the principals of sharing through reproduction of Brazilian music, literature and other production. "The Ponto Cultural," Gil had written upon their introduction, was "a type of anthropological 'do-in,' massaging the vital, if currently sleeping or dormant, points of the cultural body of the Country" (Ministério da Cultura 2011).

Indeed, during his tenure as minister, Gil fought long and hard for these sleeping cultural organs to awake, often through declarations critical of top-down cultural creation. He suggested that market and online music exchange systems be reframed as sharing or peer activity rather than piracy, arguing that "social change starts when [communities] understand cyberspace as a territory of their own, when they understand uploading before they ever heard of downloading," and that these communities "recognize the digital technological devices as cultural performance tools, as a source of diversified references, as a platform for esthetic creation and re-symbolization of their experiences" (Ito 2008). A musician and artist himself, Gil's newest album at the time featured a song nimbly adapting a canonical samba about technology, social cohesion and communication, "Pelo Telefone," into "Pela Internet,"[4] in doing so firming the Internet's role in Brazilian cultural identity and transnational connections.

Uruguaiana

With the election of President Dilma Rousseff in 2010, a member of Lula's Partido dos Trabalhadores, elite Brazilian attitudes shifted dramatically. The forceful intervention in Uruguaiana would represent an important public coup for the Rio de Janeiro police at a time when the city was being gutted, cleaned and prepared for the upcoming World Cup and Olympic Games in 2014 and 2016, respectively. Trumpeting the temporary closing of a market which would soon be replenished of its pirate goods probably did not dramatically alter anybody's life, nor really rearrange the limits between the legal and illegal. Rather, it was an invocation of power that could be understood in a salient and tactile spatial sense. Identifying piracy with the invasion of a particular public sphere, as the police movement accomplished, was part of a broader campaign to criminalize this alternative social imaginary of pirates, where practical – if small-scale – assaults gnawed at the shimmering image of Rio as the "marvelous city" and Brazil more broadly as a safe harbor for international capital in the years before the big international sporting events.

The famous pirate market at Uruguaiana, the Camelódromo, perches rustily on Rua Uruguaiana[5] at the corner of Avenida Presidente Vargas, named for former dictator Getúlio Vargas and a major thoroughfare in the sprawling city. At the other end of Rua Uruguaiana lies one of Rio de Janeiro's other famous downtown streets, Rua da Carioca, lined with old music shops and carving the city between downtown, the newly renovated Praça Tiradentes and its rapidly gentrifying surrounding neighborhood, Lapa. Buffered by two subway stops, the street is old, cobblestoned and pedestrian oriented, with small byways for motorcycles and trucks loaded with consumer goods. It has little shade except as provided by the buildings on either side, older *carioca* (native) institutions that sell consumer white goods such as refrigerators and laundry machines and fancy clothing. Whether one enters from the imposing ten-lane wide Avenida Vargas or the more genteel Rua da Carioca, Rua Uruguaiana remains open and welcoming, one of the few areas in the city with a traditional crisscrossing grid of streets named after various South American capitals. Despite its easy access from almost every part of the city, it is not an area frequented by the increasing numbers of tourists to the city.

The street's most famous denizens, the *camelôs,* are Rio's pirates and the principal informants of this essay. Named for the camel-like humps on their backs from carrying cargo, a *camelô* is best translated in English as a street vendor, though the connotation in Portuguese carries a more criminal and base connotation.

The street – named Rua Uruguaiana – and the pirate market that sits at its end – the Uruguaiana Camelódromo, or area of *camelôs* – bleed into each other, but are crucially different to understanding the city's attitude toward space and criminality. I discovered this difference on my very first trip to the market, when I spied a *camelô* selling a copy of a fall 2010 romantic comedy. His setup is the same as all the other dealers' setups: A mesh/wire-frame box fold out, with a flattened cardboard box on top. His DVDs in standard-issue plastic cases, even though the DVD inside is pirated.

I buy the film for R$10[6] after a little bit of bargaining. Fabio is very open to talking about how stores lose, but he insists that authors and creators don't lose. "It was always very expensive," he says, "and now I and my friends make it more accessible." I ask him about the movie theaters, given that I have seen at least two on the way to Uruguaiana that are showing *Nosso Lar*. "I provide a service for Brazilians who can't afford to go to the movie theater or to buy the movie directly," he answers.

Fabio is nervous, agitated and looking around for any signs of the Guarda Municipal (GM). At one point in our initial conversation he folds up his items, doing as all *camelôs* do by putting the wire frame to the side, picking up the four corners of his "tablecloth" that effectively create a net at a moment's notice. It is obvious that the GM know when *camelôs* are doing this; one can see their eyes rove back and forth as they cross the pedestrian path, swinging batons and eying their perennial nemeses. Dressed in beige-brown suits and carrying guns, but lacking the full military-themed regalia and gravitas accorded to the Polícia Militar, who normally handle Rio's drug trafficking and other major crimes, the GM are familiar with their roles in the urban ecosystem, and are tasked officially with keeping the streets clean. Hated by the *camelôs*, they are in constant contact with them and are normally one of the few police units on foot, cops on the beat in an age of distanced surveillance and technological panopticons.

The GM are one of the material, visible keys to understanding urban Rio's particular divisions and spatial interactions, and an even more interesting beginning inquiry into our question of street pirates and market pirates. They are the gatekeepers between the *camelôs* on the street and those inside the physical, tin-covered structure. "I am on the street," Fabio exclaims after they pass, "because I can't afford the police payoff inside the market. The only real difference between them and us is money, but I'm so happy I'm not stuck inside there as friends with the police."

We have set the scene, then, at Rua Uruguaiana – where Fabio the *camelô* has brought us. Let us step back and shift down the street to the Uruguaiana Camelódromo market, long a shopping destination in Rio de Janeiro where lower-class Brazilians, and especially people of color, would visit. Taking up roughly two square blocks, it sits at the end of its eponymous street. It is by all accounts a modernized market, with some sections having air conditioning. It even boasts a website.

While my original intended research subject in downtown Rio in was Brazilian-produced media such as movies and music, it was hard to miss the Uruguaiana market as breeding ground for other modes of piracy, such as counterfeit Nike shoes and luxury bags. When something was in season, or brand new, it was available at Uruguaiana at the exact same time as it was in the main stores, without delay. Famous shoes seen on an American movie star were proudly on display the next day at Uruguaiana. Strange mixtures of pirated imagery played on celebrities and their international reach.

The pirated goods were specifically tailored to a local audience, with an understanding of what Brazilian consumers wanted. Before Rio's week-long annual Carnaval celebration, for instance, I noticed the preponderance of pirated samba school shirts. Made of cheap nylon, unlike the official school shirts I had seen in the lower-middle-class suburbs of Mangueira and Portela who gave their names to the schools, these shirts were made to be worn when one's favorite band was playing during the Carnaval of 2011. There were soccer jerseys of local teams and the types of jeans that Brazilian women were purchasing that season.

Whereas *camelôs* outside the market on the street were free, in a sense, to set up where they wished, the actual market rented space by the month to its vendors, who sold everything from jerseys to evangelical music CDs, to pirated cell phones and video gaming systems. To purchase a stand inside its corrugated roof, one had to pay a fee depending on whom one rented from; generations had subleased to one another in increasingly complex, almost fractal rental agreements. One's fee also naturally depended on the location in the market, facing outward toward the many passersby incurred a higher fee. Bury your *loja* (store) in the nether reaches and border the Saara shopping district allowed the most dubious of dubious to operate, such as the cell phone unblocking technicians and PlayStation unlockers. I found much music there, both on actual CDs but also on flash (USB) drives and as burned MP3 discs. One needed to use a computer to play them or to transfer the files to a cell phone. In a few select stands, I could pick a hundred songs from a catalog of thousands and have the *camelô* burn them to CD for a mere R$8.

Here, a note: I only call the vendors inside the market *camelôs* because of its name: the Uruguaiana Camelódromo. To others, like Fabio and Maria dos Camelôs, the subject of our next section, the market was no home to *camelôs* but its very antithesis.

Rights to the City

It is a scorching Tuesday afternoon and I finally have been able to finagle a meeting with the famous Maria dos Camelôs. She works at the Centro Unido dos Trabalhadores (CUT), a labor rights organization active all over the country but with a particularly strong Rio showing. Maria is bright and warm as she invites me into her air conditioned office. She grew up poor, married early and had a child, and divorced immediately after. At age 25 she arrived in Rio, without money or a home, and began squatting in a building downtown that has since remained in the family and passed on to her grown children. After a few odd jobs around Rio, she continued to run into *camelôs* in her squats and saw how they were able to make more money while "being their own boss." It was a very open climate to her, and quite international: she recalls people from Paraguay and São Paolo, which were very compelling for someone from small town Minas. "*Camelôs* were interesting, exciting," she exclaims in between a shot of brutal Brazilian coffee, "they know the streets." According to her, in those days there was a mutual respect between the GM and the *camelôs*: whenever the GM would enter *camelô* districts, it was more for show and they would respect the rights of the *camelôs* and not destroy anything.

She became a *camelô* after a few months living in Rio and realizing the opportunities it would give her. Incidentally, she is one of the very few female *camelôs* I know.[7] In the mid-1990s, she became pregnant again and nine months in, just before Maria was about to give birth, "things in Rio began to change, the *jeito* [way of being] was no longer the same." She recalls one major operation at my insistence. She becomes increasingly agitated as she describes it:

> The GM came into a side street just off Rua Uruguaiana and caused a *briga enorma* [huge fight] in the street and threw all my things around, destroying and arresting without concern. I'm very pregnant and worrying about my child, but they leave me untouched, thank god. At that point I didn't think or care about labor rights.... I was *revoltada* [quite angry] and just scared for myself and my child.

In 2003 Maria joined CUT as a representative of the *camelôs*. Their labor, she felt, was being unrecognized. CUT offered her a stable salary in addition to health care, something she never had being a *camelô*, and having children by then was causing her to tire of the *camelô* life without security. After attending her first *manifestaçao* (protest) at Cinelandia, a plaza in Rio's downtown, over the arrest of a *camelô*, she recalls crying over the multitudes that visited: "I couldn't breathe – there were *camelôs* from Madureira [a poor northern suburb], *camelôs* from Niteroi, and I couldn't contain myself. They were all very united. I could barely speak."

It is Maria who brings us into the modern condition for the *camelôs*, all predicated on accusations of piracy. Since the last *manifestação*, she maintains, the government has created a worse condition for the *camelôs* then ever. *Camelôs* disappear to unknown locations while the GM takes all their personal belongings and wares. A large part of it is the regularization – formalization – of Uruguaiana market, she flatly asserts. This has made the *camelôs* on the street much less organized than before. They come and go, arrested or in fear and "it's just impossible to get them together."

I emphasize this difficulty in uniting *camelôs*; I too noticed this during my months of interaction with Maria, as we became friends even as our times together were filled with emergencies, job-related and personal. Like her friends, certain informants of mine would disappear for a month, arrested or sick. I would worry but had no way to contact them, as I never knew their numbers or their real names, much less their addresses. Curiously for media pirates, too, they had very little access to the Internet. Whereas most of the people I knew in Brazil pirated music and movies by downloading from the Internet, the *camelôs* would copy them via copy centers buried in old corners of the colonial downtown. I visited some of these copy centers during my time in Rio. They were old small offices with ancient DVD burners and printing devices for DVD covers. Doing complete ethnography of these locations proved impossible, however, as they were constantly moved somewhere else when the police would find them.

Whether fighting police takeover of a squatter building on Avenida Mem de Sá in Lapa or arranging press releases for CUT, whenever I was with Maria she was fielding calls from arrested *camelôs*. She was frustrated both by the system that arrests them and by them as well. She has tried to organize a *camelô* union, but nobody ever shows up at the meetings: "They only call me when they are arrested and I don't always have time for that."

I once asked her about the legal reasons pirates are arrested, by way of introduction to my research on piracy and criminalization. "People get arrested for nothing," she says, and begins imitating a police officer:

"I'm arresting you because you are in front of someone who is pirating."
If there weren't any *camelôs*, piracy would still exist. *Lojas* [stores] will
sell pirated goods. Like inside Uruguaiana [market]. Unlike the past, now
camelôs have to be anxious all the time and recognize whenever the GM
will come and go: *A GM sai da moda, entra da moda* [the GM go out of
style, come back in style].

The distinction between inside and outside the market is recurs frequently.
To the newcomer to Rio, the differences between the Uruguaiana market
and Rua Uruguaiana seem minimal. Inside, she tells me, they are not *camelôs*
even though they appear to be (and it is named the Camelódromo). This is
merely a historical artifact, she explains, but they are basically stores. They
not only are not part of the *camelôs* outside, but they do not even bother to
help them when the GM comes running after them.

Piracy and Urban Circulation

If the Uruguaiana market is not really composed of *camelôs*, why was it shut
down with so much media hype by police as an anti-piracy campaign? The
police shut down Uruguaiana not because the pirated products themselves
were bothering them; after all, according to my informants police were
being paid off to look the other way most of the time.[8] The police shut
down Uruguaiana because it presented a competing Brazilian viewpoint
to consumption, one that international capital cannot abide. Unable to
jail or imprison all street vendors, the market drew police attention as an
image rich, public relations victory that allowed people to interact with
the Brazilian state's power on a local, consumptive level. The services
the *camelôs*, both inside and outside the market, had been offering were
competing visions to state dominance over consumption, where more elite
business interests reigned.

During my fieldwork, a very famous sequel to the international hit movie
Tropa de Elite (or *Elite Squad* in the international version), *Tropa de Elite
2*, came out in the theaters. Immediately, that Friday at Uruguaiana, the
camelôs were selling it on every street corner, screaming "*Tropa* has arrived"
to a hungry, consuming audience. Stopping to note the conversations that
occurred between these vendors and the consumers, one could not help but
notice a serious conversation about both the quality of the two films and
the cinematic discrepancies between them, but a lively, invested discussion
about the qualitative approaches toward police brutality and Rio's general

corruption in the two movies. My informant Fabio declared the second movie to be "more Hollywood," if less critical of the police, while another *camelô*, Zé, assured me that being "more Hollywood" did not necessarily eliminate the criticism of the police, but it did make the main heroes look much more good and left out the "bad parts" about them the first movie showed.

Jose Padilha, director of both the first and second *Tropa* movies, famously wrote an editorial in *O Globo*, Brazil's leading newspaper, in 2007, arguing that piracy was merely a "popular term for intellectual robbery" and should be treated like a grave crime, suggested that the popularity of the first film among the pirate markets of Uruguaiana and São Paulo's similar counterpart[9] did not "make him proud," as some critics had suggested. "As a Brazilian, I cannot be proud of this," he noted, because it takes away from all Brazilian industries that rely on the author as cultural diplomat (Padilha 2007). It was with particular relish that he then proceeded to describe the security measures put in place with the collaboration of São Paulo's police upon the release of the *Tropa de Elite* sequel, including using public funds to outfit the studio with keyword-only entry doors (to monitor individual access) and cameras streaming 24-hour footage of the room on the Internet, a peculiar engagement with the expertise of the visual as a way both to shame would-be pirates as well as a direct challenge to Internet users about the voyeuristic nature of piracy (Giannini 2010).

Threaded through these accusations and conversations with the *camelôs* was an intimate engagement with Brazilian cities as variegated, hierarchized urban spaces that only criminals and police navigated with ease. The Rio de Janeiro of pirates becomes a public different from its portrayal in the movies. The *camelôs* liked to compare themselves to these criminals, but only insofar as they understood the common public space of spheres like Uruguaiana to be a welcome place for all who came. It was in these spaces, as Fabio would explain to me, "that all people could make their living" and was even international; he often would point out recent arrivals from Peru and Paraguay. Noting that these people were not exactly "friendly," he nevertheless agreed that they made the space safer for all *camelôs*. When the streets are empty, he explained to me, nobody benefits. It indeed was shivering to see Uruguaiana empty, even in the melting Rio de Janeiro sunlight.

In my work over the months I had spent meeting *camelôs* both inside and outside the formal market, I noticed the differences between popular stereotypes of pirates – cunning thieves responsible for lost employment opportunities who sat salivating at every corner in wait of new bounty – and the actual lives of the street vendors. For them, they explained in great detail, piracy was not only a way of life but a way of "serving customers" that the big studios never would understand. Moreover, everyone expressed nuanced sadness at the CD and DVD stores that had been closing around Rio and losing ground to piracy, both physical and Internet-based. "When I was a child," recalled Marcelo, "I would love to run to the windows of the CD stores on Rua da Carioca. Now, most of that is gone. But I don't think it's our fault; it's the studios fault for such *sacanagem* [abuse of power, blackmail]" for selling at such high prices.

Fabio, who had become one of my main informants in my time in Rio, had switched from selling CDs to DVDs to backpacks as the seasons demanded. He came from a poor neighborhood in the north of the city, Jacarepaguá, and had begun as a *camelô* when he was 14, ten years earlier. Like most of his colleagues, he was a mixed-race male, plainly aware not only of the indelible racism that plagued Brazilian society but the class interactions between *camelô* and police that happened in the public, circulatory systems of downtown Rio. Others I interviewed noted with sadness that times had changed for the *camelô* in Rio, because "things used to be better for us" before the 1990s. There were fewer tourists, and the general consensus was that the police treated the *camelôs* better as a result. Also, before the urban renewal processes of the late neoliberal Lula regime, the city had been somewhat more relaxed in its enforcement of piracy.

When trends came and went from Uruguaiana – such as the tattooed arm bands that were in style in early 2011 – Fabio would switch to selling them immediately. This had surprised me initially, since I had come to Brazil to specifically look at media such as music and related cultural artifacts. But the *camelôs* I would come to know had no such attachment to one particular object to sell. All of what they sold, they claimed, was to make a living first, but to be in touch with the *"povo carioca* [people of Rio de Janeiro]." Around Christmas and the New Year, I observed, the pirates were even busier than stores, both because the consumers were interested and because the *camelôs* were making up lost money for the year. Although they were formally illegal and considered on the margins, people relied on the *camelôs* for a very Brazilian cultural experience of Christmas and end-of-year shopping.

This flexibility and connection with the consumer without corporate resources points toward theorizing piracy not as parasitic on content production but instrumental in its circulation and distribution. Demand for, and familiarity with, popular pirated goods and an identity of being *"camelô* vs. police" were among the few things that united the various classes of *camelôs*, a frustration that Maria and the other organizers at CUT wrestled with daily. Of course one could make the standard argument that piracy is against the law. It would be silly to reject this claim outright. But I suggest that the anti-piracy movement sought to quash Uruguaiana because it was a material representation of Brazilian identity toward material goods and commons that could not be indexed to state growth.

Moreover, the elites that made up both outspoken piracy opponents and proponents – such as bloggers and government officials – I had been reading were focusing on the production and the initial copying in their writings, studying its origins[10] or the involvement between the author of the work and the consumer. On the other hand, focusing on the "intermediate" pirates such as the *camelôs* shifts our focus from the hegemony of target and destination, or author and consumer, and toward a more fluid understanding of space as influencing consumption, of public circulation as marking the value of an object. It is no coincidence that this movement follows very well the metaphor of the ocean and piracy that has tailed fiction fans and actual pirates for centuries. Rather than focusing on the ports of capital we focus on the transmission and suggest that apparently fixed positions such as authentic creator and passive receiver are malleable and shifting.

When walking back through the various back streets after the raid, I saw a *Globo* reporter interviewing one of the Polícia Civil. As I passed, she was answering a question about piracy's ill effects: "With piracy few gain, and everyone loses." It was hard to digest; for me, it was precisely piracy that had made Uruguaiana one of the most vital, Brazilian and yet international places in Rio, bundling together citizens and the objects they wanted with the social relations legitimate stores effaced.

Public Streets, Public Terror

In his work on politics and aesthetics, Jacques writes that politics in the 21st century only obtains when it focuses on "transforming [the] space of 'moving-along,' of circulation, into a space for the appearance of a subject: the people, the workers, the citizens" (Rancière and Corcoran 2010, 37). For Rancière, the secret successes of official political movements – such as democratically elected governments – in the long capitalist centuries lay in separating the public sphere, where usually only the privileged elite could speak to one another, from the domestic sphere where it was inappropriate to speak, or where speech acts did not really have any significance.

The police are the ultimate example of this division of appropriateness and inappropriateness. It is the police who, contrary to the subjects who Rancière celebrates, assert "that the space for circulating is nothing but the space of circulation."

But how do the *camelôs* at Uruguaiana, officially nothing more than thieves distributing pirated CDs and DVDs, disturb the police and via pirating question the role of "circulation as nothing more than circulation"? To do this we must reexamine Rancière's claims by thinking through the material interests of those who circulate. For Rancière, "dissensus" is an epistemological stance of political being. This theorizing, however, does not give us enough to understand politics as a continuous negotiation with power structures; rather, even in its radical realignment of spatial concerns with political agency it still depends too narrowly, I believe, on its predecessors in superstructural Marxism, such as Althusser, whose famous police interpellation theories Rancière directly sources. The *camelôs* do not directly speak to the police, nor do they actively create a new politics simply by existing and circulating (e.g., moving). Rancière points to this problem when he writes that

> the specificity of political dissensus is that its partners are no more constituted than is the object or stage of discussion itself. Those who make visible the fact that they belong to a shared world that others do not see – or cannot take advantage of – is the implicit logic of any pragmatics of communication. (Rancière and Corcoran 2010, 38)

It is unfortunate, but I concur, that an implicit belief in communication is almost impossible in Rancière's viewpoint, and indeed it is almost impossible in a formalized system of politics. However, it is not impossible if the logic of communication is ripped out of one-way identification – communication as a way of me communicating to you. What if, following an anthropological understanding of imbued social structure, we see other forms of embeddedness, such as circulating market materials, and buying and selling, as communication? What kind of politics can be created in these spaces?

Below I highlight a major police intervention in Rio's public sphere and how a product's circulation and remix allowed piracy to formulate a valuable narrative, and place it against the Brazil's general shifting thoughts on piracy. In doing so, I trace how legal regimes of property at different scales offer a glimpse into Brazilian understanding of cultural spaces, race and class, and the public sphere.

Rio de Janeiro's northern section, known colloquially as Zona Norte, is a diverse economic and geographic mixture of lower- and middle-class *suburbio* (suburban neighborhoods) and *favelas* (hilltop ghettos). Most of the wealthier population of Rio de Janeiro city and the state surrounding it, however, consider it simply impoverished. While not all of Zona Norte is in the same slumlike conditions depicted in popular movies such as *City of God.* many residents of Rio's southern, richer area, Zona Sul, avoid the Zona Norte and receive their news and information about this part of the city strictly through the Brazilian media, much of it controlled by the Globo news corporation. The Zona Norte reigns famously in popular imagination as a black paradise, as one of the birthplaces of samba music, and as a dirty, industrial space that is unbecoming of Rio's boozy, beachy popularity. This vision is not precisely wrong, but it is quite simplified: the Zona Norte is a place where Rio's various middle and lower classes fluidly mix, where immigrants from the north of the country interact with the twin armies of the drug dealers (who generally stick to the *favelas* themselves) and the militias composed of former police officers, who stand outside the *favelas* and in collaboration with the drug traffickers keep their residents in fear and maintain an iron barrier between the tourist-friendly Rio de Janeiro of Zona Sul. It should therefore be no surprise to anyone but the casual observer that most of the *camelôs* at Uruguaiana come from the Zona Norte, and bring their sensibilities to their marketplace at Uruguaiana, likely the most southern place in Rio they will ever travel most of their lives.

In November of 2010, owing to an alleged series of bus burnings and attempted assassinations of police, the various police arms of Rio joined together to invade several immensely powerful *favelas*, mostly in the Zona Norte, ending in a long standout in the particularly infamous Complexo Alemão *favela*. Media coverage of this invasion was notoriously biased toward the police. Magazine covers routinely compared the residents escaping police as cockroaches skittering into characteristically tiny dusty allies and television reporters approvingly discussing the beauty of Rio's police force compared to the ugly and corrupt traffickers, nimbly cloaking the involved racial demographics. Indeed, for many critical observers of Rio's long history of police brutality (e.g., Caldeira 2001), November came as a frustrating watershed moment where police violence was routinized and became socially accepted in ways it never had before.

It was in the immediate aftermath of these tense days that I found the *camelôs* at Uruguaiana selling a DVD entitled *Terror in Rio 2010*, or a different DVD with the same cover image, titled simply *Complexo Alemão*. The DVD cover featured a crudely photoshopped version of the iconic Rio de Janeiro

Cristo, the Jesus statue that hovers above the city, is lit all night, and features prominently in almost every media image of Rio in existence. In this cover, however, Cristo was backlit by an exploding wall of fire and wore a Batalhão de Operações Policiais Especiais (BOPE, or the Brazilian equivalent of the elite SWAT team) bulletproof jacket. The DVD itself showed a slightly different *Cristo*, drawn and very nearly crying, yet with the same bulletproof vest and the BOPE crossed-swords coat of arms.

I purchase the DVD for about R$10, or US$7, still the going price for a single pirated DVD in Uruguaiana. With the addition of another DVD the price goes down dramatically. I ask the *camelô* about the DVD and furtively glancing to his sides, he somberly informs me the DVD demonstrates "how the police did bad things in Complexo," like taking the TVs of people that lived there, or intimidating the *moradores* (citizens or community dwellers). I continue my walk around the market and run into another *camelô* selling the same DVD with a slightly different cover, who tells me about how the DVD is really exciting and *ligado* (fresh or hot) and, he suggests furtively, while it is very interesting, it nevertheless represents the perspective of the media. I ask him to what perspective he refers, assuming that he thinks the DVD is not sufficiently critical of police activities during the invasion. I was wrong; the *camelô* tells me the footage is entirely shot by the media. The entire "documentary," it turns out, is pieced together from images culled from the mainstream stations, both national and international, that covered the four panicky days the city was on lockdown.

Amazed at this pirate media remix, I rushed home to view the DVD. The second *camelô* was correct; it was various clips of footage brought together, sometimes inexpertly, sometimes with transitions appearing almost professional. Curiously and brilliantly, the DVD wove together transitions in apparently contradictory fashion. For example, television hosts are shown discussing how police are being kind and gentle to the population next to an officer kicking down the door of a female *favela* resident. The DVD strongly makes the point not only about how the media portrayed a story about the poor of Rio, but how the media's own images are always subject to pirating. Without any explicit narrative conceit or apparent point of view, the *camelô* pirate mix not only distributed as wide as possible the gruesome images of the invasion of Complexo Alemão, but entered it in a marketplace where the trade of images of violence bring with them a public value uncapturable by the images' "original" viewing on the television.

This is heavy stuff. Black victims and white media. With no explicit commentary, the pirate artfully chooses his images, pointing firmly at Brazil's gaping racial divides behind a curtain of "racial democracy." The music on the DVD is black – the *favela*'s funk soundtrack alternating with calmer samba music – as are the victims. A physical version of YouTube, the *Terror in Rio 2010* DVDs shine light on the ability of images, extracted from their original transmission from producer to audience, to inform and educate an alternative, pirate public. As Alan Klima muses in his excellent work on the reproduction of death images in Thai markets outside of state control,

> the pirates of the new world order become the most powerful resistance to national media control. Under the sign of death and the space of funeral exchange with the dead, the black economy thrives on a power that can no longer be controlled by the Thai military, the state, or by Disney. (2002, 144)

While a *camelô* may point out that the bloody DVD "is not fit for children" he insists on selling it at the market, boasting to one reporter (Pennafort 2010) that he sold more than 12 during lunch. Through the reproduction of the same images the media used, the pirate is able to call on his intimate connection with the city – both the *favelas* that he lives in and recognizes as living entities, configured by the residents, and the markets where Zona Sul and Zona Norte residents mix – to provide a space for a powerful media critique that is gained only in the transmission of these DVDs. For the consumers, the individual cameramen do not matter. Authenticity is likewise unimportant. Neither, I would suggest, does the Globo logo that graces the screen momentarily; if anything, it lies there as a sad testament to the waning grip on technology and distribution the major content producers enjoyed for so long. Rather it is the vicarious thrill of the market purchase that animate these pirate images, haunting Uruguaiana and inserting the dead of the Zona Norte, figuratively and spatially, into the everyday life of an area far removed from it.

The same police that were hunting down the images of their conquests are the ones involved, some of my informants note with dripping irony, in the dismantling of Uruguaiana on that long weekend in January. This was just another front on "their campaign of *faxina etnica* [ethnic cleansing]," remarked Marcio. One laughed when he told me about the cleaning out of fake goods: "It'll be back before they know it, and those *filhos da puta* [sons of bitches] won't know where to find it. Anyway, as long as people want to buy it, they'll know where to find it." Indeed, that third day of the shutdown, as I was heading back home, a man in dark glasses whom I had not seen before approached me a few blocks away from the market, on the same street. Asking me if I needed anything, he proceeded to tell me that anything I would want was still circulating in the area, just not available at the moment. What the police were doing would pass, he argued, once they had their media blitz finished.

As I turned to look behind him at the shuttered, chained market, I saw the red-shirted temporary workers walk with white garbage bags filled with high demand, counterfeit objects, shimmering in the heat. As they threw the sacks into the large unmarked white trucks, I am reminded of Steinbeck's description of the United States during the Great Depression, where oranges are destroyed with kerosene to keep up value, while the "smell of rot fills the country" (349). It is this sense of value – the name of a brand over its worth to the people who exchange it – that pirate publics call back against.

Uruguaiana's pirates, like the poor half-citizens of Rio's *favelas* that suffered the police invasion, have preyed upon the output of Brazil's media empires, incorporating alternative formats in ways that sidestep the limits of circulation proscribed by official narratives and instead woven it into a powerful critique of the society they live in. Whether through the particular *Terror in Rio 2010* DVD or through the selling of backpacks smuggled across borders, the spatial interventions of Rio's pirates push back against the limits of capital by insisting that race and class exist against the backdrop of a free market.

Piracy and Evasionary Publics

In one of my later conversations with Maria dos Camelôs, I asked her if she had hope for the future of *camelôs* as the Olympic and World Cup cleansing of the city continued. With a wistful sigh, she remarked that

> my hope is that they make some money in the future.... Make some money. The sad thing is, the *camelô* works today only to eat for tomorrow. Its really hard to organize them. Once the GM screws around with the situation they can't reorganize people. And people don't come to meetings.

These evasions of organization are due to many reasons. As I detailed above, sometimes it happens because of police intervention, or family issues. Occasionally, the *camelô* will take vacations if he feels he has made enough money that week to remain at home. Any of these is a valid excuse, to be sure. I believe, however, that may be another reason to think about the inability to organize a direct resistance to the police. This speaks to Rancière's understanding of dissensus, one that is enriched immensely by an ethnographic core. I suggest that what is interpreted as laziness by Maria or lack of responsibility on the part of *camelôs* can be a political form of disorganized resistance by simple evasion, or a moving-around of the locus of control. David Graeber (2004) discusses this in his fieldwork on the Tsimihety of Madagascar:

> To this day they have maintained a reputation as masters of evasion: under the French, administrators would complain that they could send delegations to arrange for labor to build a road near a Tsimihety village, negotiate the terms with apparently cooperative elders, and return with the equipment a week later only to discover the village entirely abandoned – every single inhabitant had moved in with some relative in another part of the country.

For Graeber, the Tsimihety – whom he considers the "anarchists of northwest Madagascar" – represent a form of decentralization that need not rely on a centrally distributed set of directives for political action. In other words, he suggests that what the state has defined as cowardice, or failed messaging, can be a creative act. Being evasive and moving around, coming together at opportune moments and then disbanding become temporary but effective mini-destructions of elite control. Like the cries of "Guarda" echoing down the street causing each *camelô* to pull his temporary *barraca* (stand) back like a sea anemone gracefully pulling its tentacles back, I suggest that the *camelô* pirates of Uruguaiana participate in these kinds of evasions, only at an urban scale. They are familiar with where police are hiding and their networks alert them to when a GM is passing and remain united in this noncause, rather than one kind of political ideology.

Slums have recently enjoyed both popular and critical attention in books (Davis 2006; Neuwirth 2004) and movies such as *City of God* and *Slumdog Millionaire* as cosmopolitan sites of resistance where incipient citizens, lacking full rights, nevertheless contribute to the cultural and political formation of the state at an urban level. In this sense, preoccupation with these slums parses neatly with classical liberal portraits of the street and the local as a site of conscious consensus, and consequently creation of the citizen subject, as Jürgen Habermas (1991) and others have famously argued. The Enlightenment citizen creation, however, focuses on classes who have property – the bourgeois storeowner, for example. Thus the man is created not by his property but by his ownership. Recent scholars such as Nancy Fraser (2005) have pushed for a reexamination of this concept, however, outlining the problems with what these neat public spheres entail, arguing instead that we must reformulate the critical theory of the public sphere in a way that can illuminate the emancipatory possibilities of the present "postnational constellation."

The danger that Fraser notes, of course, is how to viably retain the critical democratic functions of Enlightenment-related public spheres – or "assume the emancipatory democratizing functions that are the whole point of public-sphere theory." I believe the question of emancipatory and democratizing are only applicable in a local framework of participatory democracy. Piracy in Brazil, like in much of the global south, does not operate via the circuits of participatory democracy, whose very core relies on the social consent of an organized, formal public. The point of piracy is not to create networks of cosmopolitanism that merely mirror elite networks, only "from below" as if in some sort of happy liberatory space. This position, celebrated in critical literature, too often relies on elite privileges of fluidity, easy value exchange, and mutual understanding.[11]

Indeed, piracy's opposite point is that there can be uneasy networks of participation without friendship or kindness, but economic and cultural mutual understanding. These uneasy kinships come together momentarily, through the passage of material objects with histories, escaped from their intended destinations. As Brazil enters a 21st century of neoliberal statehood, with more and more international actors (e.g., the ACTA treatment) attempting to contain its publics, piracy reacts. Without an explicit statement on democratization or the neat fluid circuits of capital, it allows for strong subjects to engage directly with global forces on local scales about intellectual property and state knowledge through an expert – if lay – interpretation of property rights. Whether on the Internet or in the city spaces of Brazil, conversations about being Brazilian are taking place by a public not waiting to be heard, but conversing among itself.

Notes

1. It was rare to see the different police entities mix at one time, including the Guarda Municipal, or municipal police, which usually deals with transit and other urban issues; the Polícia Civil, which deals with criminal activities; and the Polícia Militar, the federal police unit that usually engages high-profile crimes.
2. Indeed, critics see the moral doctrine of information freedom as an anti-democratic power despite its pretensions to equalization (Coleman and Golub 2008; Morozov 2011).

3. For more on the history of Brazil and media adoption, see Kottak 1989 and Vink 1988. In its adoption and rejection – or cannibalization – of foreign content, the country has long prided itself in playing the cosmopolitan Other (Schwarz 1996; Andrade and Bary 1991; Staden and Whitehead 2008).

4. "Pelo Telefone" (loosely "By way of the phone") is a 1917 song considered by many experts to be the first samba, a surprising and proud achievement in a musical genre known for reinvention and reuse. Originally a parody of the chief of the Rio de Janiero police's rather foolish idea to call criminals before their apprehension, the song was endlessly remixed and sung with different verses highlighting both *carioca* invention and work ethic, and remained a statement on technological evasion both in its content and in form. For more, see Hertzman 2008 and Severiano and Homem de Mello 1997.

5. This essay retains the original Portuguese names and naming conventions, including Rua, meaning street, with the plural Ruas, and Avenida meaning Avenue.

6. Roughly US$6 at the time of ethnography.

7. Forthcoming work from this research will explore the gendered dimensions of piracy.

8. I never, of course, saw this for myself. Whether the rumor of police payoff was real or not matters little for our story, where the power of rumor and its agentive power says more than truth about it.

9. São Paulo, economic capital of Brazil and home to almost 25 million people, has a vibrant Uruguiana-like market on Rua 25 de Março. Sao Paulo's mayor ("mini-dictator" to his critics) has launched an even harsher campaign against the *camelôs* there, imprisoning and expelling them en masse. For more on the most recent fights between *camelôs* and Mayor Kassab, see articles in *Causa Operária* (for example, Anonymous 2011).

10. In Rio's case, most material goods such as shoes and clothing come from China through Paraguay and into Brazil from the south, while media is downloaded and copied locally. For more on these intricate networks, see the Brazil chapter in the excellent SSRC report on piracy (Mizukami et al. 2011).

11. This kind of vanguard thinking (Easterling 2007) about the possibilities of piracy can be found in everywhere from Hardt and Negri's (2004) "multitude" concept to any number of open-source software manifestos relying on decentralization as an end goal, rather than a starting point, in an alternative politics.

Bibliography

Andrade, Oswald de, and Leslie Bary. 1991. "Cannibalist Manifesto." *Latin American Literary Review* 19.38: 38-47.

Anonymous. 2011. "Camelôs se revoltam contra repressão de Gilberto Kassab em São Paulo." *Causa Operária Online*, 26 October. http://www.pco.org.br/conoticias/ler_materia.php?mat=33350.

Barbosa, Alexandre F. 2010. *Pesquisa sobre o Uso das Tecnologias da Informação e da Comunicação no Brasil: TIC Lanhouses 2010*. Trans. Karen Brito. São Paulo: Comitê Gestor da Internet no Brasil. http://www.cetic.br/tic/lanhouse/2010/index.htm.

Bourdieu, Pierre. 1977. *Outline of a Theory of Practice*. Cambridge MA: Cambridge University Press.

Caldeira, Teresa P. R. 2001. *City of Walls: Crime, Segregation, and Citizenship in São Paulo*. Berkeley: University of California Press.

Coleman, E. Gabriella, and Alex Golub. 2008. "Hacker Practice: Moral Genres and the Cultural Articulation of Liberalism." *Anthropological Theory* 8.3: 255-277.

Davis, Mike. 2006. *Planet of Slums*. London: Verso. http://books.google.com/books?id=FToaDLPB2jAC.

Easterling, Keller. 2007. "Contemplation: Pirate." In *Enduring Innocence: Global Architecture and Its Political Masquerades*. Cambridge MA: The MIT Press.

Fraser, Nancy. 2005. "Transnationalizing the Public Sphere." *RepublicArt* (March). http://www.republicart.net/disc/publicum/fraser01_en.htm.

Giannini, Alessandro. 2010. "José Padilha usou policiais paulistas para evitar pirataria de 'Tropa de Elite 2.'" *UOL*. http://cinema.uol.com.br/ultnot/2010/09/15/jose-padilha-usou-policiais-paulistas-para-evitar-pirataria-de-tropa-de-elite-2.jhtm.

Graeber, David. 2004. *Fragments of an Anarchist Anthropology*. Chicago: Prickly Paradigm Press.

Habermas, Jürgen. 1991. *The Structural Transformation of the Public Sphere: An Inquiry into a Category of Bourgeois Society*. Cambridge, MA: MIT Press.

Hardt, Michael, and Antonio Negri. 2004. *Multitude: War and Democracy in the Age of Empire*. New York: Penguin.

Hertzman, Marc Adam. 2008. "Surveillance and Difference: The Making of Samba, Race, and Nation in Brazil (1880s-1970s)." PhD diss., University of Wisconsin-Madison.

Ito, Joi. 2008. "Gilberto Gil's talk at Google Zeitgeist." Joi Ito's Web. http://joi.ito.com/weblog/2008/05/19/gilberto-gils-t.html.

Kambouri, Nelli, and Pavlos Hatzopoulos. 2011. "The Tactics of Occupation: Becoming Cockroach." Nomadic Universality. http://nomadicuniversality.wordpress.com/2011/11/26/the-tactics-of-occupation-becoming-cockroach/.

Klima, Alan. 2002. *The Funeral Casino: Meditation, Massacre, and Exchange with the Dead in Thailand*. Princeton, NJ: Princeton University Press.

Kottak, Conrad Philip. 1989. *Prime-Time Society: An Anthropological Analysis of Television and Culture*. Belmont, CA: Wadsworth Publishing.

Latour, Bruno. 1993. *We Have Never Been Modern*. Cambridge, MA: Harvard University Press.

Ministério da Cultura. 2011. "Cultura Viva » Ponto de Cultura." Ministério da Cultura. http://www.cultura.gov.br/culturaviva/ponto-de-cultura/.

Mizukami, Pedro, Oona Castro, Luiz Moncau, and Ronaldo Lemos. 2011. "Brazil." In Joe Karaganis, ed., *Media Piracy in Emerging Economies*. New York: Social Science Research Council.

Morley, David. 1995. "Television: Not So Much a Visual Medium, More a Visible Object." In Chris Jenks, ed., *Visual Culture*. London: Routledge, 170-189.

Morozov, Evgeny. 2011. "The Internet Intellectual." *The New Republic*, 3 November. http://www.tnr.com/article/books/magazine/96116/the-internet-intellectual.

Naro, Nancy Priscilla, Roger Sansi-Roca, and David H. Treece. 2007. *Cultures of the Lusophone Black Atlantic*. New York: Palgrave Macmillan.

Neuwirth, Robert 2006. Shadow Cities: A Billion Squatters, a New Urban World. New York: Routledge.

Padilha, José. 2007. "José Padilha: 'Nas ruas, gato por lebre' – O Globo Online." *O Globo*, 28 August. http://oglobo.globo.com/opiniao/mat/2007/08/28/297461668.asp.

Pennafort, Roberta. 2010. "Camelôs faturam alto com DVD 'Terror no Rio 2010' – cultura – Estadao.com.br." *Globo*, 29 November. http://www.estadao.com.br/noticias/arteelazer,camelos-faturam-alto-com-dvd-terror-no-rio-2010,647053,0.htm.

Povinelli, Elizabeth A. 2001. "Radical Worlds: The Anthropology of Incommensurability and Inconceivability." *Annual Review of Anthropology* 30(1): 319-334.

Rancière, Jacques, and Steve Corcoran. 2010. *Dissensus: On Politics and Aesthetics*. London: Continuum.

Sansi, Roger. 2010. *Fetishes and Monuments: Afro-Brazilian Art and Culture in the 20th Century*. New York: Berghahn Books.

Schwarz, Roberto. 1996. "Brazilian Culture: Nationalism by Elimination." In Roberto Schwarz, *Misplaced Ideas: Essays on Brazilian Culture*, ed. John Gledson. London: Verso.

Severiano, Jairo, and Zuza Homem de Mello. 1997. *A canção no tempo: 85 anos de músicas brasileiras. Vol. 1, 1901-1957*. São Paulo: Jardim Europa. http://www.editora34.com.br/detalhe.asp?id=71.

Strathern, Marilyn. 1996. "Cutting the Network." *The Journal of the Royal Anthropological Institute* 2(3): 517-535.

Staden, Hans, and Neil Whitehead. 2008. *Hans Staden's True History: An Account of Cannibal Captivity in Brazil*. Durham, NC: Duke University Press.

Steinbeck, John. 2006. *The Grapes of Wrath*. London/New York: Penguin.

Vink, Nico. 1988. *The Telenovela and Emancipation: A Study on Television and Social Change In Brazil*. Amsterdam: Royal Tropical Institute.

WikiLeaks. 2006. "06BRASILIA1781: Brazil: Copyright Piracy Six Months Later." WikiLeaks. http://cablegatesearch.net/cable.php?id=06BRASILIA1781andq=%3Dbr%20%3Dbrazil%20%3Dkcrm%20%3Dkipr%20criminal-activity%20intellectual-property-rights.

WikiLeaks. 2007. "#07SAOPAULO878: Sao Paulo City Official Talks about Governance, Politics, and Fighting Piracy and Other Crime." WikiLeaks. http://cablegatesearch.net/cable.php?id=07SAOPAULO878andq=%3Dbr%20%3Dbrazil%20%3Dkcrm%20%3Dkipr%20criminal-activity%20intellectual-property-rights.

3.   Piracy on the Ground

How Informal Media Distribution and Access Influences
the Film Experience in Contemporary Hanoi, Vietnam

Tony Tran

In order to understand the dynamics and inner workings of piracy, I conducted fieldwork in the summer of 2011 by becoming a participant-observer
at three pirate DVD shops in Hanoi, Vietnam. Like many foreigners who
rarely experience piracy in such an open and material environment, I was
initially amazed and intrigued by these stores' massive accumulation of
media texts. But as I began to normalize myself within the pirate shop, my
focus expanded beyond just the media itself, but also started to include
how the store and media incorporated themselves in the customers' lives.
During my time at these stores, I met Vietnamese directors and actors
trying to find films to study and librarians from local universities buying hundreds of discs for their library collections. I watched a crowd of 15
strangers gather around a television in a store to laugh over an episode of
Mr. Bean. I overheard informal reviews of films that customers brought last
week and debates over which film was the best in *The Fast and the Furious*
franchise. I heard sounds of excitement as a film finally came to the store,
as well as rants about the lack of films.

As my experiences illustrate, in the context of many developing nations
such as Vietnam, "pirate and grey-market practices have been vectors not
only of 'consumption' in a narrow sense but also of cultural participation,
education, and innovation" (Liang and Sundaram 2011, 344). Pirated media
texts in Vietnam are not just for entertainment, but are educating the current and next generation of filmmakers and media consumers. Within a
context like Vietnam, it is helpful to look at the works of Lawrence Liang
(2005) and Ravi Sundaram (2010), which approaches piracy as a form of
access and focuses on everyday forms of piracy and consumption (physical
DVDs, clothing, electronics, etc.) that commonly exist on the fringes of
global society. This framework of "piracy as access" is interested in the
transformative properties of piracy and how it can distribute knowledge,
culture, and capital in areas where official infrastructures are lacking
(Lobato 2012, 82). The act of piracy, Liang argues, is not necessarily just about
morals or an act of resistance, but one out of necessity in many developing
countries. Piracy, then, is also about "ways through which people ordinarily

left out of the imagination of modernity, technology, and the global economy [find] ways of inserting themselves into these networks" (Liang 2005, 6). Sundaram has also found piracy to be "more pragmatic and viral than the avant-garde or tactical media [and that] pirate culture allowed the entry of vast numbers of poor urban residents into media culture" (2010, 112). For Sundaram, piracy is not oppositional or countercultural, but rather a realistic strategy for survival and innovation.

Nevertheless, as piracy is a point where many people in developing nations insert themselves into global media, we must also not lose sight of its distributive properties because the "frames through which we are presented any text of message becomes a vital part of that text or message... and will change depending on the venue in which they are presented" (Gray 2011, 101). Distribution in any variety, formal or informal, is a crucial aspect of film and media studies as it controls the speed and flow of information, how information and ideologies are presented, who can access this information, and most of the financial aspects that arise from these controls. Even though distribution is central to comprehending how media works within society and culture, it has generally been an area of relatively limited study and theorization in media studies (Lobato 2007, 114; Wang 2003, 1-2). Of the significant works on the structures and mechanisms of global media flows, many works have focused on official networks, producing a Hollywood-centric viewpoint and mode of analysis. Although these works on official distribution networks have increased our knowledge of film culture and are ultimately needed, their emphasis on major Hollywood systems have ignored the "informal" and "shadow" economies that dominate much of Asia, Africa, and South America that are actually the global norm in terms of film distribution (Mattelart 2009, 311; Lobato 2012, 1-2).

This is not to ignore the power of these dominant systems, but rather to acknowledge and shed light on the diversity and depth of the myriad distribution networks that exist alongside these official channels. When informal distribution practices (like piracy) and its consumers do appear in public and academic discourses around the globe, these conversations are often limited and framed around legal and ethical debates, broad economic numbers, and enforcement practices (Liang and Sundaram 2011, 344).[1] Overall, these discourses narrowly focus on the monetary bottom line of the global media economy without addressing the roles these informal spaces play as a mode of distribution and their influence on society as circulators of cultural texts. Furthermore, by invoking the issues of legality and morality, these discourses ignore the fact that for many people around the globe, informal distribution sites are the only feasible method of obtaining media, as "the flood of legal media goods available in high-income countries over the past two decades has been a trickle in most parts of the world" (Karaganis 2011, i). In these circumstances, media piracy is not necessarily an active political decision to break the law or resist global capitalistic forces, but a ubiquitous source of access in many developing countries that is created by the social and economic constraints of the surrounding environment.

If we are to realistically explore media and its flows on a global scale, we must consider the shadowy and subterranean modes of distribution and access that commonly exist in much of the world. Although legal forms of distribution, such as multiplexes, legal DVDs, and television/cable, are becoming more common in Vietnam, a large number of US television shows and Hollywood films reach audiences' screens through the illegal circulation of media from piracy shops (IIPA 2012, 278). Considering the impact of piracy and distribution, how then does the media circulation via these pirate shops influence film consumption in a nation such as Vietnam, where formal and legal infrastructures are limited, overpriced for the market, barely established, and/or lag behind in terms of speed and popularity to other circulation methods like piracy?

This essay is concerned with questions about how a specific form of piracy (the DVD store) exists, operates, and interacts with the everyday life of consumers within Hanoi, Vietnam. As a distribution method, what kinds of knowledge, information, and capital can piracy spread and how does it organize and control them? What are its potentials and limitations in helping Vietnamese people insert themselves into media culture and modernity? Centering on the DVD shop and its products, this essay explores how pirate cultures and informal distribution circuits operate on the ground level and integrate global media texts (mainly Hollywood films) into the local society of Hanoi, Vietnam. Drawing from fieldwork conducted in Hanoi during the summer of 2011 – which includes interviews with owners and workers at multiple pirate DVD shops and obtaining employment at three stores – this essay traces and examines the physical flow of media through these store sites.[2] By exploring the interactions between media texts, store workers, customers, and the store's design itself, this essay reveals how piracy helps to shape and influence media experiences and cultures in Hanoi.

Global Film Distribution in Vietnam

In order to understand the informal shadow economies of piracy, we must first briefly look at the official structures in which they travel under. As a dominant global power, Hollywood has always had an aura that attracted global audiences and its consumption is a major symbol of cultural modernity. In Vietnam, this desire for Hollywood (and foreign media in general) is aided by the lack of a viable and popular national film industry, which from 1953 to 2003 had been mostly subsidized by the Vietnamese government (see Ngo 2007).[3] After multiple decades of disproportionate funding and output, the film industry almost became extinct in the 1990s when funding was heavily cut and few quality films were released (Marr 2003, 286). Placing art above entertainment value, these films revolved around themes of war and overt politics which did not appeal to general Vietnamese audiences, especially the nation's large and growing youth population. In 2003, the Vietnamese government began to allow films to be privately funded and this has led to a small revival of Vietnamese cinema. Moving beyond themes of patriotism, war, and politics, this new era of Vietnamese cinema began to emphasize the entertainment aspects of film, often drawing inspiration from Hollywood and other major Asian cinemas (e.g., Hong Kong, Japan, and South Korea). Nevertheless, these films still lagged behind Hollywood in terms of output, audiences, and screen time at movie theaters.

Ironically, however, the lack of Vietnamese films which generates desire for entertainment from foreign sources also creates barriers to the legal access of Hollywood films. Due to the scarcity of domestic films in the 1990s, there was little incentive to invest in or preserve movie theaters. Thus during the late 1990s and early 2000s, audiences in Vietnam had limited exhibition spaces which could adequately show films. In an endeavor to enhance and sustain the national cinema industry, the Vietnamese government enacted in 2006 the Cinematography Law which was committed to reinvesting in modern cinema venues. In order to protect its investments, however, Vietnam instituted a quota system within the law that restricted the number of foreign films to 65% of total projected films per year. With an average output of 10 to 15 Vietnamese films per year, the quota system legally only allows about 30 foreign films per year.[4]

Although there has been uneven enforcement of the exact percentage of foreign films on theater screens over the last five years, the quota system has been assisted by Vietnam's strict censorship policies and film distribution regulations, which have always been around to deny access by ensuring only a limited amount of Hollywood film are shown in cinemas (Viet Nam News 2010; IIPA 2012, 286).[5] For the Hollywood films that were released in Vietnam over the last decade, these policies and regulations generally created lengthy delays in their release dates of up to more than a year. Surveys conducted by the Viet Nam National Film Distribution and Screening Company (FAFIM) during the late 1990s and early 2000s indicated a very low attendance of movie theaters because of these delays, as 32% of people surveyed replied there were no good films at the theaters as "FAFIM is unable to import good films made within the most recent year." The survey also highlights a significant barrier between Vietnamese audiences and access to legal media: products are overpriced for the market. The survey concluded that low attendance was also attributed to "the income [of viewers]… not being enough to cover the fee for the film," as 38% of those surveyed mentioned high ticket prices as the sole reason of why they did not go to movie theaters (Hoang 2007, 267-268).[6]

In 2011 the exhibition and economic situation has improved in many aspects. Since 2003, the number of modern multiplexes has tripled and box office revenues have increased 20% annually (Frater 2011). Beginning in early 2011, Hollywood films have finally begun to be released during the same time window of major international cities. Still, Hollywood films are far from being accessible to the majority of Vietnamese audiences. In a country with 87 million people, there are only about 150 viable cinema screens in Vietnam, with most being located in the large urban centers of Ho Chi Minh City and Hanoi (Frater 2011). Ticket prices to these screens range from US$2 for older outdated theaters to US$7 for the newer multiplexes. With the average monthly wage of US$60 to US$80, visits to the cinema, especially the newer ones, most likely do not occur on a regular basis for many Vietnamese people, even with the economic improvements of the last decade (Schwenkel 2011, 133; Viet Nam Household Living Standard Survey 2010, 13).[7] And while more Hollywood films are being released in Vietnam (e.g., *Transformers: Dark of the Moon* [2011], *X-Men: First Class* [2011], *Kung Fu Panda 2* [2011]), more than two-thirds of Hollywood films never reach Vietnamese screens legally (e.g., *Harry Potter and the Deathly Hallows – Part II* [2011]).

In the realm of legal DVDs, films from Sony Pictures became available in 2008, with Warner Brothers and 20th Century Fox films arriving in 2009, and Walt Disney films in 2010 (Reuters/Hollywood Reporter 2008; Tuong 2010). These DVDs range from US$2 to US$6 in cost, but the DVD titles released are several months to years behind release dates in the United States and other Asian countries. Furthermore, the selection is very limited and seemingly random, and finding current films is very difficult. These legal DVDs can be found at several bookstores (and even in some of the piracy shops where I conducted fieldwork) but there never seemed to be a steady or organized shipment of film titles. In the summer of 2011, the newest film on DVD was *The Karate Kid* (2010) and other available titles included *Talladega Nights: The Ballad of Ricky Bobby* (2006) and *2012* (2009).

The Trajectory of Pirated Material in Vietnam

With most films priced at US$0.75 per disc and a large and constantly updated selection, it can be seen that the pirate DVD store becomes an affordable and efficient site of access for many Vietnamese people. Here, the film distribution business is "off-the-books," traveling through subterranean channels that bypass official network structures – such as global zoning and "windowing" release models, taxes, and censorship – established by Hollywood Studios and governments.[8] The specific films bought and the money used to purchase them will not contribute to any box-office revenue, nor will they determine the success or failure of a film within the Hollywood industry. Regardless, these store sites are still nodes and hubs of media distribution that have a significant impact on the circulation of global media in Vietnam.

Vietnam's pirate economy is unique in that it is a mixed economy that features both domestic and foreign-produced (mainly Chinese) DVD products, though the majority of the pirated materials in stores originate from China.[9] Unlike "burned" copies commonly found in households and smaller pirate operations, the Chinese DVDs are mass produced and professionally pressed with industrial machines.[10] These DVDs come in two major forms: DVD5s and DVD9s. Visually identical before pirate production, the main technological difference between these discs is their storage capacities: DVD5s have a maximum capacity of 4.37 gigabytes, while DVD9s have a maximum of 7.95 gigabytes. What this mainly affects is the quality of the image and sound, the content of the discs, and the final selling price. For an undiscerning viewer, a single film on DVD5s and DVD9s will look and sound very similar on standard-definition televisions. Because DVD9s have more storage space for data, however, there is less compression of digital files, sometimes resulting in clearer sound quality and less pixilated images when compared to DVD5s. This can be especially seen and heard with longer films (which contain more data) and during scenes with fast camera movement and complex sound design.

Relatedly, this data difference also affects the amount of content and features on discs. Since they have larger capacities, DVD9s are able to hold multiple films or episodes of a television program (about six to seven hours) without sacrificing much in image and sound quality. Likewise, DVD9s can also carry subtitles and audio-dubbing in multiple languages, with many even carrying the option of surround sound. Although technically the same amount of content could be compressed onto a DVD5, this would result in extremely grainy images and audio quality that would fall under the acceptable threshold of standards in Vietnam (this threshold is examined later in this essay). Thus, while DVD9 can contain various amounts of content (single or multiple films, multiple television episodes, audio-visual options, etc.), DVD5s are generally restricted to a single film per disc. Obviously all of these factors influence the final selling price, with DVD5s priced at US$0.75 while DVD9s ranged between US$1.25 and US$1.50.

These pirated materials are usually smuggled from China to Vietnam across their shared border via ground transportation (buses, trucks, train, etc.) according to my interviews with store owners and workers in Hanoi. Ground transportation is preferred as it allows smugglers to closely accompany shipments, which in turn also allows smugglers to deal with (i.e., bribe) authorities directly. When asked if these shipments take any special routes, they all replied "no" and that these packages travel on infrastructures that also transport legal materials. Once in the country, these boxes of DVDs were either shipped directly to stores or to the homes of store owners – which were often used as storage – or to middlemen suppliers who would then distribute the discs to the store by motorbike.

The films on Chinese DVD5s usually arrive in the store in the following phases of audio-visual quality: a first-edition or "camcorded" copy, a screener copy, and a final-edition copy. A first-edition copy is a film that has been illegally captured by a video camera inside a movie theater. As most know, these first-edition films have very low audio-visual qualities (which will be further elaborated later in this essay) and, depending on the theater's location, could be in various languages. Most Vietnamese customers prefer to skip this phase and wait for a better copy to appear. The next phase brings screener copies – leaked preview versions of films given to critics, film festivals, studios, etc. – which are not visually perfect and very often contain watermarks indicating their original sources (see Pulver 2012). However, these versions are generally considered watchable by customers and a considerable upgrade from camcorded versions. The final-edition DVD5s are "perfect" copies, in that the pirate disc's images onscreen are mostly indistinguishable from legal DVDs in terms of image and sound quality. These may come from uploaded digital copies of finished films or ripped from a master copy (e.g., a legal DVD). Both the screener and final-edition copies contained the film's original language and all discs usually had the option of English and Chinese subtitles.

These phases and their time lines, however, are not concrete. Some films skip straight to final editions the first week they are legally released in theaters, while others may be limited to first-edition status for months. Obviously, sometimes screener copies may appear in pirate stores before a film is released in theaters, with first editions coming afterward. As far as the store owners and workers I interviewed were concerned, there is no system to predict when and in what manner a film would reach the store as the supply of pirated media solely depended on the random errors and cracks within the legal distribution system.

During all three phases, the film titles on the Chinese DVD5s are usually limited to "new" releases. In the context of the store, the term "new" is a very complex term. In its simplest form, the term lines up with the common understanding of a new release, referring to pirated DVDs that contained films that were being recently released in theaters somewhere around the world. As long as the discs are available in the store around the general vicinity of the official release – either slightly before or after – these films are considered "new." In spite of that, it is more commonly used to describe a final-edition copy of a film that has just arrived at the store for the first time, even if the film is not considered a new release in their place of origin anymore. Hence, "new" is a relative term as even films that have been released in theaters for months could still be considered new in the pirate store. Like new releases around the world, a film title eventually loses the descriptor of "new" within the context of the store and will eventually be shifted into the "old" sections of the store. The time line of a film's demotion is dependent on many factors, such as the number of new titles arriving at the store, its sale numbers, and the total time it has been labeled as "new." In the summer of 2011, new DVD5s included *Cars 2* (2011), *Water for Elephants* (2011), and *Paul* (2011).

On the other hand, the Chinese DVD9s are available with almost every title imaginable, including classic and contemporary Hollywood, Bollywood, and European films and US, Japanese, and British television. Due to this broad spectrum of media titles, the DVD9s vastly outnumbered DVD5s. In terms of television, the discs would have multiple episodes on each disc and be either sold in box sets as an entire series or individual seasons. The majority of films on DVD9s were limited to one film per disc, but every store had collections based on cinematic figures that are popular in the US and Europe. Packaged similar to television programs, these box set collections would have multiple films per disc and be organized around a person or entity, such as Jean-Luc Godard, Federico Fellini, Will Smith, Bruce Willis, James Bond (007), and the Disney/Pixar Company. All of these media texts are in their final-edition forms because it would be illogical to produce and attempt to sell a more expensive disc with an inferior master copy such as a camcorded film. The majority of these discs are presented in their original language of production with English subtitles and many discs frequently had French, Spanish, Chinese, and Japanese subtitles and/or official dubbed voice-overs.

Shipments of Chinese discs to the stores in Hanoi generally consisted of DVD9 copies of television programs and films. Though smaller in numbers, the Chinese DVD5s consisted of mainly final-edition films, though there were occasionally screener editions and, very rarely, first editions. Some of these titles in these shipments were selected by the store owners and workers in face-to-face meetings with suppliers. When asked on how they decided on these titles, the owners and workers stated that they relied on informal sale numbers based on personal sales experiences and placed orders of films and television programs that were popular in their stores, both in terms of sales and customer requests. In addition, some workers would also look online at sites like the Internet Movie Database (IMDb.com) to see top-ten lists of popular films and television shows. In the summer of 2011, these requests included new seasons of *The Big Bang Theory* (2007-present), *Mad Men* (2007-present), and the films of Quentin Tarantino (both individually and as a collection).

Beyond their requests, the store owners gave a lot of power to the suppliers in regards to the selection of media texts. These suppliers in Hanoi, who would have supply connections to pirate sources along the border and within China, were also given a budget to buy any films or television shows that would be deemed as new within the contexts of the stores. Therefore, many of the titles in these stores are not specifically or purposely acquired, but rather randomly gathered for the sake of having a larger inventory of new materials. This explains the diversity and unpredictability of media titles in many stores, including the box set collections mentioned above and several independent films and documentaries, such as *Four Lions* (2010) which only had a limited release in the US. Overall, there seems to be a very limited method in the stores' selection process of specific titles, but more of an emphasis of simply attaining new films and television programs.

While China has a complete monopoly on the DVD9 in Vietnam, the majority of the DVD5 inventory consists of Vietnamese-produced DVD5s. Similar to their Chinese counterparts, these DVD5s are priced at US$0.75, generally contain one "new" film per disc, and follow the same pattern of phases of quality (first edition, screener, and final edition). However, what makes the Vietnamese DVD5 more popular in terms of sales than the Chinese discs are that all of these Vietnamese DVD5s had the options of turning on Vietnamese subtitles and/or a mono-dubbed soundtrack in Vietnamese (one person reading the subtitles), which is not available on any Chinese DVD5 or DVD9.

Before any of these Vietnamese-produced DVD5s fill the store's shelves, the media on these discs first start their journey within official systems of media distribution, in forms like screener/preview DVDs, Internet streaming sites, or on the screen of a multiplex. If a leak occurs, like the uploading of a DVD on a BitTorrent website, Vietnamese media pirates in Ho Chi Minh City (HCMC) download the digital files on hard drives and add Vietnamese subtitles. The source of subtitles varies with each film. If a film has already been officially released for a few weeks, the coding for Vietnamese subtitles can be readily accessed and downloaded free online. These Vietnamese subtitles are produced by Vietnamese fans and cinephiles, both within Vietnam and abroad, and can easily be added to the digital file of the film.[11] In some cases according to store owners, media pirates would hire people – mainly university students studying the English language – to write subtitles. This occurs when a pirated digital film has been downloaded, but not enough time had elapsed for fans to subtitle the film and upload the subtitles on the Internet for free. This acquisition of labor transpires because, as general rule, many pirates and store owners believe that the earlier a film appears on the shelves of stores the more copies it would sell, especially if its pirate release is close to the official release date.

Once a film is subtitled, the digital files are sent into mass production at large optical disc factories, many which are only licensed to produce blank or legal discs (IIPA 2012, 278). As a major economic and industrial center in Vietnam, the overwhelmingly majority of pirate DVD production occurs within HCMC due to its established infrastructures (e.g., high-speed Internet) and proximity to multiple factories. As the discs are in production, media pirates also produce DVD covers that accompany the discs. Original forms of pirate creativity is very limited here as the covers are simply downloaded from websites that feature official or user-created DVD cover images, such as CoversHut.com and FreeCovers.net. The only additions added are a translation of the film's title to Vietnamese and texts stating the current phase of quality of the disc and the available subtitles. Once the covers are printed on glossy paper, the covers and finished discs are packaged separately and sent to suppliers around the country.

For the delivery of Vietnamese-produced DVD5s in Hanoi, suppliers (often delivering both Chinese- and Vietnamese-produced discs) would drive up to the store about every other day and hand a worker a stack of about 50 to 100 paper DVD covers. The worker would then flip through the pile and select any covers of films that were new or needed to be restocked, as well as request specific titles not in the pile of covers. The supplier would then record the titles selected and give a receipt – which could be a Post-it note or a piece of scrap paper – to the worker. These discs would then be delivered the next day in separate components: a stack of ten DVDs of the same film and a stack of DVD covers. Once the discs were packaged with the covers, they are placed on the shelves ready to be sold. At the end of the month, receipts would be complied and a payment would be made to the supplier: each DVD5 costs 8,000 Vietnamese Dong (US$0.40) and each DVD9 costs 18,000 Vietnamese Dong (US$0.90).

While the store owners and workers in Hanoi had some ability to request specific media texts and ultimately had the power to select what media is physically sold in their stores, their power to actually select which title gets to enter pirate production is basically nonexistent. Requests for specific titles may reach up the chain of command, but there is very little direct contact between the stores and DVD producers. This is especially true regarding the Chinese-produced DVDs – none of the owners or workers interviewed knew much about their specific operations. Although there is contact between Hanoi and HCMC, the factories in HCMC do not have the capital, experience, or organizational ability to produce a diverse set of media products like China. Thus, instead of taking specific request from stores, these factories mainly manufacture mass numbers of new and popular films that are low risk and can be moved quickly in order to stay profitable.

This approach has produced a domestic pirate production that is very uniform and in line with mainstream global media, with all of the stores in Hanoi having very similar products (the unusual products mainly originate from China). As very little production actually occurs within Hanoi – there are some very small-scale burning operations – the stores are mainly importers of media texts and, therefore, subject to whatever materials are sent their way by the producers of pirated materials. Nevertheless, as a popular space where transnational texts meet Vietnamese consumers for the first time, the pirate stores' main power exists in the fact that they are physical entry point into media that helps shape how film and television are being introduced to audiences in Hanoi.

Selling Piracy: Life on the Sales Floor

To closely engage with the pirate store, I began working at three stores in Hanoi. All of these stores operate openly in the public and are housed in brick and mortar locations, catering to both local and foreign customers. For each store, I worked three to four times a week in four-hour shifts, alternating between mornings, afternoons, and night/closing hours. As a person of Vietnamese descent, I was mostly able to pass as a worker. During my time at the stores, I wore clothes I brought in Vietnam and spoke very little to all customers (both local and foreign) and limiting my speech to one word answers such as "yes" or "no" in both Vietnamese and English. During my time at these stores, I carried out informal interviews with the owners and workers, observed and participated in daily duties, and observed the consuming habits of customers who entered the store.

Although these stores were operated by different people, my work experiences and observations at these sites were surprisingly very similar to each other. My main job when there were no customers was to prepare the DVDs for sale: fold a DVD cover, place a disc into a disc sleeve, put everything into a plastic sleeve, seal the entire package, and shelve it. For discs with newly released films, we would test them on a TV to look at its audio-visual qualities and available subtitles in preparation for questions asked by customers. Similar to the discs we packaged, this job was full of repetition. On average, every worker packaged a minimum of a hundred discs per shift, though the exact amount would vary based on the time of the day and the number of customers. If I did finish a batch or wanted to take a break from that task, I helped tidy up the stores (sweeping, dusting, etc.) or organize the discs on the shelves. In some cases (like rainy days – motorbike is the main mode of transportation) these were the only things we did and the only data I collected. Other duties where I only observed involved the selecting of films from a supplier as mentioned above, taking inventory of the store to see what films or television box sets needed to be restocked, and basic cash duties.

The more interesting aspect of my job was in sales. At these stores, I was informally trained by several workers. Some had been working full-time at these stores for years, while others were university students who worked part-time. By interacting with many English-speaking tourists and having access to a large media library (they can borrow films for free), many workers had very good English skills without any formal training. During the first week of my employment, the workers gave me a very quick run through of what duties needed to be done during the sales process. This included quickly locating specific title requests, plugging the new releases to customers, answering specific questions (which will be elaborated below), providing prices for products, and testing out media on a DVD player and TV located at the front of the store.

Although they greatly ranged in size, all the stores would place new releases toward the front of the store. As time passed, these older "new releases" would be incorporated toward the back of the store. The older section would be organized based on various genre and star categories, such as war, documentary, French, Brad Pitt, Anne Hathaway, and Quentin Tarantino. These sections were created by the workers based on their interactions with customers in the store. When a significant number of requests for a genre or star/director occurs, the workers would create a space on the shelf dedicated to this category, which would be denoted with label (black marker on a piece of masking tape). In many ways becoming an informal archive, these categories show the history of popular culture in Hanoi and illustrate how audiences in Vietnam frame and request media. In my sales experiences, the sections on war, European cinema, and documentary were aimed more toward foreigners and tourists and generally these films did not have Vietnamese subtitles. The organization of mainstream Hollywood films, however, appeared to be based on the labels that suited the needs of the workers and the Vietnamese customers; they tended to focus primarily on the stars in the films rather than any genre considerations.

Due to the informal nature of the workplace, most workers were able to create their own filing and categorization system and adapt it to make it more efficient for them as they worked. This informal environment also allowed a lot of open communication between workers to locate films. In many cases, the systems were not exact and the workers only knew the general location of the film, but with years of practice, the act of flipping through discs quickly and talking with each other provided an illusion of speed. Moreover, many of the workers were cinephiles; they constantly consumed films both at home and work, which gave them a vast knowledge of actors, directors, and global film history. While those on the outside (including myself) may never fully understand their seemingly random organization, by combining their knowledge of films and the underworkings of the pirate distribution system with their own created organization system, these workers knew their stores and products well. This, in turn, allowed them to locate films and answer questions quickly as a team.

The new release section, on the other hand, did not have any concrete organization, with the main category simply being just "new." Considering the new releases were at the entrance of the store, this was the area where most Vietnamese customers went to first. This is also where the workers and store owner wanted the customers to be. First, the films in the new release section had the most copies that needed to be sold. In the older sections, the stores generally had about 5 or fewer copies of a specific film, but in the new releases, each film had about 40 or more copies with Vietnamese subtitles. Secondly, the new releases, and DVD5s in general, were the most profitable product with an 87.5% markup, compared to only a 39% markup for DVD9s. It can be seen then that the stores' business and physical structure encourage new releases as the primary media product most available for sale and circulation. Store owners were mostly interested in customers buying new releases, and so many customers were directed toward this section.

Selling new releases to Vietnamese people was easy as there were two main questions: "What is new?" (*gi moi?*), which as discussed before, referred to any media that had just arrived at the store (but not necessarily new in its global existence), and "Is it pretty yet?" (*dep chua*), referring to the visual and audio fidelity of the media product. For the question "What is new?" I would just point at and tap all of the "new" films. After I had highlighted the new films, many customers would quickly glace at the covers and have verbal reactions based on the pictures of Hollywood stars, such as a Vietnamese male stating, "Oh, his films are good, they fight a lot" when referring to a Jason Stratham film or a Vietnamese woman commenting, "She's a good actress" when picking up a Kiera Knightly film. While many foreigners noted the often hilarious grammatical mistakes of the DVD covers in the store, my observations indicate that not many Vietnamese customers noticed or seemed to overtly care that the cover contained misspellings or that the production credits of *127 Hours* (2010) was on the DVD cover of *Rio* (2011). In this context, these errors have less resonance because instead of reading the language on the covers, I found the most common action of Vietnamese customers would be to intensely read the images.[12] Picking up the plastic bag containing the disc, they would quickly flip the DVDs to look at the back of the cover, focusing mainly on pictures because many could not fully read and understand the English texts (and its errors) on the DVD covers. Nonetheless, many did seem to fully understand the standard Hollywood genres being presented and their associations with Hollywood stars and I rarely was asked the question "What is the film about?"

A simple glance at a DVD cover (similar to what many people around the globe do) easily shows why genre and Hollywood stars have become a major factor in the selection process. In the DVD cover of *Battle: Los Angeles* (2011), the visuals succinctly establish the film as a sci-fi military action film. Even within this very specific subgenre, the cover accomplishes this task by reducing the genre into its most basic iconography. In the case of *Battle: Los Angeles*, these images include: military personnel, military equipment and weapons, explosions, spaceships, and projectiles from space. It should be no surprise that Hollywood stars also play a dominate role in DVD cover images (also indicated by the organizational system heavily based on actors).

From my experiences of selling *Love and Other Drugs* (2010), many Vietnamese customers (mainly female) recognized Anne Hathaway. Occasionally, this recognition was expressed directly with her name; however, the majority of Anne Hathaway references occurred indirectly by referencing her past works, including *The Princess Diaries* (2001) and *The Devil Wears Prada* (2006). Another example is Ryan Gosling, whose presence on the DVD cover of *Blue Valentine* (2010) invoked many romantic memories from *The Notebook* (2004) for several female Vietnamese customers. As this implies, the pirate DVD covers (and the eventual consumption of the text) begins the process of associating film actors and genres. In the particular example of Anne Hathaway, there is a common thread of films dealing with themes of romance and love, as well as hints of female-oriented narratives. What is most interesting about these reactions to movie stars and their previous roles is that piracy most likely performed some function in creating and encouraging these language systems based on celebrities, their public personas, and genres they are associated with. Even with the variability of media experiences in Hanoi, these language systems based on Hollywood stars and genres would not be as coherent if these pirate shops were not distributing pirate texts in these specific physical formats, especially in a country with limited legal avenues to Hollywood films.

After a film is selected off the shelf, the next question in every store would be if the film's image is "*dep chua,*" which literally translates to "Is it pretty yet?" Here, customers are asking if the visual image of the film is "pretty" or clear; in other words, "What is the visual quality of the film?" Of course, this refers to the three phases of quality that most films go through, with first editions labeled as not pretty, final editions as pretty, and screeners somewhere in between. This question indicates a couple of points. First, the causal and widespread use of "*dep chua*" show how piracy has incorporated itself so much into the everyday Vietnamese life that an almost slang-like phrase to refer to a film's audio-visual qualities has developed. Second, it shows customers are at least somewhat aware of piracy's limitations that not all films come directly to the shelf in perfect quality. In fact, the phrase's frequent use illustrates that the Vietnamese to some extent are always expecting some form of breakdown or error in their media. Due to this expectation of errors, workers were very honest in answering the question of whether a film was visually good because there was no reason to lie since it is common knowledge that films come into the store in a wide range of fidelity and this was not necessarily the fault of the store. In this case, being honest and straightforward about a film's quality produced more trust between the pirate stores and their customers, resulting in repeat customers.

The frequent presence of errors also required businesses to have a very open return policy with free exchanges (another reason why lying about quality is a pointless action). Sometimes customers would receive flawed discs where a film's ending was missing or that was scratched and unplayable. But even though people would return for a free exchange, they were never mad at receiving a bad quality disc and in many ways, it was a very relaxed and nonchalant exchange/refund experience. Similar to many people in developing nations, Vietnamese people seem to be more accustomed to the failure and decay of technology and infrastructures; as Larkin (2008) and Sundaram (2010) have noted in different contexts, the majority of the world's experiences with technology and time are filled with breakdowns and interruptions, and not the clarity and speed of the "real-time" information era. The reality is that roads are filled with potholes, buildings crack and erode constantly, and power is lost around the city indiscriminately. Events like these happen in greater intensities and in much more visible ways that Vietnamese people have built up a large tolerance to these failures, which carries over to experiences with media.

In fact, the only times I saw customers "mad" were when they were complaining about how long a film was taking to arrive at the store (or become "pretty") or the lack of new films, often expressed with disappointed sighs, tsks, and in a few cases, loud grumbling. There were also several times when people got angry when we did not have films that were not even released in the United States yet, like *Captain America: The First Avenger* (2011), as the perceived wait signaled another sign of being left behind. The lack of reaction to the technological failures in relation to the anger expressed over the lack of films highlights the importance of time and the speed of the "new" in contemporary Vietnamese society. It seemed that the potential to experience newness always trumped the possible failures that come with piracy.

The demographic that clearly illustrates this is those who purchased first-edition films. These customers – mainly young men – would usually have an encounter with the film before they enter the store in forms such as billboards, Internet trailers, television commercials, etc. In other words, they have already experienced and brought into the hype of Hollywood advertisements and are generally specific about what they desire. Considering the unpredictability of a pirate film's progression through the three phases of quality, these customers would purchase a film because they are unable to wait for a final edition (or even a screener copy) and willing to encounter error in order to access the newness of media. Although their experiences can be lackluster (this will be discussed in the next section), they all seem to obtain some form of pleasure by being one of the first people in Hanoi to see the film, even in a blurry form. Watching a first-edition film also resolves some of the questions they had about the film's characters and plots, at least enough until they are able to purchase a final-edition copy (which many did).

Newness also overpowered the film's aesthetics. When selecting a film, there never seemed to be much consideration of what the film was about or any contemplation about a text's artistic traits. I had many occasions when I pointed to films like *Meteor Storm* (2010), a made-for-cable movie on the SyFy channel in the US, and they were usually taken just by the fact that they were new to the store. This example seems to suggest that "taste" and "pleasure" in this context emphasize speed and time over the actual aesthetic properties of a media text and this is partly due how the store organized these films. Usually while blockbuster films are being presented on the big screen in the multiplex, "straight-to-DVD" films pass over this stage, appearing immediately in store shelves and discount bins. In the United States, distribution clearly separates these two types of films. In the pirate store, however, there is no physical separation as Hollywood blockbusters appear next to films like *Meteor Storm* – in this case, *all* films are straight-to-DVD. While lacking major Hollywood celebrities, these B-films do not carry the stigma of coming from a discount bin, but share the same qualities of speed and newness found in many Hollywood films. This emphasis of speed and newness is perhaps created by the pirated films themselves.

Discussing the concept of piracy and time in India, Liang and Sundaram argued:

> The social life of piracy occurs at this intersection of anticipation – now often measured in days or weeks – and aspiration to belong to the modern, to inhabit the space of global time represented by and through the movies, where things are not perpetually breaking down or delayed. (2011, 351)

While the quality or breaking down of a media text may be a deemphasized component in customer satisfaction in Hanoi, this creates a focus on the aspect of the "delayed" as an obstacle to both the fantasy world of films and the literal technological future of reality. In this sense, the piracy shop becomes one large waiting room for media – and to an extent, cultural modernity – and this room is often filled with impatient customers.

While time is an important component of the "waiting room," the material and spatial dimensions of the room are also critical in understanding wider discourses of society. Studying the layouts of actual waiting rooms, Anna McCarthy's *Ambient Television* showed how rooms that were the "unmarked universality of everyday experience" were actually imbued with site-specific politics and social discourses (2001, 198). In her work, she drew on the geographical concept of "scale," which primary "addresses the differences that range from global to local" (ibid., 10). According to McCarthy then, "scale is thus an inherently political concept... [as] determinations of what counts as 'local' are imbued with power" (ibid., 10). Furthering her point, McCarthy cited Neil Smith, who stated geographical scale "defines the boundaries and bonds the identities around which control is exerted and contested" (1992, 62). Using the state of homelessness to illustrate the politics of scale, Smith stated that homeless people are powerless because they are only limited to their local environment (the street) and unable to access further up the chain of power to the institutional level. For them to move up in society would require classed aspects such as money, home ownership, and employment, which, of course, are out of reach for homeless people.

The concepts of scale and its relationship to power and politics can certainly be applied in the context of the piracy shop. Considering the piracy DVD shop has media from around the globe (and labeled sections like French, German, Japanese and Korean), we can see the shop as a scaled model of world, with the media products as a representation of global cultures and power; thus, Hollywood films dominate the store, while Vietnamese cinema is hidden in the margins under the products of the West.[13] What is important here is the issue of *language* (usually in the form of subtitles) because language controls a major boundary between the local and global and the ability to access global cultural capital. At all of the stores in Hanoi, the majority of films with Vietnamese subtitles were limited to the front of the store in the form of new releases, forming the "local" area of the shop. This could be seen as a positive from the point of view of a Vietnamese person, as the "local" included the newest and biggest blockbuster films and all the cultural capital these films carry. However, for many Vietnamese people, they are confined only to the "local" space of the new releases and unable to completely navigate and access the other "global" sections of media, which make up a considerable percentage of the available media for sale. Even though Vietnamese customers are able to access the Vietnamese films in the store that many foreigners cannot, this section was one of the smallest in the store and, as mentioned before, the least desired among Vietnamese people (in fact, these films were generally requested by foreigners and tourists, ironically making this section aim more toward global audiences).

Although Vietnamese customers can enjoy an updated selection of contemporary films, finding a specific film with Vietnamese subtitles becomes more difficult as the film leaves the "new" category. As previously discussed, accessible forms of global film and media exists mainly in the present for non-English speaking customers – as time passes, accessible media for Vietnamese customers becomes increasingly fragmented, delayed, or lost as it is no longer profitable to produce and stock older film titles with Vietnamese subtitles that are less in demand. The Vietnamese customers who wanted older films took greater risks as it was based on luck if the store had a version with Vietnamese subtitles. There were multiple instances where customers were told the store did not have any subtitled copies and perhaps a copy would show up in the next shipment, leaving them in a state of limbo. In some sections, like documentary or European cinema, the odds were very small if a subtitled version even existed to begin with, and in terms of television, it was even less likely as almost all of the television selection were Chinese-produced DVD9s that had no Vietnamese subtitles.

Even though this essay's framework has placed the piracy shop as a site of access, I want to stress the shop is not a neutral conduit of media and, like any form of distribution, it imposes particular conditions and ultimately is an unequal site of access and power distribution. If we visualize the boundaries and space in which Vietnamese customers are able to move within (mainly the new release section) and connect that spatial area of accessible media with politics and power, it can be seen that Vietnamese customers who only speak Vietnamese are limited in their cultural and economic power as they are unable to fully escape the space of "local" (Vietnamese-subtitled) media. Likewise, they are also unable to completely link up on the "global" level of (unsubtitled) media. I do not wish, however, to create a strict binary as the potential for access and negotiation is present and this situation is superior to having no media at all. Still, the full experience of consuming and comprehending global media is a restricted and incomplete form of access for many in the pirate store.

Here, as mentioned above, language becomes a key component of understanding global media. Language is certainly a classed commodity in this context as the Vietnamese people who spoke English were usually better educated (often studying abroad) and wealthier than most Vietnamese who did not have a firm grasp of the English language. A manifestation of this class division between Vietnamese people appeared physically in the store, as English-speaking Vietnamese (as well as most foreigners) were able to access and navigate throughout the store without the obstacles of language. From my field notes:

> A Vietnamese woman, in her mid-30s, drove up in a sliver Mercedes-Benz and entered the store. Speaking Vietnamese, she requested *Jaws* (1975). After I located it (with the help of Anh Hai), I gave her a Chinese-produced DVD9 and told her it did not have Vietnamese. She shrugged off my comment and said, "No problem" in Vietnamese. She eventually brought *Jaws 2* (1978) and *Jaws 3* (1983) (both without Vietnamese subtitles) and a few DVD9 new releases, which also do not have subtitles.

Her position in the upper-class and the power that arises from it is easily transferred into the store as she was able to browse and access texts from around the globe effortlessly and without delay, calmly shrugging off my comment about language.

This economic difference also extends to the physical products of piracy. With the Vietnamese-produced DVD covers, there may be some success in the erasure of its past in the basic visuals, but this attempt to conceal its pirate origins is ultimately thwarted at the level of the disc in both visual and physical terms. The Vietnamese DVDs are pressed with a monochromatic and faded image, often of the same image of the DVD. Although the pressing is of higher quality than "home-made" burned DVDs, a quick inspection will reveal thin plastic layers being held together by irregular layers of adhesive that has usually spilt over the edges of the DVD. Compared to the colorful and detailed covers, the actual discs fall short in comparison. Still, while the covers are visually similar to the "official" covers, the physicality of the covers subverts any attempt to completely expunge its history as a pirated text as this flimsy paper is eventually stuffed into an equally flimsy plastic bag. The cover is then prone to tears, folding, and wrinkling due to its malleability and the lack of any protection.

This lower-quality materiality is further noticeable when the Vietnamese-produced products are compared to Chinese-produced products. These Chinese-produced covers are equally as ripe with errors and the Chinese characters obviously give away their origins. From a material standpoint, however, the Chinese versions seem much more professionally constructed with sleek DVD covers and discs when compared to the Vietnamese pirate versions. The Chinese covers for the DVD5s are made of durable cardboard paper which are much sturdier than the flimsy paper covers of the Vietnamese-produced covers. For the DVD9s, the materials are of even better quality, with covers that could be opened with even more images on the inside of the cover. Additionally, instead of a thin, clear plastic sleeve, the DVD9s are placed in a durable, padded, and colored plastic sleeve. At the level of the discs, the Chinese versions are extremely precise in their details and honestly could "pass" under an undiscerning eye as an official DVD – in some cases, these discs are complete with warnings about copyright infringement!

Pirated television texts are also very similar in this regard of physical difference, but perhaps in more stark terms. First, the television selection with Vietnamese subtitles is extremely small – the only "new" program during the summer of 2011 with subtitles was *Nikita* (2010-2013), which most likely only existed due to the presence of the lead actress, Maggie Q, who is part Vietnamese.[14] Within this very limited selection, the Vietnamese-produced discs are packaged in a similar manner to the films, except with multiple discs shoved in one plastic sleeve. Chinese-produced discs, however, are packaged in very visually and physically nice box sets made up of hard cardboard and fabric lining. When set next to each other in the store, there is clearly one version that is physically superior to the other.

I do not wish to argue that the difference of thickness of a plastic sleeve or cardboard is necessarily a major factor in people's media consumption, but the difference of materiality does play at least some minor role in how Vietnamese people give value to cultural objects. For instance, some Vietnamese customers *do* notice this material difference. From my field notes:

A male Vietnamese customer in his 30s comes into the store and tests a Vietnamese DVD5 version of *Rio*. He hands me the film and I remove it from the plastic bag and test it out on the TV. It is a "perfect" version and he is fine with it. As I take out the DVD from the player, he asks if he could take the cover of a Chinese-produced DVD5 of the same film. I look over at Anh Hai and point to him (Anh Hai). The customer re-shouts his question and Anh Hai just nods. So I swap the discs and put the Vietnamese DVD5 in the thicker, Chinese cover of *Rio*. I assumed this was because of the quality difference between the covers, but for a second opinion, I asked Anh Hai why he thought the customer wanted to do that and he replies, "Because it looks better."

Here, the visuals of the DVD covers basically look the same. But this action of swapping covers seems to suggest that there is some valuing of the physical properties of media materials. Thus, the look and feel of media texts are permeated with dimensions of class and cultural capital. Drawing on the notion of local and global space again, in this example a customer is trying to link up with the more global selection, but he is unable to do so because of language barriers. However, he negotiates and attempts to fulfill this action of upward mobility by imitating the "global" disc's physical appearance as much as possible, even if the cover has no effect on the actual media text.

Exchanging media packaging is virtually impossible within the realm of television programs because of the extremely limited availability of TV programs with Vietnamese subtitles and the fact that the box sets came presealed from China. More directly related toward notions of class, though, was the issue that the physical packaging restricted who could buy the program based on financial circumstances, adding another layer on top of the obstacle of language. These box sets often contained several seasons and considering the store charged by the disc, the box sets were usually out of the price range of many Vietnamese people and aimed more toward tourists. From my field notes:

> Today a Vietnamese woman in her 20s wanted to buy a box set of *The X-Files*, which had 9 seasons and 20 discs, coming out to about US$25. When I told her the price, she asked "Why so much?" I shrugged. She then asked if she could get a discount and I pointed to Anh Hai. She walked over and asked for a discount. He said no. She said "please" a few times, but Anh Hai seemed to just ignore her and say no. She asked if she could buy just one season but he told her it doesn't work that way. She left without buying anything.

As this example and section has illustrated, the distributive mechanisms and physical aspects of the store and piracy play a key role in helping to establish (and limit) the film experience in Hanoi. But as customers leave the store with pirated media, piracy continues to influence the film experience as the images of the discs appear onscreen.

The Pirate Film Experience: The Aesthetics of Piracy

Within the selection of Vietnamese-subtitled films and television programs available for Vietnamese customers, this method of distribution delivers a wide and complex variety of cinematic experiences at the textual level. While there have been many theorists that have explored the sensorial and identity-forming experiences of cinema (see Sobchack 1992 and Hansen 2000), these works has always assumed the technologies of film were at their optimal levels. However, as Brian Larkin has astutely pointed out:

> What is less discussed is how technology influences through its failure as much as its success. The inability of technologies to perform the functions they were assigned must be subject to the same critical scrutiny as their achievements. Breakdown and failure are, of course, inherent in all technologies, but in societies... where collapse is a common state of technological existence, they take on a far greater material and political presence. (2008, 219)

As this essay has shown, though piracy is in many ways very inventive and more efficient than legal business infrastructures, it is also inconsistent and prone to errors and failures: discs may have scratches; DVD covers may have misspellings; and/or the subtitles may lag or be translated incorrectly. With the shift to VCDs and DVDs, transferring films without degrading images is much easier than it was with analog technologies. However, there are still imperfect pirate DVD copies, usually within the first week of a film's official release, and these first-edition discs usually consisted of movies that have been filmed in cinemas. While not popular in terms of overall sales number, the stores would usually sell all of the first-edition discs within the first week of it being available and sometimes the stores would order additional copies. Replacing the wait that most Vietnamese hated was the pirate aesthetics that pervaded these first-edition films in which these customers would have to traverse.

In the realm of the pirate text, narrative gaps and audio-visual static were common. For instance, a first edition of *Transformers: Dark of the Moon* (2011) omits the introduction sequence of the film. After the credits and title are shown, the film smoothly skips 12 minutes into the film (i.e., the skip occurs at a natural transition point and not mid-scene). This introductory section has some critical moments that connect this film to the previous installments of the *Transformers* film franchise and also sets up key narratives and plot points for the first half of the film. While this large narrative gap does not make the film become entirely unreadable, there are some possible areas of confusion because of this loss of information and compounding this confusion is that the narrative skip is not abrupt or overtly noticeable, especially for a first-time viewer. This structuring of sequences is not a conscious action of creativity by an editor to construct a storyline or the film as a work of avant-garde editing, but is determined by technological errors and failures in the pirate distribution process. In other words, the pirate distribution system impacted and altered the narrative of *Transformers: Dark of the Moon* and how some Vietnamese audiences consumed the film.

Additionally, these pirate aesthetics in first-edition films go beyond affecting just narrative comprehension, as they also influence the larger sensorial experience of watching films. Watching *Transformers: Dark of the Moon* in a movie theater can be an overwhelming experience. Throughout the film, Michael Bay uses slow motion shots to emphasize the mechanical morphing of the Transformers and the clash of metal and robots in large action sequences revolving around destruction. These scenes are visually spectacular and busy in their details, especially in the third installment as computer graphics particular to *Transformers* have had time to develop over three films.

Instead of the experience of visual and audio spectacle and excess, the viewers of these first-edition films are presented with underwhelming images of coarse pixels and audio static. The piracy experience is quite the opposite of an "authentic" movie experience: bodies move toward the screen in order to discern hazy details; eyes squint during action sequences to make out where one body ends and another starts; heads turn to the speaker to search for sound effects. Previously clear images of a Transformer eviscerating a building are now a massive blob of gray fuzz, while sound is roughly ejected from speakers. The countless hours spent designing and rendering these special effects (as well as the millions of dollars) were wasted on Vietnamese audiences as this specific *Transformers* experience is one filled with either disappointment or disregard. Here, the pirate store and its products create a film experience that is fragmented, disjointed, and imprecise, both in visual and narrative terms.

The quality of images and sound, however, go beyond influencing just the sensorial experience of film as these sounds and images (or lack thereof) are linked to formations of identities. Speaking about negative representations of minority groups on screens, Pratibha Parmar has stated that:

> Images play a crucial role in defining and controlling the political and social power to which both individuals and marginalized groups have access. The deeply ideological nature of imagery determines not only how other people think about us but how we think about ourselves. (Cited in hooks 1992, 5)

While Parmar is speaking in a different contexts, I feel her argument of how imagery affects how people see others and themselves can be applied to the images of the pirated text and their level of quality; instead of just degrading representations in Hollywood films, pirate texts also contain *degraded* images, which can be seen as a reflection of viewers' own identities and economic statuses in a developing nation such as Vietnam.

The absence of the "First World" Hollywood experience is not difficult to notice during a viewing of a first-edition film because the pirate aesthetics are constant indicators of the film's existence as an illegal and informal product, which in turn reinforces the spectator's own situation. While Hollywood films like *Transformers* are able to conceal the circumstances of their production, first-edition pirate films are self-reflexive in that they bring attention to their status as a constructed media product through their aesthetics. Most first-edition films began with clicks and static caused by the setting up of the camera in the movie theater, with the hand of the "cameraman" clearly seen within the frame as he adjusts the camera's framing of the screen that is playing the film that he is filming. The action of filming a film within a movie theater is somewhat disorienting because the camera(s)'s exact subject and subjectivity is thrown into doubt and confusion – this is not a direct experience, but is instead a mediated event with film. This is not to argue, however, that spectators of these first-edition films fully mistake the pirate image for the "real" film's image; rather, because the pirate camera generates an imperfect replication of a Hollywood experience (or its imagined perceptions), the pirated text frequently brings attention to its own means of production. Thus from the start of a first-edition film, the presence of confusion allows audiences to recognize and confirm that this experience is not a Hollywood film, but a *film* of a Hollywood film. There is never any doubt at the textual level that this disc is not an official copy, but a cheap knockoff that the viewers have to buy because of their current economic situation.

As this illustrates, the redundancy of pirate filming – such as filming a film – creates multiple layers of subjectivity and space. Besides confusion, these layers also produce a sense of emotional detachment and textual distance, which prevent viewers from fully immersing themselves into the fantasy world of the film. Beyond the degraded images of the film, many first-editions films increase this distance by literally inserting another world between the audience and the film, that of the movie theater in which the illegal filming is taking place. This insertion of another space forms a sense of double Othering – not only are the images of the original film presenting a space that Vietnamese audiences can rarely inhabit (the story world of the film), but the addition of the movie theater produces another space that is out of reach for many Vietnamese people. While parts of the fantasy world of the film could be easily dismissed or downplayed, the space of the movie theater has a more significant impact because it is not a fictional construct. Watching and hearing people in the movie theater – either an audience member walking to a seat after the film has started or the audience laughing and talking over the film's dialogue – puts the spectator of the pirate film physically, economically, and culturally on the outside in a real and concrete world.

These layers can also exist in other forms, such as subtitles and voiceovers that are added after the pirate "filming" process. In the case of one version of *X-Men: First Class* (2011), the screen has Russian subtitles, English subtitles, Vietnamese subtitles, and the space of the movie theater in which it was filmed, pushing the viewer farther away from the original and official image (with the option of a mono-dubbed Vietnamese narrator providing an additional layer). Here, the Russian subtitles are technically part of the real image (the film was recorded in a Russian movie theater), but the English subtitles are digitally added after the recording process and cannot be removed from the screen, while the Vietnamese subtitles and voice-over can be turned on or off. These layers act as barriers that separate the viewer from the image, and in order to reach the image to consume the film, viewers must traverse the complex terrain that pirate aesthetics create.

In many cases, by the time viewers reach the image, the sensorial experience of watching a Hollywood film (and its resulting cultural capital) has largely eroded and has turned into a secondhand experience. In this instance, the original film has already been "used" in a previous time and space, making this film-within-a-film a media hand-me-down that has been passed down to a younger and less-developed nation. Thus, piracy produces a paradox as it allows the Vietnamese people to be modern and participate in a global cultural event, but it does this while reaffirming their lower status and position in the global hierarchy. Piracy, in the case of the first-edition film, constantly reminds spectators through abrupt jump-cuts and blurred images that access to a true Hollywood film experience is still limited.

Conclusion

During my last week in Hanoi, I began to question owners over what their future plans were for their stores. One owner complained how sales have been slowly falling and she does not see a bright future for her business. She is not sure of the exact reason of this decline, but she thinks it is probably due to people starting to download films from the Internet. She tells me that after the store sells most of its products, she is eventually going to invest in a bar and music club because that appears to be a more stable type of business. When I ask her about the legal future of the pirate store and if it will last much longer, she just shrugs and says she does not worry about that and that the police only want money. For her, leaving the piracy business is not about legality or ethics, it is purely business. I believe she sees the digital shift in the future and that shift is what motives her to move toward to a more "legitimate" business, not a desire to escape the "illegal" lifestyle.

Another owner seems less aware of the approaching digital tide of piracy, but he appears calm about the future of his business and projects several more years. His actions outside the store, however, suggest he also does not see a future in physical piracy, at least not in his family business. His children, both in their lower teens, are fluent in English, and he has told me he hopes they get "high-level" jobs either in Vietnam or "nice" Southeast Asian countries like Singapore when they eventually graduate from college. For him, the pirate shop is a means to support his children's education and it seems he would consider his highly educated children taking over the "family business" as a step backward. This does not necessarily mean he considers his own actions as illegitimate, but the pirate store's overall trajectory is not respectable as a career in technology or international business.

Currently, these stores are in a state of limbo just like physical media piracy in general, at both at the level of Vietnam and the global economy. As noted above, the shift from physical media to digital media will occur and will eventually affect all methods of distribution (legal and illegal). From the viewpoint of legal enforcement, there is increasing attention on physical media piracy as more laws are being passed and raids increase in Vietnam (National Assembly of the Socialist Republic of Vietnam 2006/2010, article 28; IIPA 2012, 278-279). In other words, physical piracy is being squeezed from several directions.

Still, piracy in general will remain important and evolve and adapt much like the owners of the stores. While the current physical materials of media may become rarer as time moves on or shift to different modes of physical storage and distribution (e.g., microchips, external hard drives, etc.), the pirate products and infrastructures created by these pirate networks will modify themselves for the future. Because they are so malleable, these infrastructures do not have to stay within the pirate realm; as Larkin (2008) and Lobato (2012) have noted, pirate infrastructures in Nigeria now distribute *legal* copies of films. Besides thinking about the potential for the future, these pirate pathways are interesting because they are layers of history and unearthing these pathways can reveal much about how materials and cultures have moved in the past and present. In the context of Vietnam, Hollywood stars, narratives, and cinematic styles traveling through pirate networks have helped shape film and media culture in Hanoi. In the end though, like the fuzzy image on the screen, piracy is an ambivalent object; it is a source of freedom and limitations, as well as an intricate system of conflicting desires and hopes that both allows and denies access to global information.

Notes

1. See Albanese 2007; Chaudhry and Zimmerman 2010; and Phillips 2005. In the realm of public policy there are numerous reports released by several organizations, such as the International Intellectual Property Alliance which releases annually the Special 301 Report on copyright protection and enforcement.
2. All names and store names have been changed.
3. I am following the history of the Vietnam's cinema history in relation to the Socialist Republic of Viet Nam (the current government). Before the fall of Saigon, South Vietnam did have a separate film industry.
4. The Cinematography Law has since been amended twice since 2006. In 2010, the foreign film percentage allowance was raised to 80% (Viet Nam News 2010).
5. Analyzing the 2011 release schedules of MegaStar Theaters and Galaxy Theaters (two major multiplex chains in Vietnam), there were about 60 foreign titles. While the majority of the films were from Hollywood (about 40), the number of foreign titles also included films from other countries, such as China, South Korea, and India (Bollywood). In 2010, Hollywood studios released 141 films (Block 2011).
6. These surveys were conducted in major cities in Vietnam, where most of the wealth and income are located. If rural areas were included, the percentages would mostly likely be much higher.
7. This paper will use the exchange rate of 20,000 Vietnamese dong for 1 US dollar, which was roughly the rate during 2010-2011, although it fluctuates often. Due to ineffective tax collection system and massive informal cash flows, it is difficult to get a precise number for the average income, though most estimates of monthly income are around the US$60 to US$80 range in urban areas.
8. Usually the only "tax" encountered are payoffs for local police.
9. For works on specifically on Chinese piracy, see Wang 2003 and Pang 2005.
10. A burned disc and a pressed disc can be distinguished by looking at the data side of a disc: burned discs are colored (with some having colored rings) while pressed discs are silver.

11.   The subject of "fansubbing" is a growing interest of study within media studies, mostly in the area of fans subtitling anime. For a starting point, see Lee 2011.

12.   Also, as mentioned before, while these covers are selected by Vietnamese pirate producers, they had a limited role in actually creating these images.

13.   In this case, Vietnamese films are literally hidden under the products of the West as there were usually box sets of television shows on top of the "Vietnamese section."

14.   Also available with Vietnamese subtitles (though in fragmented seasons) were *Lost* (2004-2010), *Prison Break* (2005-2009), and *24* (2001-2010). Although not shown in China, these shows were very popular with Chinese audiences and fansubbing groups, which may have prompted Vietnamese pirates and fansubbers to follow China's lead.

Bibliography

Albanese, Jay S., ed. 2007. *Combating Piracy: Intellectual Property Theft and Fraud.* New Brunswick, NJ: Transaction Publishers.

Block, Alex Ben. 2011. "Global Box Office Soared to Record High of $31.8 Billion in 2010." *Hollywood Reporter,* 23 February. http://www.hollywoodreporter.com/news/global-box-office-soars-record-160740.

Chaudhry, Peggy, and Alan Zimmerman. 2010. *The Economics of Counterfeit Trade: Governments, Consumers, Pirates, and Intellectual Property Rights.* Berlin: Springer.

Frater, Patrick. 2011. "CGV Makes Mega Play in Vietnam." *Film Business Asia,* 8 July. http://www.filmbiz.asia/news/cgv-makes-mega-play-in-vietnam.

Gray, Jonathan. 2011. "Mobility through Piracy, or How Steven Seagal Got to Malawi." *Popular Communication* 9.2: 99-113.

Hansen, Miriam Bratu. 2000. "The Mass Production of the Senses: Classical Cinema as Vernacular Modernism." In C. Gledhill and L. Williams, eds., *Reinventing Film Studies.* New York: Oxford University Press, 332-350.

Hoang, Tran Doan. 2007. "Today's Public Film Demand." In V. D. Pham, ed., *Vietnamese Cinematography: A Research Journey.* Hanoi, Vietnam: The Gioi Publishers, 262-270.

hooks, bell. 1992. *Black Looks: Race and Representation.* Boston, MA: South End Press.

IIPA. 2012. *2012 Special 301 Report: Vietnam.* Washington, DC: International Intellectual Property Alliance.

Karaganis, Joe, ed. 2011. *Media Piracy in Emerging Economies.* New York: Social Science Research Council.

Larkin, Brian. 2008. *Signal and Noise: Media, Infrastructure, and Urban Culture in Nigeria.* Durham, NC: Duke University Press.

Lee, Hye-Kyung. 2011. "Participatory Media Fandom: A Case Study of Anime Fansubbing." *Media, Culture, and Society* 33.8: 1131-1147.

Lessig, Lawrence. 2004. *Free Culture: How Big Media Uses Technology and the Law to Lock Down Culture and Control Creativity.* New York: Penguin Press.

Lessig, Lawrence. 2008. *Remix: Making Art and Commerce Thrive in the Hybrid Economy.* New York: Penguin Press.

Liang, Lawrence 2005. "Porous Legalities and Avenues of Participation," *Sarai Reader 5*: Bare Acts, 6-15.

Liang, Lawrence, and R. Sundaram. 2011. "India." In Joe Karaganis, ed., *Media Piracy in Emerging Economies*. New York: Social Science Research Council, 339-398.

Lobato, Ramon. 2007. "Subcinema: Theorizing Marginal Film Distribution." *Limina* 13: 113-120.

Lobato, Ramon. 2012. *Shadow Economies of Cinema: Mapping Informal Film Distribution*. London: British Film Institute.

Marr, David. 2003. "A Passion for Modernity: Intellectuals and the Media." In H. V. Luong, ed., *Postwar Vietnam: Dynamics of a Transforming Society*. Lanham, MD: Rowman and Littlefield, 257-295.

Mattelart, Tristan. 2009. "Audio-visual Piracy: Towards a Study of the Underground Networks of Cultural Globalization." *Global Media and Communication* 5.3: 308-326.

McCarthy, Anna. 2001. *Ambient Television: Visual Culture and Public Space*. Durham, NC: Duke University Press.

Monlux, Nicholas R. 2009. "Copyright Piracy on the High Seas of Vietnam: Intellectual Property Piracy in Vietnam Following WTO Accession." *AIPLA Quarterly Journal* 37.2: 135-174.

MPAA. N.d. "Copyright Information: Why We Care About Copyright." Motion Picture Association of America website. http://mpaa.org/contentprotection/copyright-info.

Ngo, Phuong Lan. 2007. *Modernity and Nationality in Vietnamese Cinema*. Edited by Aruna Vasudev and Philip Cheah, and translated by Dang Viet Vinh and Nguyen Xuan Hong. Indonesia: Galang Press.

Pang, Laikwan. 2005. "Global Modernity and Movie Piracy." Sarai Media Lab, *Contested Commons/Trespassing Publics: A Public Record*, Delhi: Sarai Media Lab, 2006, 40-50,

Pulver, Andrew. 2012. "Burn after Viewing: DVD Screeners Are Part of Award Season – and Piracy." *The Guardian*, 9 February. http://www.guardian.co.uk/film/2012/feb/09/bafta-oscars-dvd-screeners-piracy.

Phillips, Tim. 2005. *Knockoff: The Deadly Trade in Counterfeit Goods: The True Story of the World's Fastest Growing Crime Wave*. Philadelphia: Kogan Page.

Reuters/Hollywood Reporter. 2008. "Spidey and Bond DVDs Headed to Vietnam." Reuters, 6 May. http://www.reuters.com/article/2008/05/07/film-vietnam-dc-idUSN0643088920080507.

Schwenkel, Christina. 2011. "Youth Culture and Fading Memories of War In Hanoi, Vietnam." In K. M. Adams and K. A. Gillogly, eds., *Everyday Life in Southeast Asia*. Bloomington: Indiana University Press, 127-136.

Smith, Neil. 1992. "Contours of a Spatialized Politics: Homeless Vehicles and the Production of Geographic Scale." *Social Text* 33: 55-81.

Sobchack, Vivian. 1992. *The Address of the Eye: A Phenomenology of Film Experience*. Princeton, NJ: Princeton University Press.

Strangelove, Michael. 2005. *The Empire of Mind: Digital Piracy and the Anti-Capitalist Movement*. Toronto: University of Toronto Press.

Sundaram, Ravi. 2010. *Pirate Modernity: Delhi's Media Urbanism*. New York: Routledge.

Tuong, Vi. 2010. "Phát hành DVD phim của Disney tại Việt Nam." *Saigon Times*, 19 July. http://www.thesaigontimes.vn/Home/vanhoa/sinhhoatvanhoa/37799/

Viet Nam Household Living Standard Survey. 2010. *Results of the Survey on Household Living Standards 2008*. Hanoi, Vietnam: General Statistics Office.

Viet Nam News. 2010. "Gov't Regulation Supports Local Films." *Viet Nam News*, 28 June. http://vietnamnews.vnagency.com.vn/Life-Style/Film/200965/govt-regulation-supports-local-films.html.

Wang, Shujen. 2003. *Framing Piracy: Globalization and Film Distribution in Greater China*. Lanham, MD: Rowman and Littlefield.

4.   Honorability and the Pirate Ethic

Jonas Andersson Schwarz

Introduction

The term "peer-to-peer" (P2P) implies a flat topology, but despite the apparent lack of hierarchy that characterizes online "pirate" archives of digital content, certain hierarchical tendencies are found to arise in tandem with them. According to Derrida (1995), an archive is always dependent on someone – or even some*thing*[1] – upholding it. Even the fleeting "an-archives" (Ernst 2008) of the online realm are dependent on some form of orchestration, some act of denomination and place-holding. Moreover, when observing the communities arising alongside such orchestrational hubs (or "strategic sovereigns") (Andersson 2009), familiar patterns of eulogizing behavior are seen among its adherents, putting into place a mode of reverence that is actually hierarchical.

I have studied a range of different online data collections – one of them a wondrously deep, torrent-based cinephile archive of rare films whose name I have to leave out due to anonymity (see Andersson Schwarz 2015 for a further elaboration on this case study). Others include the P2P music-sharing application Soulseek and the web-based text archives Aaaaarg and Avaxhome. They vary significantly, but they all allow for sharing of intellectual property on a significant scale, without permission from the copyright industry. I will show how these online archives relate to issues of hierarchy. By doing so, I will critically engage with proponents of commons-based approaches to cultural content, such as Benkler (2002) and Medosch (2008), as I am detecting a virtuous, honorable ethos that unfolds within commons-based meritocracies. Despite not being based on traditional command-obey structures, certain strategies for coordination and administration come into play, serving a regulatory role by appeasing the users, thus simultaneously acknowledging the administrators as the rightful upholders of the archive. The existence of such an ethos contradicts simplistic dismissals of hierarchy.

Complexity

It would be hard to argue for a "pirate ethic" in the singular form – as the term "pirate" has a range of connotations and uses, many of which being unsettled and controversial. Despite this obvious demographic variety, a possible interpretation of a "pirate ethic" could be a *uniform set of values* shared by such a motley crew, akin to what Himanen (2001) or Raymond (1996) describe regarding hackers. "Black hat," "white hat," "grey hat" – hackers come in various guises, yet these authors specify some common characteristics, or shared values.

As this article addresses what could be called meshwork/heterarchy/distributed[2] forms of organization versus hierarchical/bureaucratic[3] forms of organization, a paradox arises. The epistemological problem of how to specify the generic sentiments that would be common to pirates (or hackers, for that part) is similar to the ontological problem of finding out what makes coherence possible in wildly heterogeneous, heterarchical meshwork aggregates. As Manuel DeLanda (1998, 280) writes, "ecosystems are examples of self-consistent aggregates, since they link together into complex food webs a wide variety of animals and plants, without reducing their heterogeneity." We could equally regard the Internet as an ecosystem that allows for a baffling level of heterogeneity and playful disregard of hierarchical modes of organization. "Besides centralization and decentralization of control, what defines these two types of structure is the homogeneity or heterogeneity of its composing elements" (ibid.).

Still, unifying elements do exist. A shared property of that which is exchanged online is, for example, the digital nature of the shared files. If they were not digitized, the goods would not be possible to exchange in the ways they are. In this sense, the Internet is based on a protocol logic (Galloway 2004); a totalitarian, binary order. There are other abstract protocol logics that seem to allow for a similarly paradoxical coexistence of radical heterogeneity through systemic totalitarianism: e.g., the market system (with money as its prime expressive constituent), and cellular mitosis (combined with a range of other biological life forces).

A key analytical problem is that systems are interconnected and partially overlapping. The concept of "piracy" is far larger than merely online file sharing. It would be overly grand to lay claims to describing a shared ethics in its entirety. However, if we restrict our analysis to a more system-oriented, contained sphere of exchange, some particularities might appear.

> Indeed, one must resist the temptation to make hierarchies into villains and meshworks into heroes, not only because, as I said, they are constantly turning into one another, but because in real life we find only mixtures and hybrids, and the properties of these cannot be established through theory alone but demand concrete experimentation. (DeLanda 1998, 284)

The freedom to upload copyrighted content onto a dedicated service – such as Avaxhome or the Pirate Bay – is not devoid of responsibility. I would argue that this freedom comes with an obligation to act in a way that *the intended public deems as honorable*, regarding access to the content. This notion of virtue can be applied both to the individual users and to the site administrators; the responsibility of the latter arguably being more extensive than the former. In order to make any sense, the notion of what counts as honorable behavior has to be shared by a larger community. Arguably, a measure of its relevance is how wide a variety of groups it manages to cross. The process of deeming certain behaviors as honorable relies on different modes of justification (Boltanski and Thévenot 2006) which can, in turn, comprise different publics or audiences, to which different behaviors will be differently understood and assessed in terms of responsibility. Another example of the notion of honorable behavior – or "sensible stewardship" (Andersson 2011) of a media ecology – can be connected to what has been labeled file "integrity" (Liang et al. 2005); that is, the upkeep of indexes where the files linked to are not corrupted, damaged, containing viruses, etc. Historically, this has varied wildly on different file-sharing networks. The attentive weeding-out and upholding of content on BitTorrent owes to an investment of care – arguably, in and of itself, an example of honorable behavior.

Hence, I will start with outlining different ways of envisaging such "pirate' forms of organizing media content; novel forms of orchestrating horizontal file exchange, or of indexing media artifacts in ways that combine traditional hierarchy (statistical ranking, listing according to numerical importance, etc.) with *heterarchy* (ways of relating elements to one another without a priori ranking; cf. Bauwens 2007). In my reading, heterarchy relates to maintaining archives by different principles of horizontal sharing, mutual interplay, lack of command-obey structures, and – in a more philosophical view – the ability to sustain parallel simultaneous modes of logic or different standpoints, coexisting and resulting in new categorizations and asymmetries arising in a bottom-up fashion.

Archive

Derrida (1995) points out that the word "archive" comes from the ancient Greek word *arkheion*, referring to the residence of superior magistrates (the *archons*). At the root of the word archive (*arkhē*) lies a double meaning; simultaneously "commencement" and "commandment." As De Certeau

(1984) has shown, the ability to *state the law* requires a location, a *topos* from which decree could be issued. Without stable domicile – both in the spatial sense and the linguistic – no real authority. "At the intersection of the topological and the nomological, of the place and the law, of the substrate and the authority," Derrida (1995, 10) continues, "a scene of domiciliation becomes at once visible and invisible."

> It is thus, in this domiciliation, in this house arrest, that archives take place. The dwelling, this place where they dwell permanently, marks this institutional passage from the private to the public, which does not always mean from the secret to the nonsecret. (Ibid.)

Archiving, Derrida emphasizes, always entails the power of *consignation*; assigning residence, putting into reserve, but also *con*-signing as in *gathering together signs*. He is careful to note that the distinction between secret and nonsecret is not the same as that between private and public.

Reynolds sees today's Internet-addled mediascape as a "delirium of documentation" (2011, 26) extending beyond institutions and professionals to more spontaneous amateur archive creation. He quotes Huyssen (2000) who has called the last decades of the 20th century a "memory boom" where the archival mindset is seeping out into every zone of culture and everyday life. Reynolds conjures a feverish rush to upload:

> Nothing is too trivial, too insignificant, do be discarded.... The result, visible above all on the Internet, is that the archive degenerates into the anarchive; a barely navigable disorder of data debris and memory-trash. (Ibid., 26-27)

He relates this to Derrida's term "archive fever": "In French, *mal d'archive* contains the concept of both illness and evil. For Derrida, there is something morbid and sinister at the core of the archival impulse" (Reynolds 2011, 26-27): compulsive, repetitive, and nostalgic, a desire to return to the origin, the archaic. Derrida relates this desire to what Freud has called the "death drive" (Derrida 1995, 13). The act of locating memory outside of the own, lived body (a form of *hypomnema*, Derrida argues) is to give in to the logic of repetition, which remains, according to Freud, indissociable from the death drive. The Eros of collecting is always tainted by a reminder of how archives contain the *undoing* of living memory, by imbuing memories in coded form into mnemonic devices. Thanatos reigns: Archives remind us of how they are not only in a state of constant entropy (libraries are always, ultimately razed) but also act as prostheses (we become dependent on memory devices, while at the same time these prostheses not only aid our own lived memories but act to raze them as well). Derrida points to how we are *en mal d'archive*: in *need* of archives (1995, 57) – a burning desire. At the same time, he argues, the archive is at once revolutionary and traditional:

> It keeps, it puts in reserve, it saves, but in an unnatural fashion, that is to say in making the law (*nomos*) or in making people respect the law…. It has the force of law, of a law which is the law of the house (*oikos*), of the house as place, domicile, family, lineage, or institution. (Derrida 1995, 12)

The keeper of the archive is the keeper of a realm. This is, at heart, an authoritarian role. Even in an ostensibly "flat," heterarchical realm, someone has to manage the encircling, the organizing principle of classification and making-retrievable. Even in so-called "folksonomies" – said to be typical of the present digital world (Shirky 2005) – where taxonomy is achieved not by imposing predefined categories but by voluntary collective tagging, there is, I would argue, an authoritarian role: Someone would necessarily have to designate the rules for the practice, as well as the *topos* where the practice takes place. Collective tagging relies on collective agreement, which in turn assigns both *nomos* and *topos*. The role of being the upholder of this archival function can be approached in various ways; Latour (2005, 52-55) uses the narratological term "actant," borrowed from Greimas (1966). The actant is a functional operator, which (in the event of labeling) becomes embodied as an aggregated macro-actor (Latour and Callon 1981) consisting of the veritable assemblage of actors required for this particular agreement. Note that Latour would include both human and nonhuman actors; human actors decide to assign, yet this can only be achieved by making nonhuman actors act as carriers of the assignment (importantly, these also exert various forms of resistance of their own).

Consequentially, someone always makes the original act to *assign residence* for the archive. Even if the referents of an index are scattered, temporarily fleeting and never guaranteed to be in place, the index has to reside somewhere. Whereas files on P2P networks are held by local computers acting as peers, the index which lists these files is commonly held to be more stable, centralized, hosted on web servers or the like. Torrent indexes serve the role of consigning links to material held in private residences (personal computers) but made public, through the process of "seeding" content. For unauthorized indexes of copyrighted literature, like Aaaaarg and Avaxhome, the index is similarly upheld by being placed on web servers, where links are found which point to material located elsewhere: In the case of these latter two services, the links most often lead to other web-based, so-called cyberlockers (e.g., Mediafire, Rapidshare, or Megaupload). In Andersson (2012b), I take a cue from Benkler (2006: 93) by comparing the superabundant pools/reservoirs of content engendered by cyberlockers to blood donation (Titmuss 1971).

System

The sites and networks investigated for this article – the above-mentioned ones, but also Kazaa and Soulseek – all vary in terms of how rigidly they organize information.[4] This rigidity can be envisaged as a measure of hierarchy. Ernst (2008) underlines the ever-shifting character of archives; we should rather see them as ongoing performances (activities) than permanent givens (*topoi*). This information superabundance – nonhierarchical and decentralized to the point of appearing spontaneously emergent, ever-changing, and never fully overseeable – can somewhat provocatively be defined as an "an-archive" (ibid.). Traditional archivist practice has *storage* and *transfer* as its default settings. However, this emphasis is now shifting from cultural memory toward a situation of *permanent transfer*, Ernst argues. When all information can be stored, the paradoxically an-archivist dimension of the Internet reveals itself: "Cyberspace has no memory. Cyberspace is not even a place, but rather a topological configuration" (ibid., 92). For the Internet, the archive is just a metaphor. In fact, Ernst argues, no products are actually archived; what is distributed is *access* rather than space.

One can relate the conceptual dynamic between hierarchy and heterarchy by contrasting these tendencies (access, speed, permanent transfer) with two ideal properties within mathematics, namely *entropy* (chaos, disintegration) and *negentropy* (redundancy, order). Still, hierarchy is never fully redundant and heterarchy is never fully entropic, since any information structure would entail a balancing of redundancy with entropy.

The concept of heterarchy was originally developed by the cyberneticist Warren McCulloch (1945). Crumley (1995, 29) defines heterarchy as "the relation of elements to one another when they are unranked or when they possess the potential for being ranked in a number of different ways," whereas Stephenson (2009: 6) sees it as "an organizational form somewhere between hierarchy and network that provides horizontal links permitting different elements of an organization to cooperate, while they individually optimize different success criteria." It is important to note, however, that

Stephenson's definition of a heterarchical bureaucracy is that each heterarchy in fact "consists of at least three (or more) separate hierarchies, each with its own *raison d'être*, but which, in turn, must collaborate with each other to accomplish a collective good more complex than any one hierarchy can manage on its own" (ibid.). The p2pfoundation Wiki (Bauwens 2007) gives a puzzling definition, drawing on the late Gerard Fairtlough (former CEO of Shell Chemicals UK) where heterarchical systems are understood to share power (for example, a board that votes to decide issues, or different branches of government that have checks and balances through separation and overlap of power), whereas "responsible autonomy" (ibid.) would be a purer form of self-organization, having no inherent structure, yet distinguishing itself from anarchy by holding decision-makers responsible for the outcomes of their decisions. Fairtlough emphasizes that hierarchy, heterarchy and responsible autonomy comprise a *triadic* approach to organization.[5]

Interestingly, Von Goldammer et al. (2003) note that McCulloch too was interested in C. S. Peirce's attempts at developing a triadic logic, while at the same time being appreciative of the philosophy of dialectics, inherited from antiquity via Kant and Hegel. In his 1945 paper, McCulloch introduces what is termed a *diallel* – a logical circle (*circulus vitiousus*; "arguing in a circle") or logical contradiction – which, Von Goldammer et al. argue, is something that standard, Aristotelian physical logic simply does not cater for. As formal logic only applies to physical states (something *is* or *is not*), the third position (that something would *simultaneously* be and not be) can only be formulated by recursion to processual logic.[6]

> We can assert that paradoxes (or antinomies or a *circulus vitiosus*) cannot be measured in a physical sense. Paradoxes only occur within our interpretations of particular situations; they are never part of the description of physical systems nor of physical states. (Von Goldammer et al. 2003)[7]

One example (used by these authors) is how, in the following sentence, a word processing program will immediately discover the two syntactical errors but *not* the third, the semantical error: "*This sentence contains three erors.*" Evidently, the mental category "error" can be approached by the human brain on different processual levels, accommodating paradoxes in an entirely different way than mathematical, sequential reasoning would. Note also how the semantical error cannot be ranked in a hierarchical sense against the two syntactical errors. Surely, the human brain accommodates it by acknowledging asymmetry – yet it does not, however, operate by simple linearity, but rather by encircling or by mentally assigning phenomena to overlapping sets. A heterarchical mode of reasoning means that different logical standpoints (or domains) are maintained simultaneously, having equivalence. "It is the parallel simultaneous mediation of the different standpoints that enables our brains to maintain (dialectical) contradictions" (Von Goldammer et al. 2003) until sublation (*Aufhebung*) is reached, enabling a decision. In this sense, circular process logic is entirely different from linear formal logic. Yet, paradoxically, despite being composed of binary machines, computer networks (in their aggregate form; that is, considering also their externalities) manage to entail such circular logic. As Thacker and Galloway (2007, 62) note: Networks are dynamic, and only exist through process. "Networks are only networks when they are 'live,' when they are enacted, embodied, or rendered operational" (ibid.).

The two archival practices of heterarchy and hierarchy need not be opposed, but could rather be seen to reinforce one another. Sean Dockray, one of the architects behind the literature-sharing service Aaaaarg, has noted that when people digitize books and make them instantly duplicable, this makes for *promiscuity* rather than a discriminatory logic of either/ or. New structures of organizing information arise through a bottom-up fashion, and reinforce older, top-down ones. Still, I would like to address how new, systemic side effects appear to emerge, acting to steer cognition in certain ways that engender new, previously unforeseen hierarchies. One such paradoxical asymmetry is the affect and judgment that the users are directing toward the keepers of the archives. As soon as any form of responsibility is disclosed – as soon as spokespersons or representatives are to be found – it is as if the anonymity of the exchange is belied by the tacit, honorable mode of address cropping up.

Both hierarchical and heterarchical processes of archiving require active labor, especially so in an era of digital storage where data has to be migrated constantly (a familiar problem for librarians and archivists). Nodes on P2P-based file-sharing networks come and go, constantly jetting in and out, on and off. Moreover, the illegality of the entire operation also adds to its fickle nature, networks sometimes being closed down in sudden raids or evasive maneuvers. While the classic library ideal – centralized, hierarchical, overseeable storage – could be said to allude to an Alexandrian ideal, the more decentralized, scattershot, unreliable, and nebulous nature of the an-archive could be said to be Babylonian. Especially so when considering the less highbrow forms of content often catered for by such migratory, badly labeled, fickle means of storage: pornography, novelty pop tunes, bad movies. Schlocky and lightweight products that users might never have paid money for to begin with – yet download anyway, out of curiosity and novelty.

Integrity

Pollution, early on a very common problem on unmoderated P2P networks, has been addressed in the system design of some of the more recent networks. BitTorrent distribution, for example, involves human moderators who weed out damaged or polluted files. Hence, since the emergence of BitTorrent in 2005, pollution is less of a problem than it was on, for example, Kazaa or LimeWire.

Snickars and Vonderau (2010) and Reynolds (2011) have described YouTube as "a field of cultural practice" (Reynolds 2011, 59) typical for the present media an-archive due to its noisy, superabundant, semi-regulated, highly convenient but sometimes polluted character. While being largely dependent on the output of the mainstream corporate entertainment industry – since a lot of the material on YouTube is simply rebroadcasted audiovisual entertainment and news clips – endless varieties of much more esoteric, obscure, user-generated material also exists; underground music, art, film, animation, and different forms of recordings of performances. It is a disorganized, messy public reservoir, offering a stupefying range of content – from ultra-obscure live footage to extremely widespread, viral "funny clips." Often the image and sound quality is crummy, and plenty of duplicates and "damaged copies' persist, Reynolds notes (drawing on Hilderbrand 2009). This helps inducing a kind of Google-addled, associative "drift," Reynolds argues, reminiscent of that described by Carr (2010), where "artifacts from different eras are jumbled promiscuously and linked by a latticework of criss-crossing associations" (Reynolds 2011, 62). Still, "elsewhere on the Web, all kinds of official organizations and amateur associations are assembling well-managed cultural databases whose contents are available to the general public" (ibid.), such as the British Library, the National Film Board of Canada, and organizations like UbuWeb.

Similarly, metadata resources have been common since the inception of the public web, often built in Wiki-like ways: examples include the Internet Movie Database (IMDb.com, launched in 1990) and Discogs (launched in 2000). These are user-driven, collectively managed information databases currently rivaling any established public or proprietary database in depth and comprehensiveness; highly reliable and with low degrees of misinformation. Still, these resources do not contain any audiovisual content, except occasional "snippets" of video or sound in order to preview artifacts (often provided by YouTube).

Private torrent communities – e.g., the cinephile site explored in Andersson Schwarz (2015) – operate as highly sophisticated archival resources. The anonymized site in question, for example, hosts a 30,000-strong community of cineasts – each one personally invited by at least one of the other users – who use the service as both a collective knowledge resource and as a noncommercial place for exchange of the actual movies. Some of the similar, invite-only torrent communities of the same era (most notably OiNK and TV-Links) have been forcefully shut down. Arguably, one of the reasons this particular site has been able to avoid litigation since its inception in 2005 is that it adheres to a rather strict content policy: *"Only arthouse, classic, cult, rare and alternative material allowed,"* their forum rules explicitly make clear; a policy that has been in place since the beginning. Furthermore, *"no mainstream, blockbuster or recent Hollywood/Bollywood films allowed. No uploads of ongoing TV series. No mainstream porn."* Alongside this rigorous policy, the site administrators actively feature a curatorial selection labeled "Masters of the Month," showcasing everything from Iranian cinema, 1950s science fiction, or Hammer films to avant-garde jazz, Krzysztof Kieslowski, or Marguerite Duras. Sometimes the selections are rather scholarly; in November 2010, the monthly feature was on the literature, music and cinema of the Weimar Republic, and at other times comprehensive collections of ethnographic cinema, Soviet montage, as well as the documentaries and animation of above-mentioned National Film Board of Canada have been showcased.

It is testament to the relatively small communities of devoted fans who congregate on these types of sites that the rate of pollution is extremely low, and that many users devote significant labor to archival care. After all, this community is comparatively tiny, with around 5,000 daily visitors. Contrastingly, Soulseek – which used to have a rather significant user community with over a million registered usernames and 100,000 users logged on during peak hours – was despite its size considered to be mainly catering for alternative, nonmainstream material outside of the purview of the Recording Industry Association of America and thus remaining largely scot-free in the eyes of legal authorities (Mennecke 2003). With its simple user interface (reminiscent of the original Napster interface) and few formal filters for quality or genre, Soulseek does not require extensive metadata or comprehensiveness; the degree of missing, incomplete, badly rendered or polluted files hence varying greatly. From time to time, precarious yet impressively comprehensive collections are still made available (see Fig. 4.1).

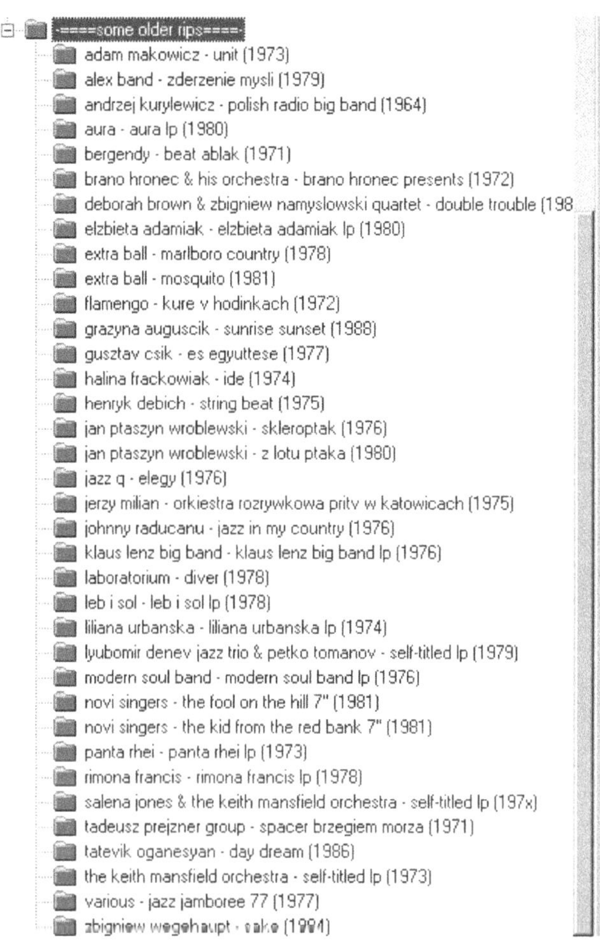

Fig. 4.1: Screen dump of a user making available several rare Polish jazz albums on Soulseek, 14 February 2008

Case: Aaaaarg

Another connoisseur-oriented file-sharing service that has garnered considerable attention in the academic community is the collective literature-sharing site Aaaaarg. Currie (2010) describes it as "a sundry collection of critical documents – many of them highly treasured theoretical classics, others obscure anarchic tomes and legal texts – presented in a simple, sleek alphabetized index of.pdfs." The archive was launched in 2001, attracting increasing public interest in recent years; Dockray agreeing to several interviews (Myers 2009; Currie 2010; Fuller 2011). He regularly emphasizes the necessity of keeping Aaaaarg as simple as possible regarding both metadata and its file-quality threshold:

> The dominant sensibility of Aaaaarg at the beginning was the highly partial and subjective nature to the contents and that is something I would want to preserve, which is why I never thought it to be particularly exciting to have lots of high quality metadata – it doesn't have the publication date, it doesn't have all the great metadata that say Amazon might provide. The system is pretty dismal in that way, but I don't mind that so much. I read something on the Internet which said it was like being in the porn section of a video store with all black text on white labels, it was an absolutely beautiful way of describing it.... There are movie sharing sites that are really good about quality control both in the metadata and what gets up; but I think that if you follow that to the end, then basically you arrive at the exported version being the Platonic text, the impossible, perfect, clear, searchable, small – totally eliminating any trace of what is interesting, the hand of reading and scanning, and this is what you see with a lot of the texts on Aaaaarg. You see the hand of the person who's read that book in the past, you see the hand of the person who scanned it. Literally, their hand is in the scan. This attention to the labour of both reading and redistributing, it's important to still have that. (Dockray, in Fuller 2011)

Aaaaarg gets shut down periodically, regularly migrating and shifting form. In March 2009, a new website was launched; in April 2010, after book publisher Macmillan had complained to the site administrators, the ability to download e-books directly from the site was suspended and instead external links to Mediafire and similar cyberlockers were introduced. The URL address was also changed, from http://a.aaaarg.org/to http://aaaaarg. org/. This move, decentralizing the operation by beginning to host the actual files elsewhere, is synchronous with similar movements in the file-sharing world at the time (Andersson Schwarz 2013, 132ff). In late 2013 the site was intermittently down, and a complete redesign of the interface was launched in early 2014.

Regarding usability and accessibility, Aaaaarg displays an ambiguous stance, to say the least. It permanently questions the Alexandrian ideal of selection, elision, and attributable authorship, while its users often seem to conspicuously establish norms of intellectual aloofness, glossolalia, and obscurantism. In many ways, sites like Aaaaarg are not a total free-for-alls, but rather the opposite: Quite clear norms for operation are established, either by making clear demands and setting thresholds like the private torrent sites, or by leaving the actual platform ostensibly open and the interface plain, yet invoking an expectance of a certain etiquette of sharing. Making the topology of the site as minimalistic as possible diverts the task of marketing and circulation to the users. A "certain kind of readerliness" (Fuller 2011) is made possible, where users can participate in tying associative connections around the archive; extraneous connections of metadata, comments and links. The making of discourses[8] in this sense becomes visible, traceable – but only so in the present, not over time. A lot of the discussions around the actual operation are now lost to oblivion.[9]

All of my examples – Aaaaarg, Soulseek, and the cinephile site – serve to erect rather specific discourses (i.e., systematic claims to validity). The selection offered by each service is rather narrow, manifesting very particular taste and genre preferences. There is, for example, hardly any management literature available through Aaaaarg, just as there are vast genres (especially more popular forms) of music and film that the latter two P2P communities simply will not make available. Different publics carry different interests, and discourse is steered in certain directions. Like Marcell Mars's (2013) discussions on "the public library as infrastructure' – where sites like Aaaaarg, Monoskop, textz.org, LibGen, and UbuWeb are taken as examples – a certain idealism of creating possibilities for new counterpublics seems to underpin each venture. Dockray explains how Aaaaarg docks into his general concept of the Public School in his interview with Fuller:

> SD: The original community was very American and European and gradually people were signing up at other places in order to have access to a lot of these texts that didn't reach their libraries or their book stores or whatever. But then there is a danger of US and European thought becoming central. A globalisation where a certain mode of thought ends up just erasing what's going on already in the cities where people are signing up, that's a horrible possible future.

> MF: But that's already something that's not happening in some ways?

> SD: Exactly, that's what seems to be happening now. It goes on to translations that are being put up and then texts that are coming from outside of the set of US and western authors and so, in a way, it flows back in the other direction. This hasn't always been so visible, maybe it will begin to happen some more. But think of the way people can list different texts

together as "issues" – a way that you can make arbitrary groupings – and they're very subjective, you can make an issue named anything and just lump a bunch of texts in there. But because, with each text, you can see what other issues people have also put it in, it creates a trace of its use. You can see that sometimes the issues are named after the reading groups, people are using the issues format as a collecting tool, they might gather all Portuguese translations, or The Public School uses them for classes. At other times it's just one person organising their dissertation research but you see the wildly different ways that one individual text can be used. (Fuller 2011)

Fuller argues that this would create a form of paratext, a meta-index, out of the organizational practice of *encircling*; arguably a typical example of how hierarchization comes into being also in very "flat," heterarchical ecologies.

Honor

One should not conflate the hierarchy of formalized, institutionalized command structures with the inherent hierarchization that comes with the holism of human cognition. Wilber (2000, 25ff) argues that the ideal of heterarchy is misleading, as human cognition operates by constantly making associations, connections, categorizations, and distinctions. This is analogous to Lyotard's (1993) distinction between human and inhuman (see Sim 2001). Further, hierarchy should not by definition be thought to be linear and dominating, according to Wilber, as hierarchy could just as well be seen as *sets* or various magnitudes of wholes, encircling each other (letters integrating into words, integrating into sentences, integrating into paragraphs; cf. the reading circles in the discussion on Aaaaarg above). The order of magnitude need not imply causality or inherent value.[10] There is always asymmetry – yet, Wilber argues, that does not necessarily imply privilege. The analogy to McCulloch's concept of heterarchy should be obvious.

The asymmetry of varying importance can of course be measured statistically. The Google PageRank algorithm has made apparent that different web pages have vastly different popular impact. Certainly, the Internet is premised on a heterarchical information exchange – everyone enters on equal terms. Yet, someone is always "more equal' than the rest, to paraphrase the common aphorism. This phenomenon was observed by Enzensberger (2003) already when assessing the budding amateur exchange of audiovisual content made possible by personal video recorders, 40-odd years ago. "Open" infrastructures quickly become susceptible to corruption, hostile takeovers or strong-arm actors who can bypass the background noise, the low-level chatter of masses occupying themselves with ceaseless mutual exchange. This is why all of my examples above thrive on certain forms of closure rather than openness; maintaining control of one's own server infrastructure is to maintain a form of "autonomous zone" (Bey 1991) that can establish more or less permanent counterpublics. Still, if left to be isolated, unknown to the wider public, and devoid of popular appeal, amateur production could always be quite easily neutralized politically, Enzensberger argues.

Enzensberger never mentions Hardin's (1968) lament on "The Tragedy of the Commons," a text that has been equally influential. In the contemporary debate on "pirate politics," Hardin's stance has, however, been questioned and even directly opposed:

> Every commons, Hardin argued, would sooner or later be destroyed because all participants essentially acted as rational, utilitarian profit maximizers and the self-interest was higher then concern for the common resource. Research by the political scientist Elinor Ostrom (1990) however showed that Hardin's findings were only true under specific conditions and that other conditions existed where collective commons management was indeed possible. (Medosch 2008)

I will not expand on this debate at any further length here, but suffice to say that the optimistic presupposition that the "endless" space online would be disproved by noting that the attention span of human beings is, after all, limited and can be saturated. Further, there is cognitive asymmetry in the ways human beings (largely subconsciously) assess and encircle differing regions of the surrounding mental ecology according to different criteria. This is neatly mirrored in the world of sociology by, for example, Boltanski's recourse to how people formulate criticisms and justifications by referring to shared conventions, sometimes mutually incommensurable (Boltanski and Thévenot 2006). Paradoxes are accepted, subconsciously, to different degrees depending on one's standpoint and one's intellectual investment in the regime of justification in question. What is dismissed in an industrial mode of arguing and reflecting can be tacitly accepted, without even blinking, in a domestic mode of reasoning. One such example is the glitch between saying and doing, when it comes to tenured academics who in principle defend the idea of a public library but in practice stay silent when sites like Aaaaarg go down – either in order not to divert too much public attention to these valuable resources or, simply, in order not to appear too dependent on such resources, as they are seen as both illicit and associated with the economic poverty and precariousness of postgrad studenthood. It relates to a double-bind of salaried academics, in that they are not dependent on the (in any event, meager) book royalties of conventional academic publishing – yet they are dependent on being published in the conventional ways in order to maintain "impact" and credibility.

Moreover, the primary justificatory regime that many academics operate within is that of an *archivist mode* of interpreting culture (see De Kosnik 2012, for the correlation between collectors and pirates). Here, file sharing is, in many ways, seen as a way of maintaining or safeguarding a sprawling, living archive of cultural content, yet there is a certain negligence toward the conditions for production outside of the salaried model described above. In other words, academics operating within an archivist mode of justification are in many ways misaligned with cultural producers operating within a *unionist mode* of justification particular to the cultural industries (cf. Boltanski and Thévenot 2006, 16). It probably adds to this misalignment that many cultural studies scholars are more interested in media audiences and the particular situatedness of such audiences (a *civic mode*, highlighting civic access, consumer freedom or even populism) than they are in established professional cultural production (cf. Andersson Schwarz 2013, 19).

Ever the optimistic pundit, arguing for the viability and radical potential in bottom-up modes of organization, Benkler (2002) emphasizes free software and P2P production projects as being radically different from production models organized around command-obey hierarchies. Still, while these phenomena are driven by aggregated, voluntary participation, they nevertheless tend to entail compensation systems, he admits; a form of non-monetary recognition of each participant's *virtue*. Benkler and Nissenbaum (2006) recognize this as a shared feature of several peer-production projects (e.g., Slashdot, SETI@home, Wikipedia). The communities of production for these sites would less commonly address the particular, atomistic actions of individuals than they address the actual social standing of individuals within their particular community of shared norms and justifications; their *ethos* as it unfolds over time.

> Where the basic unit of moral evaluation for rival frameworks is individual actions (or action-types), the basic unit of moral evaluation for virtue ethics is the person (or soul or character), an entity persisting over time. (Benkler and Nissenbaum 2006, 404)

Benkler and Nissenbaum primarily refer to the actual ground-level users/participants of peer-production projects. It is worth noting how the potentially transient migratory behavior of users online seems to foster a particular ethic which puts the appeasement of users before virtually any other considerations (except the continued overall technical functioning and upkeep of the network). As I will show below, this is the axis on which the popularity of site administrators and owners hinges, as the benchmark question seems to be: *Are they optimizing the user experience?*" Due to the horizontal nature of the Internet and the informal nature of the communicative exchange, often cloaked by (semi)anonymity and a shared dedication to the continued upkeep of the actual exchange taking place, participants can be found to display a certain intransigence regarding the integrity and sovereignty of the particular hub, network or community they belong to.

> It is nonetheless clear that peer projects [like Wikipedia] require a range of "leadership" functions involving coordination, recruitment and administration. Free software project maintainers must welcome new participants and facilitate the integration of their contributions; evaluate and criticise proposals to ensure they do not degrade the quality of the project; keep the project dynamic (discussing and summarising ideas); and ensure discipline (by conferring privileges, arbitrating disputes and excluding troublemakers). The catch is that, with the exception of the last actions, which are of a strictly administrative or judiciary nature, none of these tasks lend themselves to a command-obey relationship. In fact, maintainers must take care not to antagonise or disappoint participants by not meeting their expectations, failing to pacify conflicts and establishing unrealistic objectives... or participants will exercise their exit option and desert the project. (O'Neil 2011, 2)

The "hacker ethic" (cf. Levy 1984; Himanen 2001) claims to mistrust centralized authority by swearing itself free from "bogus" criteria such as degrees, race, age, or position. Still, O'Neil (2011, 4) argues, "charismatic hacker authority is based on the extraordinary skills of a person" – something which in the case of Wikipedia is imbued on its much-admired founder, Jimmy Wales. Although manifest demographic factors like the above-mentioned do not seem to have direct bearing on the authority of leading administrators, moderators, founders or programmers, the skills involved are directly reminiscent of another set of character traits:

They must remain charismatic in the eyes of their audience. O'Neil invokes Weber (1978, 241):

> Charismatic authority derives from the gift of grace: from a higher power or from inspiration. It rests on the qualities of an individual personality, by virtue of which he or she is deemed extraordinary and treated as endowed with superhuman or at least specifically exceptional powers and qualities. (O'Neil 2011, 4)

Besides the common emphasis on technical operability, a common trope in the correspondence offered by administrators of P2P sites would the moral recrimination toward extraneous parasitical sites or services that abuse the good name of one's own, implicitly more defendable site. In a user message heralding a software update for the Soulseek client (Fig. 4.2), the administrators take an extremely humble and disarming approach, yet dismissing the commercial ethos of other, implicitly less noble file-sharing sites. Another example comes from Soulseek developer Nir Arbel's comments in 2008, in response to a more compulsory update of the software client:

> I would also like to take this opportunity to address some of the lies that have been spread about our lifestyle and the money we make off Soulseek. We live from hand to mouth. A few months ago we had to let go of sierracat, our system admin, despite his excellent work, because we could no longer afford his services. We are pretty heavily in debt. We are fighting a legal battle in France. We are not poor nor starving, but neither of us drives a fancy car nor could we begin to afford one if we wanted to. I don't like discussing money issues, but I feel it necessary to defend ourselves from accusations that are, and have always been, patently untrue. with that, I would like to thank you all for using Soulseek and making it a significant, if not hugely popular or successful experience. Thanks. (Slsk 2008)

No matter how sloppy, leaky and noisy the archive is (that is, the extent of which it in fact borders to be an an-archive), the upholder of the archive must remain in good regard with his fellow coarchivists. No matter how amateurish, abstruse, or noncommercial the entire operation is, it rests on the same principle that Derrida (1995, 59) observes; a paternal and patriarchic principle of the archive, reminiscent of the *nomos* of law, of institution, of domiciliation, of filiation.

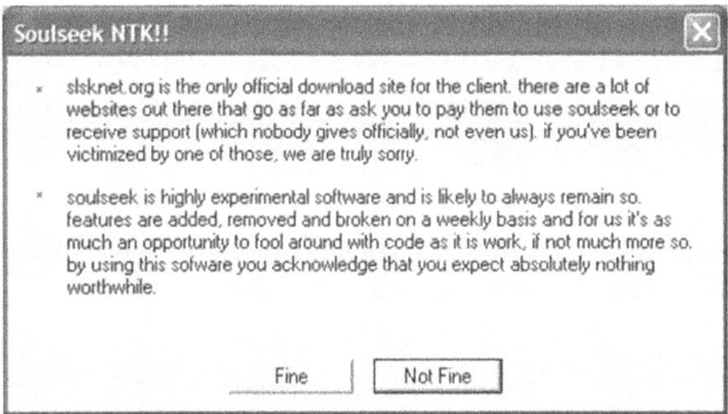

Fig. 4.2: Screen dump of a message from Soulseek administrators to users of the application, 11 November 2006

In the late 19th century, a renegotiation of economic value was formulated by John Ruskin. His was a direct antithesis to those Victorian contemporaries within political economy who measured economic worth in merely monetary terms. For Ruskin (1997), especially in his essay "The Roots of Honour," it was clear that political economy of his time failed to deal with the relation between the employer and the employed in terms of justice, empowerment, and equitability – values that were not directly measurable by means of a strict monetary interpretation of economy. What Ruskin did was to show how there are alternative forms of capital; other forms of value than those made apparent by simple market mechanisms. This legacy has of course been largely recuperated by the labor movements of the 19th and 20th centuries, fighting for the inclusion of civic interests into financial policy and, to a significant extent, succeeding. However, we are still a long way from seeing the inclusion of what classical economists label "externalities" into equations of financial policy; most tellingly, the natural environment is only gradually beginning to be taken into account. Besides the vast field of economic sociology, this has been explored by authors more central to critical theory, such as Callon (1998) and Bourdieu (1984) – the latter famously recognizing fields where specific forms of alternative capital are accumulated, such as different forms of cultural and social capital[11] – but also in discussions on "intangible goods" (Polanyi 1944; Titmuss 1971) and "gift economy" (Mauss 2002; Hyde 2007). These latter exponents will not be discussed further here; see Andersson (2012b) for a further application of these concepts to online file sharing.

Honorability, in Ruskin's sense, is a more narrow concept than sheer virtue; it carries at its core an ethic of sacrifice, of stretching oneself further than the rest, and thereby risking to forgo those things that are hold very dearly for most people: one's freedom, one's source of income, one's reputation in "established" society, or even one's life. Ruskin differentiates between the *honorable* and the *mundane* – where the former is the fighter/warrior/ martyr "whose mission is to die" (1997, 175). This is the role of the hacker, artist, entrepreneur, trickster, tinkerer and, indeed, criminal, who sacrifices his/her ordinariness on the altar of honor. Sacrifice lies at heart of the reputational economy of the martyr, but also trustworthiness, verisimilitude, and authenticity – and equally, charisma, wit and a memorable appearance ("faciality"; see below). At the same time, honorability goes both ways: Honor is bestowed also on those taking sides, those who exculpate the tragic actor.

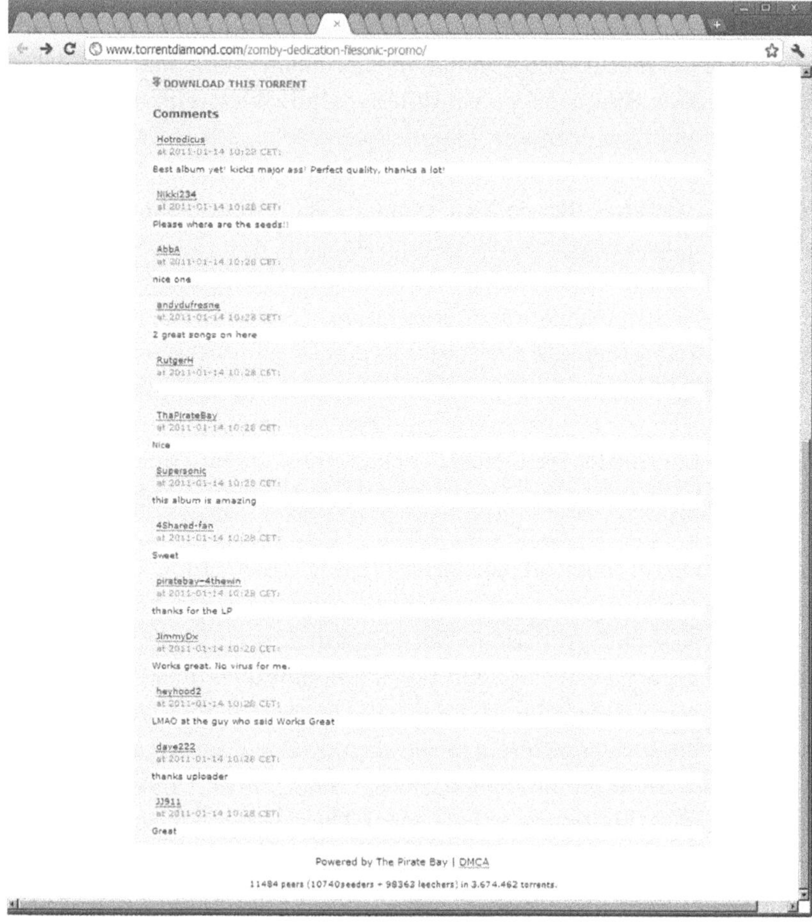

Fig. 4.3: Screen dump of a fake site (Torrentdiamond) appearing as a Pirate Bay clone, 6 August 2011

In the file-sharing world, the first example that comes to mind is the deliberately provocative stance taken by The Pirate Bay administrators (2003-2009) – an approach that indeed resulted in prison sentences and lifetime economic exile (cf. Andersson Schwarz 2013). This discursive stance, combined with the aesthetic style of punk and nonconformism, helped shaping a profile of The Pirate Bay administrators as assertive hardliners. Despite now being run by unknown administrators – Swedish court orders barring the original trio from managing the site – the Pirate Bay as a site still appears to maintain high visibility and popularity in the file-sharing world; perhaps even more so after the highly publicized Pirate Bay trial in 2009. The fame held by The Pirate Bay is indeed so strong, that fake sites rip off its graphic design in order to falsely appear to be "legit" among unassuming file sharers, even sporting false user comments (Fig. 4.3).

Case: *Avaxhome*

The popular file-sharing community Avaxhome began its life as Avaxhome.ru in 2001, was put down in 2008 and subsequently returned, using the domain suffix.ws until December 2011 when it moved to the domain avaxhome.bz, and in May 2014 to the domain avaxhm.com. The Avaxhome network claims to have 230,000 unique daily visitors and features an extensive collection of copyrighted material, uploaded by its users. The content is uploaded by letting invited users make their own blogs – where each post normally consists of links to whichever artifacts the user chooses to upload, primarily e-books. The posting of "publications' must contain links to content, and the content must be hosted on third-party hosting sites (cyberlockers), in a similar fashion to the way many MP3 bloggers link to their uploaded albums or songs.[12] The network pays lip service to legal agreements like DMCA by having comparatively authoritative information on how they respond to copyright infringement claims by taking down links as soon as possible.[13]

Avaxhome is ad-financed, seemingly driven by shrewd business sense, especially when noting its ambitions to function as a news network (avaxnews.net) featuring visual curiosities collected from all over the world. Its "administrator blogs" (later discontinued) featured an "Avax" blog[14] containing a disparate mix of attention-grabbing images and links to attendant services in the grey economy ("Russian Girls," "MiliWoman," "AirHostessWoman.com," cracked software site "AvaxSoft," etc.) mixed with populist contests (*"Best places to travel!"*) and seemingly genuine film and music recommendations; all in Russian and broken English, clad in garish graphic design. Its Facebook page sports over 11,000 likes and posts similar daily news images.[15] Before Facebook changed its architecture in March 2014 to make fan pages less transparent, one would find on it a mixture of general praise from fans, requests for "invitation codes," and fans giving solutions to technical problems. Most of these comments were by males, many of them having non-Western names. Italy is an outlier among its fans, accounting for 13.6% of its fanbase.[16]

Are these editorial contraptions a way to put a human face on what would otherwise remain a rather nebulous assemblage of aggregated users? When investigating Avaxhome in 2011, one of the administrators appeared to be a particular individual (originally from Ukraine but residing in Israel) who blogged on Avaxhome, and has both a Twitter feed and a Facebook page, which even shows images of this real person, connected to the AvaxNews site. While his affiliation to Avaxhome is less obvious today, his Twitter page still links to the network.

Avaxhome's e-book section is often mentioned alongside other e-book sharing outings (Library Genesis, Monoskop, Aaaaarg), aligning a lot of its offerings with an educational angle, however admittedly far more mainstream than that of Aaaaarg or Monoskop. With all of the sites listed above, the orchestration of the actual file exchange is designed to be neutral, nimble and discreet, while being embedded in larger information infrastructures of links, descriptions, and comments. Like with the current incarnation of The Pirate Bay, the administrators of the cinephile torrent site that I investigated remain totally anonymous. In contrast, the administrators of Avaxhome – and Soulseek as well – are not as enigmatic (at least in a historical perspective; through long-term engagement I have been able to find out who they are). The more highbrow, intellectually ambitious outings of Aaaaarg, Monoskop, and UbuWeb have much more public administrators and spokespersons. As soon as the identity of the architect is somewhat disclosed, this is seen to come with great public approbation for having the kudos to run it, but at the same time it does put the administrator in the target of those who seek to police such exchange. Interestingly, the attendant scale of secrecy can be paralleled with the degree of popular appeal held by each site; the often mainstream, Hollywood-type material offered in torrent indexes is highly policed by the likes of the Motion Picture Association of America and the Recording Industry Association of America, while only some of the material available through Avaxhome and Soulseek would be in the purview of active policing by such actors. Only very little of that which is offered on the academic literature sharing sites is actively targeted; the multinational book publishers also have considerably smaller means than the movie, music, and games industries.

Tragedy

The utopian ethic of a universal library is found in an exclamation that has been common on various torrent sites: *"If we all seed just 1:1, give at least what we take, this torrent will NEVER DIE!"* As in Ray Bradbury's *Fahrenheit 451* (1953), where each character memorizes one piece of literature as all printed books have been banned, the P2P network provides the ability for each citizen to keep their favorite movie or book in potential circulation.

Yet *Fahrenheit 451* is a tragedy; the future depicted dystopian rather than utopian. What today's nonsanctioned, illicit archives of content prove is an imminent incapacity within contemporary society to progressively utilize digital technology for archival ends; the modern-day archivists of UbuWeb, Aaaaarg, Soulseek and The Pirate Bay are indeed sacrificing their own time and their own labor in order to achieve what institutional actors currently do not seem to manage. As is manifest on the unruly, loosely regulated web, open systems often become prone to corruption and/or saturation. Yet, many of them manage to operate despite high degrees of pollution and disorder. The reasons for this are always particular; they are most likely found in a fragile assembly of users, interfaces, system structure, administrators, and societal context. The worst examples of online an-archives all seem to be attributable to a critical mass of anonymous, autonomous-but-*not*-responsible (Bauwens 2007), *nonvirtuous* (Benkler and Nissenbaum 2006) users flooding the network with useless artifacts. Still, it owes to the software interface whether this flooding would in fact have a critical effect on the usability. Flooding quickly becomes problematic on infrastructures with practically nonexistent search functions (e.g., Gnutella, Chatroulette) or search functions that give too many false positives (e.g., Kazaa, MP3 aggregators), whereas services with good search functions (e.g., YouTube, torrent indexes) suffer less from that particular problem.

Open infrastructures are easily held victims to users with poor judgment or lack of consideration, as with the example of the photographic evidence from a Swedish murder trial being uploaded by a user and subsequently indexed on The Pirate Bay (Andersson 2009). Here, the administrators' ability to remain the venerated "keepers of the realm" was put to test, as they had to balance the concerns of the user community with the concerns of the general public. While maintaining the stance that the service was merely a neutral carrier and did not filter anything except outright immoral and damaging material such as child pornography, they had to make a publicist decision where the right to air legal documents (which are by default public in the Swedish legal system anyway) had to be weighed against the potentially damaging consequences for the victims involved in the case. Nonsanctioned content providers like the ones described in this essay are in this sense balancing a tightrope between appeasing the own user base and official society.

As noted earlier, this makes for a precarious situation. The architects behind Aaaaarg are not even sure that what they are presenting is an in any way permanent solution. Alternative archiving online is very much an ongoing *performance*, a never-fully stable state of affairs. Just as file-sharing communities, formed around highly commercialized products (mainstream films and computer games) effectively become sitting targets for the copyright industry and affiliated legal authorities, sites can go down, or gradually peter out (by lack of user support, migration to other forums, or becoming swamped by the "wrong" forms of artifacts or people). This can be another reason for the *mal d'archive* felt online. As Dockray points out, "a lot of the mania isn't driven by just the need to have everything; it's driven by the acknowledgement that the source is going to disappear at some point" (Fuller 2011).

> Aaaaarg is definitely not a futuristic model. I mean, it occurs at a specific time, which is while we're living in a situation where books exist effectively as a limited edition. They can travel the world and reach certain places, and yet the readership is greatly outpacing the spread and availability of the books themselves. So there's a disjunction there, and that's obviously why Aaaaarg is so popular. Because often there are maybe no copies of a certain book within 400 miles of a person that's looking for it, but then they can find it on that website, so while we're in that situation it works. (Ibid.)

Yet, this might be a view which actually only retains relevance when limiting the analysis to certain sectors, genres or media forms. Within Bengali language content, a site like BanglaTorrents might operate as a novel intervention. Within J-pop, JPopsuki might similarly do so. Within the particular field of dissemination of critical theory, Aaaaarg might similarly be seen as an intervention. But when taking a macro view – trying to conjure all the various forms of sharing and exchange that are allowed to take place over the Internet – this ongoing cacophony arguably looks more like an emergent condition in its own right, rather than an intervention (cf. Andersson 2012a). Yet, as Thacker and Galloway (2007) point out, there is something deeply disturbing with a cacophony which lacks center, as it disrupts our deeply engrained human sensibility of acknowledging who is friend or who is enemy.

> A swarm attacks from all directions, and intermittently but consistently – it has no "front," no battle line, no central point of vulnerability. It is dispersed, distributed, and yet in constant communication. In short, it is a faceless foe, or a foe stripped of "faciality" as such.... What sort of ethics is possible when the other has no "face" and yet is construed as other (as friend or foe)? What is the shape of the ethical encounter when one "faces" the swarm? (Thacker and Galloway 2007, 66)

Conclusion

In this essay, I have tried to show how reconciliation with the heterarchical tendencies of P2P networking and the an-archivist tendencies of digital promiscuity takes several manifestations. Following Ruskin (1997), one mode of justification which is perhaps more expository to file sharing than to read it merely through the political economy of money, is to juxtapose file sharing with the moral premise of "doing unto others as you would like them to do to you" – a mutual obligation of honor and virtue. This is also implied in the dictum "If we all seed just 1:1, give at least what we take" described above. Following Benkler and Nissenbaum (2006) the moral implication of this can be read as virtuous. Since "user popularity" is the lifeblood of any site or object of civic exchange, the promiscuity of the digital object is compelled to be channeled in as commendable a way as possible, from an end-user point of view. Importantly, the ways this promiscuity tends to be manifested lend the *indexing site* that is being used to attain both *nomos* and *topos*; it becomes singular and attributable, susceptible to being invoked with great affect.

Bey (1991) has formulated the space occupied by pirates as "temporary autonomous zones"; a form of utopian space outside of conventional state jurisdiction, expedient for alternative, autonomous economies. Historians like Braudel (1996) and Serres (2007) have acknowledged that piracy is as old as history itself; the establishment of alternative *topoi* need not necessarily be violently oppositional toward officialdom. However, the necessary element of noncompromise involved means that there is always a degree of sacrifice when deliberately taking a separate path, especially when this path lies outside the realm of legality. As Selman (2008) notes, the martyr-like intensity of pirate life makes the privateers external to the state:

> The "warrior god" is a radical exteriority to the State form.... The State may attempt to reign in the power of the war machine, as it did with the privateers, but it can never encompass it – governments were perpetually at risk of attack from the same privateers they supposedly employed. While Sir Francis Drake and Captain Henry Morgan may have received knighthoods for their part in war in supposed times of peace, just as many were hung for the same actions. (Selman 2008, 28)

She emphasizes the nomadic, nonpermanent nature of this external life – a precarious existence – and moves on to discuss pirate space as "deterritorialized space" (Deleuze and Guattari 1986), consisting of "temporary autonomous zones" (Bey 1991) and "heterotopias" (Foucault 1986). These are spaces marked by temporality, possibility, passage, exposure, and deconstruction (Selman 2008: 33-34) – but I would, however, raise a word of caution, as these elusive spaces after all seem to have a remarkable potential to take on what Thacker and Galloway (2007) label "faciality," namely the boundedness to place and to certain individuals that Derrida (1995) acknowledges as pivotal for the archive, regardless of how anarchic it might appear at first. If its nexus of orchestration is stable enough – more long-lasting than the flickering of occasional nodes in the periphery – and attributable to some entity other than the blind, faceless swarm, its systemic agency as "warrior god" begins its consignation – and what materializes is precisely that which lends itself to be assigned as friend or foe; a heroic, yet thereby tragic actor.

Notes

1. Any actor, human or nonhuman, which exerts power and generates effects can be said to have agency. This is a definition of "actor" that I take from actor-network theory, which in turn is founded on narratology and relational ontology.
2. Deleuze and Guattari (1987) label these "self-consistent aggregates."
3. Deleuze and Guattari (1987) label these "strata."
4. Peer-to-peer is by its very definition anti-hierarchical. However, hierarchy is often sought in order to solve problems of, for example, searchability. Soulseek acts like Napster in that its catalog, or index, is located on central servers. The Fasttrack protocol (Kazaa) uses so-called supernodes, a hybrid

between centralization and distribution, whereas an example of a network with an entirely distributed index is Gnutella. For BitTorrent and cyberlockers, the index is hosted on regular web servers, acting as a separate layer added to the distributed P2P exchange.

5. Selman (2008) similarly recognizes how spatial imagination can involve a "third space" (Soja 1996) or heterotopias (Foucault 1986).

6. If Kittler (1997) or Ernst (2008) can be said to see the distinction between RAM and ROM as a determining principle for digital an-archives – the veritable carrier medium or "submedia space" (Groys 2003) – it is telling that the notion of heterarchical processing, according to McCulloch (1945), is so far removed from the actual way a Turing machine operates.

7. This would hold also for the most famous of paradoxes in the physical realm; the wave-particle dualism, as it too is a result of our thinking and appears as a paradox "because physics excludes the thinking subject and any subjectivity from within the formal description" (Von Goldammer et al. 2003; cf. Barad 2007).

8. See Laermans and Gielen (2007) for a Foucauldian reading of Ernst.

9. E.g., the debate on the Aaaaarg discussion board around the move to begin providing alternative means of access to the material, http://a.aaaarg.org/discussion/12427/going-underground (no longer accessible).

10. This should be familiar to anyone who has experience of programming languages, where objects and classes, labels, and ontologies are generated. It is also connected with Badiou's (2005) translation of set theory into a philosophy of being, objects, and events.

11. Importantly, these forms of capital are not subject to the same potentials for financial hoarding/accumulation as labor capital expressed in monetary form would be. Arguably, they could be converted into such capital – but not without considerable difficulty.

12. See http://avaxhome.ws/faq.html for rules and description of their posting process.

13. See http://avaxhome.ws/dmca.html.

14. See http://avaxhome.ws/blogs/Avax.

15. http://www.facebook.com/pages/AvaxHome/121754914527366.TYPOGRA-PHY?

16. According to Socialbakers.com (June 2014).

Bibliography

Andersson, Jonas. 2009. "For the Good of the Net: The Pirate Bay as a Strategic Sovereign." *Pirate Philosophy* 10: 64-108.

Andersson, Jonas. 2011. "The Origins and Impacts of Swedish File-Sharing: A Case Study." *Critical Studies in Peer Production* 1 (June).

Andersson, Jonas. 2012a. "Not Necessarily an Intervention: The Pirate Bay and the Case of File-Sharing." In Kevin Howley, ed., *Media Interventions*. New York: Peter Lang.

Andersson, Jonas. 2012b. "The Quiet Agglomeration of Data: How Piracy Is Made Mundane." *International Journal of Communication* 6: 585-605.

Andersson Schwarz, Jonas. 2013. *Online File Sharing: Innovations in Media Consumption*. London and New York: Routledge.

Andersson Schwarz, Jonas. 2015. "Catering for Whom? The Problematic Ethos of Audio-Visual Distribution Online." In Virginia Crisp and Gabriel Menotti Gonring, eds., *Besides the Screen: The Distribution, Exhibition and Consumption of Moving Images*. London: Palgrave Macmillan.

Badiou, Alain. 2005. *Being and Event*, trans. Oliver Feltham. New York: Continuum.

Barad, Karen. 2007. *Meeting the Universe Halfway: Quantum Physics and the Entanglement of Matter and Meaning*. Durham, NC: Duke University Press.

Bauwens, Michel. 2007. "Responsible Autonomy," P2P Foundation wiki. http://p2pfoundation. net/Responsible_Autonomy.

Benkler, Yochai. 2002. "Coase's Penguin, or, Linux and the Nature of the Firm." *Yale Law Review* 112.3: 369-446.

Benkler, Yochai. 2006. *The Wealth of Networks: How Social Production Transforms Markets and Freedom*. New Haven, CT: Yale University Press.

Benkler, Yochai, and Helen Nissenbaum. 2006. "Commons-based Peer Production and Virtue." *Journal of Political Philosophy* 14.4: 394-419.

Bey, Hakim. 1991. *TAZ – The Temporary Autonomous Zone, Ontological Anarchy, Poetic Terrorism*. New York: Autonomedia.

Boltanski, Luc, and Laurent Thévenot. 2006. *On Justification: Economies of Worth*, trans. Catherine Porter. Princeton, NJ: Princeton University Press.

Bourdieu, Pierre. 1984. *Distinction: A Social Critique of the Judgement of Taste*, trans. Richard Nice. Cambridge, MA: Harvard University Press.

Bradbury, Ray. 1953. *Fahrenheit 451*. New York: Harper Collins

Braudel, Fernand. 1996. *The Mediterranean and the Mediterranean World in the Age of Philip II*, trans. Siân Reynolds. Berkeley, CA: University of California Press.

Callon, Michel. 1998. "Introduction: The Embeddedness of Economic Markets in Economics." In Michel Callon, ed. *The Laws of the Market*. Oxford: Blackwell.

Carr, Nicholas. 2010. *The Shallows: What the Internet Is Doing to Our Brains*. New York: W. W. Norton.

Crumley, Carole L. 1995. "Heterarchy and the Analysis of Complex Societies." *Archeological Papers of the American Anthropological Association* 6.1: 1-5.

Currie, Morgan. 2010. "Small Is Beautiful: A Discussion with AAAARG Architect Sean Dockray." Masters of Media website, University of Amsterdam, 5 January. http://mastersofmedia.hum. uva.nl/2010/01/05/small-is-beautiful-a-discussion-with-aaaarg-architect-sean-dockray/.

De Certeau, Michel. 1984. *The Practice of Everyday Life*, trans. Steven Rendall. Berkeley, CA: University of California Press

De Kosnik, Abigail. 2012. "The Collector Is the Pirate." *International Journal of Communication* 6: 529-541.

DeLanda, Manuel. 1998. "Meshworks, Hierarchies and Interfaces." In John Beckman, ed., *The Virtual Dimension: Architecture, Representation, and Crash Culture*. New York: Princeton Architectural Press.

Deleuze, Gilles, and Félix Guattari. 1986. *Nomadology: The War Machine*, trans. Brian Massumi. New York: Semiotext(e).

Deleuze, Gilles, and Félix Guattari. 1987. *A Thousand Plateaus*, trans. Brian Massumi. Minneapolis: University of Minnesota Press.

Derrida, Jacques. 1995. "Archive Fever: A Freudian Impression." *Diacritics* 25.2: 9-63.

Enzensberger, Hans-Magnus. 2003. "Constituents of a Theory of the Media." In Noah Wardrip-Fruin and Nick Montfort, eds., *The New Media Reader*. Cambridge, MA, and London: MIT Press. Originally published in 1970 in the *New Left Review*; also translated by Stuart Hood in *The Consciousness Industry: On Literature, Politics and the Media*, New York: The Seabury Press, 1974.

Ernst, Wolfgang. 2008. *Sorlet från arkiven: Ordning ur oordning*, trans. Tommy Andersson [Orig: *Das Rumoren der Archive: Ordnung aus Unordnung*, 2002]. Stockholm: Glänta produktion.

Foucault, Michel. 1986. "Of Other Spaces." *Diacritics* 16.1: 22-27.

Fuller, Matthew. 2011. "In the Paradise of Too Many Books: An Interview with Sean Dockray." *Mute: Culture and Politics after the Net* 4/5. http://www.metamute.org/en/articles/in_the_paradise_of_too_many_books.

Galloway, Alexander. 2004. *Protocol: How Control Exists after Decentralization*. Cambridge, MA: MIT Press.

Greimas, Algirdas J. 1966. *Sémantique structurale*. Paris: Presse universitaires de France.

Groys, Boris. 2003. "What Carries the Archive – and for How Long?," trans. Stephen Kovats. In J. Brouwer, A. Mulder, and S. Charlton, eds., *Information Is Alive: Art and Theory on Archiving and Retrieving Data*. Rotterdam: V2_Publishing/NAI Publishers, 178-193. Originally published as the introduction to B. Groys, *Unter Verdacht: Eine Phänomenologie der Medien* [Under suspicion: A phenomenology of the media], Munich and Vienna: Carl Hanser Verlag, 2000.

Hardin, Garrett. 1968. "The Tragedy of the Commons." *Science* 162.3859: 1243-1248. http://www.sciencemag.org/cgi/content/full/162/3859/1243.

Hilderbrand, Lucas. 2009. *Inherent Vice: Bootleg Histories of Videotape and Copyright*. Durham, NC: Duke University Press.

Himanen, Pekka. 2001. *The Hacker Ethic and the Spirit of the Information Age*. London: Vintage.

Huyssen, Andreas. 2000. "Present Pasts: Media, Politics, Amnesia." *Public Culture* 12.1: 21-38.

Hyde, Lewis. 2007. *The Gift: Creativity and the Artist in the Modern World*. London: Vintage.

Kittler, Friedrich. 1997. "There Is No Software." In J. Johnston, ed., *Literature, Media, Information Systems*. Amsterdam: GB Arts International. Originally published as "Es gibt keine Software" in F. Kittler, *Draculas Vermächtnis: Technische Schriften*, Leipzig: Reclam Verlag, 1993. English translation originally published in *Stanford Humanities Review* 1 (1989): 81-90.

Laermans, Rudi, and Pascal Gielen. 2007. "The Archive of the Digital An-Archive." *Image and Narrative: Online Magazine of the Visual Narrative* 17 (April). http://www.imageandnarrative.be/inarchive/digital_archive/laermans_gielen.htm.

Latour, Bruno. 2005. *Reassembling the Social: An Introduction to Actor-Network-Theory*. Oxford: Clarendon

Latour, Bruno, and Michel Callon. 1981. "Unscrewing the Big Leviathan: How Actors Macro-Structure Reality and How Sociologists Help Them to Do So." In K. Knorr-Cetina and A. V. Cicourel, eds., *Advances in Social Theory and Methodology: Toward an Integration of Micro- and Macro-Sociologies*. Boston: Routledge and Kegan Paul, 277-303.

Levy, Steven. 1984. *Hackers: Heroes of the Computer Revolution*. London: Penguin Books.

Liang, Jian, Rakesh Kumar, Yongjian Xi, and Keith Ross. 2005. "Pollution in P2P File Sharing Systems." IEEE Infocom, Miami, FL, March.

Lyotard, Jean-François. 1993. *The Inhuman: Reflections on Time*, trans. Geoffrey Bennington and Rachel Bowlby. Cambridge: Polity.

Mars, Marcell. 2013. "Public Library (as infrastructure)," GitHub repository, 24 September. https://github.com/marcellmars/letssharebooks/blob/master/PublicLibrary.md.

Mauss, Marcel. 2002. *The Gift*. London: Routledge [orig. 1954].

McCulloch, Warren S. 1945. "A Heterarchy of Values Determined by the Topology of Nervous Nets." *Bull. Math. Biophys.* 7: 89-93. Reprinted in W. S. McCulloch, *Embodiment of Mind*, Cambridge, MA: MIT Press, 1988.

Medosch, Armin. 2008. "Paid in Full: Copyright, Piracy and the Real Currency of Cultural Production." In A. Hadzi and J. Andersson, eds., *Deptford.TV Diaries Volume II: Pirate Strategies*. London: Openmute.

Mennecke, Thomas. 2003. "SoulSeek Interview." Slyck.com, 26 December. http://www.slyck.com/news.php?story=356.

Myers, Julian. 2009. "Four Dialogues 2: On AAAARG." SFMOMA Open Space, 26 August. http://blog.sfmoma.org/2009/08/four-dialogues-2-on-aaaarg/.

O'Neil, Mathieu. 2011. "The Sociology of Critique in Wikipedia." *Critical Studies in Peer Production* 1 (June).

Ostrom, Elinor. 1990. *Governing the Commons: The Evolution of Institutions for Collective Action.* New York: Cambridge University Press.

Polanyi, Karl. 1944. *The Great Transformation: The Political and Economic Origins of Our Time.* Boston, MA: Beacon Press.

Raymond, Eric S. 1996. "How to Become a Hacker." Continuously updated web article. http://catb.org/~esr/faqs/hacker-howto.html.

Reynolds. Simon. 2011. *Retromania: Pop Culture's Addiction to Its Own Past.* London: Faber and Faber.

Ruskin, John. 1997. *Unto This Last and Other Writings*, ed. Clive Wilmer. London: Penguin.

Selman, Brianne. 2008. "Pirate Heterotopias." In A. Hadzi and J. Andersson, eds., *Deptford.TV Diaries Volume II: Pirate Strategies*. London: Openmute.

Serres, Michel. 2007. *The Parasite*, trans. L. R. Schehr. Minneapolis: University of Minnesota Press.

Shirky, Clay. 2005. "Ontology Is Overrated: Categories, Links, and Tags." Clay Shirky's Writings about the Internet. http://www.shirky.com/writings/ontology_overrated.html.

Sim, Stuart. 2001. *Lyotard and the Inhuman*. Duxford: Icon Books.

Slsk. 2008. "New Beta-Client Available – Soulseek Network Community Forums." Forums. slsknet.org, Nir Arbel posting as alias "nir." http://forums.slsknet.org/ipb/index.php?showtopic=18639andst=40.

Soja, Edward W. 1996. *Thirdspace: Journeys to Los Angeles and Other Real and Imagined Places.* Oxford: Blackwell Publishers.

Stephenson, Karen. 2009. "Neither Hierarchy nor Network: An Argument for Heterarchy." *People and Strategy* 32.1: 4-7.

Thacker, Eugene, and Alexander Galloway. 2007. *The Exploit: A Theory of Networks*. Minneapolis: University of Minnesota Press.

Titmuss, Richard M. 1971. *The Gift Relationship: From Human Blood to Social Policy.* London: London School of Economics Books.

Snickars, Pelle, and Patrick Vonderau, eds. 2010. *The YouTube Reader.* National Library of Sweden, Mediehistoriskt arkiv 12.

Von Goldammer, Eberhard, Joachim Paul, and Joe Newbury. 2003. "Heterarchy – Hierarchy: Two Complementary Categories of Description." Vordenker, Institute for Cybernetics and Systems Theory e.V., August. http://www.vordenker.de/heterarchy/a_heterarchy-e.pdf.

Weber, Max. 1978. *Economy and Society: An Outline of Interpretive Sociology.* Berkeley: University of California Press [orig. 1922].

Wilber, Ken. 2000. *Sex, Ecology, Spirituality: The Spirit of Evolution.* Boston, MA: Shambhala Books

5.   Modchips

How Hardware Hacking Constitutes Grey Markets, User Participation, and Innovation

Mirko Tobias Schaefer

User Appropriation

When a company releases a software application or a software-based product it often actually enters a new phase of development. Skilled users will modify, change and develop the technology further, to suit it to their needs or they might even adapt it for completely different uses, uses which are often unintended and unimagined by the original developer. For most software-based electronic consumer goods one will find easily modifications and related developer communities online.[1]

Video game consoles and their handheld equivalents are extremely popular consumer devices and constitute a valuable and highly contested market. The business models of video game consoles revolves around generating revenues from licenses for third-party developers, selling add-ons for the console such as controllers, remote control and other devices. Increasingly, access to network services and virtual goods become important in generating revenues. The hardware costs provide little or no margin for revenues and often even require vendors to subsidize the initial purchase for the customer. Therefore any appropriation that bypasses the possibilities of generating revenues from licensed software and other add-ons is critical for the vendors. However, users quickly appropriate the design through hacking and reengineering in order to modify the consoles and to execute other than vendor-approved software, and also to play copied games. From playful do-it-yourself modification and homebrew software development to professionalized production of modified processors, so-called modchips, game consoles constitute the emergence of an entire ecology of developer communities, web platforms, production and distribution channels for modified and further developed devices. It led to the emergence of a grey market for modification so-called modchips that enable users to circumvent the original design limitations.[2] This article describes the dynamic interactions between companies, gaming enthusiasts, hackers, and modchip producers in a grey market.

When Microsoft entered the heavily contested market for video game console with its Xbox in 2001, it quickly found the console to be hacked and modified (Huang 2002, 2003; Takahashi 2006, 56-59; Schäfer 2011, 82). The technical specification matched a small computer, which does not come as a surprise given Microsoft's background as the market leader for PC operating systems.[3] A quickly emerging scene of various communities with the most different motives for hacking the Xbox went to work. A group of dedicated Linux enthusiasts, called Xbox Linux Project tried to port the open source operating system onto the proprietary hardware. Other teams focused on developing so-called homebrew software, self-made applications that were not provided by Microsoft.[4] Xbox Media Center became one of the most popular applications for the Xbox, turning the game console into a fully fledged media center for films, video clips, music, and, of course, games. It supports the archiving of media files on the Xbox's hard drive. Other developers provide games or emulate those from outdated platforms for the Microsoft game console.

But in order to do so, the users had to bypass the Microsoft security features that allowed solely the execution of vendor-approved software. The box had to be modified. In general there are two possibilities to modify an electronic consumer good, either through adding a piece of modified hardware, that bypasses or overruns the original processor or a piece of software that adapts the preinstalled firmware. For both solutions, the "hard-mod" or the "soft-mod," the original device needs to be analyzed concerning eventual exploits that can be used to overrun the system and to execute other than vendor-approved code. Walt Scacchi describes the modification of game consoles as

> an expression of game players who are willing to forego the "protections" and quality assurances that console developers provide through product warranties, in order to experience the liberty, skill and knowledge acquisition, as well as potential to innovate, that mastery of reverse engineering affords. (Scacchi 2010)

While communities such as the Xbox Linux Project invested great efforts in the development of a so-called soft-mod, an entire market for so-called modchips emerged. A modchip is a device that is frequently used to circumvent the limitations implemented by the vendor and it allows to execute any software code, including copied games.[5] Producing and distributing modchips as well as the actual practice of modifying a game console has been criminalized in a global and concerted action of the leading manufacturers,

Microsoft, Sony and Nintendo. These corporations took considerable effort to represent modchips and their distribution as intellectual property infringement. Through framing it as piracy and exaggerating the potential harm through claiming that money laundering and even terrorism would be tied to modchip production and distribution and the copying of games the corporations successfully motivated law enforcement to ban these practices and enforce the copyright law. However, a further analysis of the emergence of a grey market for modchips reveals that the problem of modchips is located in the nature of computer technology and the flawed business model employed by the companies, and that practice of hacking video game consoles actually provides innovation.

An Intertwined Ecosystem

In August 2005 ten development kits of the Xbox 360 video game console appeared to be stolen from warehouse in Germany.[6] Development kits are not the off-the-shelf consumer units but are specially designed for licensed third-party producers, such as game developers, to test their software to the technical specificities of the video game console. With only a few weeks to the official market entry of their new game console Xbox 360, Microsoft was immediately on high alert. From industrial espionage to blackmailing, all kind of scenarios appeared to be possible. Mandated by Microsoft, German private investigating firm Prevent AG went to work tracking down the stolen kits. What followed had been quite sensationalized described by mainstream media. Images of the technical components of the stolen kits were posted to the website of the SmartXX team, a group of developers specialized in modification chips for the old Xbox. When Prevent's managing director called upon the help of the Austrian criminal investigation department on Friday, 2 September 2005, he presented the case as very urgent; he painted the potential damage for his clients in very dark colors. Convinced that they are confronted either with a case of blackmailing where the consoles were being held for ransom or with industrial espionage, Austrian investigators managed to receive swiftly the necessary authorization and raided the house of a SmartXX member on Sunday, 4 September. They secured two of the stolen development kits. Simultaneously authorities were investigating traces in Germany and the UK which led to further interrogations and the retrieval of the remaining development kits. It appeared that the total of the stolen devices had been initially delivered by an unidentified person to a gaming shop from where several had been sent to another gaming shop.

From there development kits were distributed to several members of the modding and Xbox hacking scene.

What had started out as an industrial espionage thriller became quickly recognized as a accidental occasion where highly valuable devices where sold to gaming shops and from there to hacking enthusiasts. As one of the involved shop owners said: "It was simply the wow-effect of getting your hands on an unreleased console." The hackers, apart from earning kudos for being first to open yet another box, were driven by their curiosity to investigate technical design. Microsoft did not press charges and allegedly even paid the hackers' expenses for lawyers.[7] The report of German police station Siegburg, one of the investigating units, concludes that an organized criminal action appears to be unlikely. "Evidence rather indicates an accidental abduction of the devices." It remains inconclusive, the report goes on, whether the devices had been delivered to a gaming shop or whether they have been distributed deliberately into the hacker scene to constitute a competitive advantage for an unknown third party.[8]

However, the case of the stolen Xbox 360 development kits reveals a dense network of various participants with different motivation. It shows how intertwined the various participants are. Their actions constitute rather a tangled network than clearly defined entities. Gaming shops were at the time an important entrance point for unskilled users to get their gaming devices modified. Having stolen brand new game consoles, and very unlikely being unaware of their actual design as development kits, the thief probably was simply hoping for potential buyers and approached therefore shops selling gaming devices.

From there the devices trickled down into the scene of hackers and modchip developers. The Austrian member of the modchip-producer team SmartXX was also contributing to the Xbox hacker project Xbox Linux Project, which had no commercial interest in hacking the box. One of the two interrogated English citizens was a member of the prominent modchip team Xecuter. The various scenes of gaming enthusiasts, game console hackers, homebrew software developers, and modchip producers appear to be intertwined; often their websites link to each other, but there are also personal overlaps of individuals contributing to several projects and communities. My earlier research on Xbox hacking showed that communities, modchip developers, and homebrew software developers were widely connected through links leading from community websites to development teams and modchip resellers (Schäfer 2011).[9]

Within this scene it remains a persistent rumor that there are also unacknowledged ties to the game console industry. Common users find information on how to modify a gaming console through community websites such as Xbox-Scene. The web platforms for gaming enthusiasts are also the spaces where hackers and common users meet and can exchange thoughts and ideas. Webshops distributing modchips often advertise their services on community websites. Reviews of modchips as well as complete tables which chip matches which console and which version of a vendor's firmware are also posted to community websites.

The possibilities a modded console provides to users has constituted a large demand in modchips. The ability to hack and modify a console has been recognized as a crucial factor in users' decision to purchase an Xbox (Schulz and Wagner 2008, 12). The same seems to be true when looking at the enormous success of devices such as the Nintendo Wii, the PlayStation Portable, or the Nintendo DS. All devices show a dynamic and vivid ecosystem of community web platforms, a large variety of available homebrew software and the Nintendo Wii and Nintendo DS see a steady production and continuous upgrade of modchips. The modification of an electronic consumer-device allows consumers to expand the possibilities of their property and to unlock the actual potential that is provided in the technological qualities of the device but deliberately limited by the vendor through design decisions.

The inherent possibility of modifying the technology or turn it into something different then intended by the original designer called hackers into action. Through reengineering, hacking, and the playful exploit of bugs or insufficient security features, the hackers found possibilities to override the original design and appropriate it. But hacking an electronic consumer device requires skill, time, and dedication many common users do not have. By transforming a hack into a software application or a piece of hardware the tiresome process of hacking becomes formalized and is available as commodity for a larger user group. In the case of modchips, a value added chain emerged, where the domain of game console hackers provides the intellectual labor of hacking and reengineering as well as designing the piece of hardware, which itself will be mass produced and then distributed through web shops.

Zooming into the Grey Market of Modchips

Production

Although their production and distribution often is in violation of intellectual property laws, modification chips are produced on a large scale and respond to user's desire to do different things with gaming devices than the vendors intended.[10] Profound knowledge is necessary to produce a working alternative chip: Knowledge of the specifications of the targeted product, often acquired by reverse engineering the device. It appears natural that enthusiast game console hacking communities of technology-savvy gamers and computer science students show an overlap with the professionalized but yet very informal networks of modchip producers. Those links became visible in the mentioned case of stolen Xbox development kits. However, the level of professionalism of modchip producers is visible in the resources necessary for serial production of a chip.

According to a former member of the modchip producer SmartXX, pre-production can cost up to US$50,000. A former modchip producer revealed that development and production costs can easily add up to US$25 per unit, which are sold for US$28 each. The minimum number of units built for a generation of modchips are approximately 40,000. With sales between 300,000 and 400,000 modchips for the first Xbox, the interviewed modchip producer is estimated to have gained a market share of 35% at the time.[11] This investment and the prospects of revenues force the modchip producers to employ encryption technologies to prevent their hack from being copied by so-called cloners. Cloners are, often Asia-based, producers who simply copy the modchip design and then reproduce it massively. Websites of modchip producers often display warnings about reproductions that allegedly are inferior to the original design.

Producing a modchip is therefore a double cat-and-mouse game. On the one side game console companies try to disable the functionality of modifications through firmware updates which mostly affect so-called softmods, they try to stifle the diffusion through lawsuits against distributors and to adapt the hard- and software of newer versions of their consoles. This often requires the modchip producer to appropriate the initial modification appropriately.[12] On the other side the modchip producer competes with cloners who seek a way to bypass the intellectual labor of reengineering and hacking and attempt to copy the modified design.

In web shops and on developer's websites and community forums are many examples how the modchip producers themselves respond to cloning. The WiiKey for the Nintendo Wii states on its website that it is only original when sporting a hologram. Displaying an "authorized reseller" icon next to the logo of popular modchip producers is another way of winning the consumers' trust. The modchip producers display lists of "authorized resellers" on their own websites. Other websites warn dramatically of potential damages when using a cloned modchip. Similar rhetoric is true for the commercial vendors of the original game console. They also warn users not to modify their devices because it could damage them. "To brick" a game device means that after modification and due to a new firmware update the entire apparatus becomes as dysfunctional as a brick.

Modchip designers attempt to provide a solution for modification that is easy to implement. If the installation of the modchip requires technical skills it could stifle its diffusion. Each new version of a modchip attempts to simplify the process. Modified chips for the Nintendo Wii required soldering. A soldering rod is not necessarily the basic equipment of gaming enthusiasts, and many producers therefore promoted "solderless modding' or emphasize that there are only four cables to solder to predefined solder points. Advertised as "plug and play" chips, the most recent generation of Wii mods do not require any more handicraft work.[13]

Distribution

Modchips are available for all popular consoles, ranging from the Xbox and Xbox 360[14] to the PlayStation 2,[15] Wii, and Nintendo DS.[16] They are mostly available through mail order distributed through webshops and directly through the developers. Developers prefer to ship directly to customers because they can then profit from a higher margin. As a member of the scene said, the majority of the paid market price usually remains with the distributors who demand discounts from the developers. Hong Kong-based mail-order shop Lik Sang had been one of the biggest distributors of modchips for all popular consoles, but had to discontinue this line of business because they lost a lawsuit against Sony over the modchip distribution. Other companies such as Taiwan-based Friend Tech even developed a complete redesign of the original Xbox, and added a new processor, a bigger hard drive and many other features. Countless web shops in Europe and the US distribute modchips for all kinds of gaming consoles. Figure 5.1 sketches the network of modchip distribution.[17] They are mostly modchip resellers, such as Ozmodchips.com, Consolesource.com, Modchipcentral. com, Modnet.no, or Consolepro.nl. Some are solely distributing online, others, such as Gamefreax are both a web shop and an actual brick-and-mortar store. Modcontrol is a community site revolving around modchips.[18] Modchip producer Team Xecuter appears as a well-connected node in the network, and so do the websites representing popular modchips, such as x360usb.com, a Team Xecuter product for modding the Xbox 360, or the Wasabi modchip (wasabi.net.cn) or the WODE Jukebox (wodejukebox. com) for the Nintendo. Clearly visible are the connections of those sites to distributor sites, such as Consolepro.nl, Rejoy.se, Modchipcentral.com, and others.

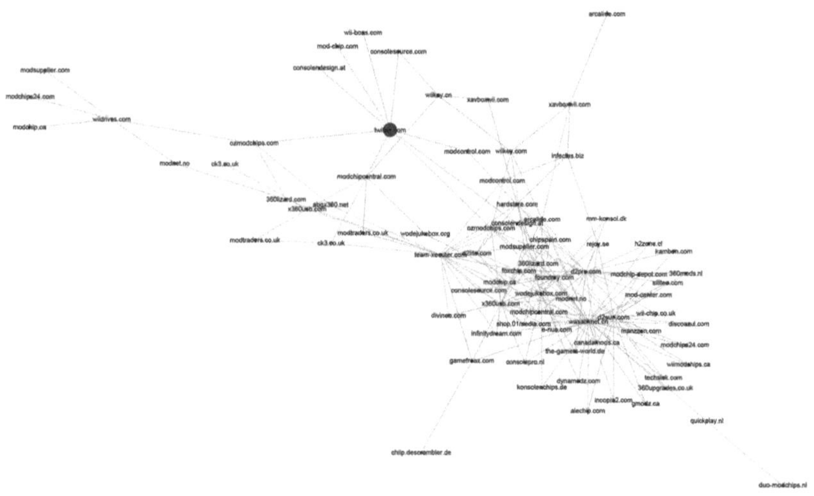

Fig. 5.1: Network of modchip producers and modchip distributors, 2011
(Data collected with Issue Crawler, visualization with Gephi)

An entire grey market has emerged due to the demand for modchips, which
are sold in large quantities. The value supply chain starts with the hackers
providing the knowledge for a work-around of the original design, and they
also develop the design for a modchip, which is then developed through a
manufacturer and then distributed through mail order. Modchip producers
and distributors are often confronted with legal charges filed by Microsoft,
Sony, and Nintendo, who argue that modchips are primarily used for playing
copied games.

Warez and Homebrew Software

The main reason for modifying a game console is naturally related to
software. This affects four areas of software use: the possibility to produce
backup safety copies of the purchased games, the facility to execute nonli-
censed software, often called "homebrew software," the circumvention of
region codes, and the playing of copied games. Creating backup copies of
purchased games is a legal activity as is the creation and use of homebrew
software. Attempts to circumvent regional limitations imposed by system
of regionally licensed copyrights is a logical consequence of regional price

differences in a global market, where users easily can purchase the lower-priced titles online. Reliable figures on download numbers are difficult to obtain; not only are the many industry conducted surveys biased, but retrieving proper download numbers of illegally distributed software is close to impossible to obtain. Surveys use estimates that vary widely.[19] Nevertheless, playing copied games seems to be the prime motivation for game console modification.

Copied games, so-called "warez," are distributed through P2P file-sharing networks and warez servers. Platforms distributing homebrew software therefore deliberately prohibit the distribution of illegal warez through their channels. While the distribution of copied games appears to the original vendors as a direct threat of their business model, homebrew software developers distance themselves explicitly from piracy and rather emphasize the added value their applications provide. Platforms such as DS-Scene.net for the Nintendo DS or the legendary Xbins server for the original Xbox warn their users that they will be banned for any illegal uploads. Consequently homebrew developers do not attempt to monetize their software for the modified devices. A lively homebrew scene had quickly emerged for the original Xbox, the PlayStation Portable and the Nintendo DS, providing many useful applications that expanded significantly the original design. The already mentioned Xbox Media Center allows users to play DVDs from the Xbox, a feature that required – for the unmodified design – the additional purchase of a remote control. The Xbox Media Center did not only turn the Xbox into a media center for video and music files, it also rendered the add-on device, the remote control, obsolete. Very popular software applications for the modified Xbox were the dashboards. A dashboard is a graphical user interface for navigating and operating the various features of the gaming console. A modified console is much more than a machine for playing pirated games, through modification the owner adopts the commodity as her own apparatus, a process that exceeds the predefined options of customizing that companies provide as a pseudo-individual choice.[20]

Commercial vendors try to discourage users from modifying their consoles through stripping them of warranty rights. Microsoft even excludes modified consoles from connecting to its online network Xbox Live and its related services. In 2009 an astonishing 600,000 Xbox 360 consoles were excluded from accessing Xbox Live.[21] In the case of the first Xbox these attempts of excluding modified consoles from the corporate network led to the emergence of completely independent networks such as Xlink Kai. Operating completely beyond the corporate structure, this network even allowed the game consoles of other vendors to connect. A Microsoft Xbox user could play a game against a user operating a Nintendo GameCube. Modchip producers reacted to the latest exclusion of users from the Xbox Live.

Another strategy to prevent exclusion from the network was to build in a switch that allowed the modchip to be turned off when connecting to Xbox Live.[22] While this required quite some tinkering recent modchips for the Xbox 360 provide the turn off option for an Xbox Live-compatible mod. This development is another example for how the modchip producers transform the community-developed hacks into a design feature of a commodity. But quite similar, the commercial vendor can adopt user appropriation to improve the design, as the implementation of many homebrew software applications into the Xbox successor Xbox 360 showed.

Game Console Modding and Its Consequences

As I have explained extensively in my work on participatory culture (Schäfer 2011), the appropriation of corporate design through users meets three different reactions; I have labeled them *confrontation*, *implementation*, and *integration*. Those dynamics are recognizable in the modchip ecology as well. They unfold in a popular and political discourse, in technological design and in legislature.

Confrontation

Confrontation describes the attempts of commercial vendors to label user appropriation as undesirable, illegal, or even dangerous. Additionally, design features aim to stifle user appropriation while the use of intellectual property laws are used to criminalize any appropriation that might endanger the business model. Microsoft's swift reaction to the purloined Xbox development kits is an example for confrontation. Nintendo's lawsuit against Lik Sang's modchip distribution, or Sony's lawsuit against Paul Owen's distribution of the so-called Messiah modchip in the UK show how user appropriation is addressed as copyright infringement (Lim 2008). Accordingly, third-party platforms (such as eBay) outlaw modchips in their terms of use.[23] In their defense, modchip producers and distributors inherently refer to the legendary Betamax case, *Sony Corp. of America v. Universal City Studios, Inc.* (1984), where the court ruled that producers of video tapes can't be held liable for copyright infringement. However, in *Sony Computer Entertainment, Inc. v. Paul Owen & Others* (2002) the court decided that the modchip intentionally provided a circumvention of copyright protection and no exception to infringement was applicable (Lim 2008).[24]

The US Immigration Customs Enforcement (ICE) conducts large-scale operations in order to shut down web shops that trade in modchips. The 2007 "Operation Tangled Web" was one of the biggest raids against the modchip distribution network in the US.[25] Raiding allegedly over 30 locations, the operation was officially targeted against a network of intellectual property piracy. However, many of the websites that were target of the operation, such as Modchipstore.com, are still operating, and many of the alleged businesses for game console modification turn out to be the rather nonprofit activities of skilled game enthusiasts who modify consoles in their local community. While these, often juvenile delinquents, face hefty charges in the US, many web shops remain unaffected from the ICE's activities.[26]

Despite many court decisions that declare the distribution of modchips illegal, it is not difficult to purchase and install these devices, and they are consequently widely used. With their large-scale operations and their quick seizure of addresses that hosts websites used for distributing modchips, copied films, games, etc., the ICE has established herself as the law enforcement arm of the copyright industry.

The copyright industry's influence in pushing for more a more industry-friendly legislature is also visible in international affairs. At least one of the notorious WikiLeaks Cablegate messages addresses the legal status of modchips.[27] The public discourse narrative that is adopted from copyright industry PR is repeated in the public statements of the law enforcement authorities when announcing and justifying their extensive activities against the modchip scene. Former assistant secretary of Homeland Security and Immigration and Customs Enforcement (ICE) Julie L. Meyers stated after the 2007 raids: "Illicit devices like the ones targeted today are created with one purpose in mind, subverting copyright protection."[28] The Homeland Security press release states that modchips stood to cost copyright-holding industries an annual loss of US$250 billion. The figures sketching the alleged losses created through modchips are impossible to verify and can be regarded as completely made up (Schäfer 2011, 134).

The copyright industry (that is, the software, music, and film industries) have developed a reputation for supporting their argument with dodgy figures and biased research (Patry 2009, 30-34; Goldacre 2009). What is visible in the press statements of the ICE and other law enforcement authorities, as well as in the rhetoric used by politicians to set an agenda for a tighter copyright law enforcement and Internet regulation, is actually the spin of the copyright industry.

Using all platforms of public discourse to describe the rather natural process of copying files as criminal activity, the copyright industry defends a system of media content control drawing from the industrial age. However, as Patry has pointed out convincingly for the music industry, this moral panic is created to divert attention away from a business model unfit for a digital economy (2009). This is partially true for the game console producers as well. However, there is an interesting observation to make. While the game console companies engage in concerted activities against the modchip production, they do not completely follow the music industry's hysteric approach. The moral panic displayed in public discourse is more cautious. The game console vendors might be even aware of the benefits of providing a hackable product: A hackable console is more attractive to users and can simply through this accidental feature gain a higher market share (Schulz and Wagner 2008). Other positive side effects of piracy could be the reduction of taxable revenues and the increase of tax allowance for losses created through illegal downloads (Scacchi 2010, 13).

There is even evidence that homebrew software draws at least the interest of corporate software developers (Schäfer 2011). There are persistent rumors within the community of game console hackers that the Xbox development kit of the original Xbox 360 console might have been leaked deliberately into the community. There is no proof for an explicit cooperation between hackers, homebrew developers, and the corporate decision makers. But the dynamics of implementation and integration show that corporations do learn from user appropriation.

Implementation

As implementation, I describe the process of successfully implementing user activities into software design and new business models. The Xbox 360 implemented many features that have initially emerged as homebrew software applications. Microsoft shipped the Xbox 360 with an implemented development kit that turned any user into a legal third-party developer and with its online network marketplace, Microsoft also provided a distribution platform. The lively homebrew software scene that developed hundreds of applications for the original Xbox withdrew almost completely from the Microsoft platform with the advent of the Xbox 360.

While the participation of those developers might have been rendered obsolete through providing many equivalents of the applications that have been initially produced as homebrew software, other reasons for the dwindling interest of hackers and programmers into the Xbox might have been Microsoft's.NET software framework that appears to be unattractive for developing applications as several members of the former developer's scene expressed. They also find a mandatory fee to pay for distributing applications for free through Microsoft's marketplace deeply unattractive. Hacking the Xbox 360 took quite some time but was eventually achieved and modchips are available as well.

Integration

The process of integration is not yet adopted in the area of video game consoles. Integration describes a collaborative effort of company and community to cocreate a commodity. Often this commodity is available for free, such as Google Maps. Here, Google provides an infrastructure and a set of technologies and enables its users to employ their data and geographical mapping information for further uses. The community participates through developing the application further and therefore improves it significantly. This has been described convincingly and in detail, supported by a large number of example cases that the active participation of users benefits the corporate effort and improves and even innovates the original design. The computer game industry integrated user participation through providing editing tools for game modification (Nieborg 2005; Nieborg and Van der Graf 2008). The game industry insists that any derivative of their games is still protected by their copyrights and therefore successfully prevents a commercial exploitation of game mods. This is similar to homebrew software that as unlicensed software cannot be sold.

Apple succeeded in integrating user appropriation into its smartphone platform iPhone by setting up the app store. While Apple grants users the freedom to develop software applications and to distribute them even commercially through the corporate network, they reserve the unlimited possibility of monitoring and regulating the user's productions.[29] Maybe smartphones can serve as an example for the video game console of how to integrate users. That would require the gaming console vendors to rethink their business model and to monetize the gaming platform differently than through licenses.

Prospects of a Grey Market

Since 2005 some things have changed in the modchip universe. The aspect of installing a piece of hardware has been altered to an extent where it is even for novice users possible to modify a game console. While gaming equipment shops have not only been the primary resellers for modchips, they have also been the first address where a user would turn to for game console modification. With the latest generation of modchips and flash-cards, modifying a game console became significantly easier. Even novice users are now able to do that.

What script kiddies are to hackers, flashers are to the professional "tuner." Common users now offer modification at a much reduced cost and they advertise it in user fora, promoting their services in the signa-ture of their postings. Websites such as the German Wer-Flasht-Wo.de (translation: Who-flashes-where) provide address lists per region in order to help users find the nearest skilled user to get help with tuning their gaming device.[30] The brick-and-mortar retailers who provided the modchip installation service see themselves as being prevented from delivering a service that generated steady revenue as well as becoming a target for legal action. Since they run official businesses and pay taxes, they can easily be held responsible for the items they sell. Securing their market one cease-and-desist note at the time, the big corporations send their lawyers to muscle the shop owners out of the market. With each note another item will be removed from the range of products. The service of modification is increasingly taken over by teenage users helping other users for some extra pocket money.

The grey market of modchips is in a way a steady companion of the game console market. The user communities, hacker teams, and modchip producers, following various motivations, interact in an environment based on appropriating corporate designs. The strategies used by Sony, Microsoft, and Nintendo show that they do not stand to lose in the dynamic ecosystem that surrounds and accompanies their products. They achieved an almost global prohibition of distributing copied software and managed to criminalize downloads in many countries. Selling modchips as a busi-ness has been pushed into the fringes of legality. However, purchasing modchips, downloading pirated games, or modifying a gaming device for whatever reasons remains an easy thing to do. Nevertheless, there are benefits to the modchip universe. Not only might hackability lead to a higher market penetration, an active and enthusiastic community of skilled users actually serves as an extended research and development department to an alert company. The biggest burden for the companies is an ill-suited business model depending on licenses for games rather than revenues generated from the gaming platform itself, related services, and access.

Notes

1. Modifications of the electronic vacuum cleaner Roomba can be found at Roomba robotic vacuum cleaner (www.roombacommunity.com); a Linux operating system for the iPod hacked (http://ipodlinux.sourceforge.net); Aibopet provides the AIBO community with modifications at (http://www.aibohack.com); a forum for PlayStation Portable mods is PSPmod (www.pspmod.com). For almost any device an online forum for modifications is available.

2. Modchip is colloquial for "modification chip." Modchip allows users to execute any software on a game console, including copied games.

3. The Xbox was equipped with an Intel Celeron 733 MHz processor, 64 MB of RAM, an 8 or 10 GB hard disk, a DVD drive, and a network interface, and a stripped-down version of the Windows 2000 kernel served as its operating system.

4. The term "homebrew software" refers to software that was not programmed by a regular company but by members of user communities. Very active platforms for homebrew software are PSP Hacks (www.psp-hacks.com), PSP-Scene (http://pspscene.net/forums/) for the PlayStation Portable, and DS-Scene (www.ds-scene.net), for the Nintendo DS.

5. Modchips are available for almost all common video game consoles.

6. All information about the SmartXX case are retrieved by the author through interviews with several persons involved in the case, either as defendant or investigator. The author further more received a file consisting of documents (e-mail exchange between the private investigators and police authorities; interrogation files, memos and protocols from the German and Austrian authorities). The file has been sent anonymously to the author. In interviews with members of the modchip scene, as well in interviews with detectives participating in the investigation, the contents of the documents could be verified.

7. A statement by SmartXX forum administrator Hamptitampti claims that Microsoft is paying their lawyers and has withdrawn from pressing charges; see "Stolen 360 Developer Kits, SmartXX Speaks Out," post, Xbox360Info.com forum, 5 October 2005, http://www.xb360info.com/xbox/news/168.

8. From the concluding report on the case (Vermerk, 28 November 2005, Landrat Siegbrug, Kreispolizeinehörde). Translation by the author. The document is part of an anonymously delivered zip file consisting of various documents about this case.

9. The research published in Schäfer 2011 includes case examples of modifications of the Microsoft Xbox and the Sony AIBO; the projects on which the research focused date from 2005 to 2008.yyy

10. Karaganis emphasize that no figures and research are available that sketch the actual size of the modchip market. Their writing implicates that the in-

dustry's claims concerning financial losses caused through modchips might exaggerate the actual diffusion of modchips (2011, 50-51).

11. These figures relate to the modchips for the original Xbox. It is noteworthy that these figures are quite different from those reported by Karaganis, who refers to 60,000 modchips that have been confiscated during Operation Tangled Web, the biggest law enforcement operation against modchip distributors in the US (Karaganis 2011, 50).

12. A good example for the changes in game console and the effect on modchip production is the overview of existing Wii modchips at Wikipedia: http://en.wikipedia.org/wiki/List_of_Wii_modchips.

13. FlatMod, FlatMii, Wasabi DX, WiiKey Fusion, DriveKey, and the WODE Jukebox.

14. Known teams of Xbox modchip producers are: Aladdin Chip Team, Duo X2, OzChip Team, SmartXX, Team Omega, Team OzXodus, Team SpiderXS, Team Xecuter, Team X-Changer, Team X-Chip, and Team Xodus.

15. Well-known teams of PlayStation 2 modchip producers include: Infinity Team, Matrix Infinity, Messiah Team, Modbo Team, MXL2 Team, Ninja Team, and Ripper Team.

16. Nintendo DS modchips.

17. For recent mapping of the modchip resellers I assembled a list of modchips from various gaming community sites, such as Xbox-Scene, and from Wikipedia. Using the websites of modchip producers as starting points a crawl with the issue crawler (Rogers) produced a list of websites linked to the initial list of modchip producers. The network mapping was then created through a visualization in Gephi.

18. Note that this crawl is only representing a fraction of the actual reseller market. Somehow many links are ignored, or not taken into account due to absence in the sample of starting points.

19. For a critical analysis of the industry-presented figures, see Julian Sanchez, "750,000 Lost Jobs? The Dodgy Digits behind the War on Piracy," *Ars Technica*, 7 October 2008, http://arstechnica.com/tech-policy/2008/10/dodgy-digits-behind-the-war-on-piracy/. For a thorough analysis of file sharing and record sales, see Felix Oberholzer and Koleman Strumpf, "The Effect of File Sharing on Record Sales: An Empirical Analysis," *Journal of Political Economy* 115.1 (2004): 1-42.

20. Although this chapter discusses only modchips it is important to mention that users also modify the cases of their gaming devices. This case modding is also provided professionally and therefore constitutes another niche in the ecology of gaming consoles.

21. "Microsoft Disconnects Xbox Gamers," *BBC News*, 11 November 2009, http://news.bbc.co.uk/2/hi/8354166.stm.

22. See a tutorial by Captain Dunsel posted to Xbox-Scene: "Adding Mod Chip Enable/Disable and BIOS Flash ROM Write Enable/Disable Switches to Your XBox (vo.6)," http://www.xboxscene.com/articles/endisable.php.

23. See eBay policies: http://pages.ebay.com/help/policies/mod-chips.html.
24. Intellectual Property Case Search System: http://www.ipo.gov.uk/ipcass/ipcass-alphabetical/ipcass-alphabetical-o/ipcass-sony.htm.
25. "Fed's Mod Chip Raid Ended a $2.5 Million Piracy Operation," *Game Politics*, 24 November 2008, http://www.gamepolitics.com/2008/11/24/feds039-mod-chip-raid-ended-25-million-piracy-operation.
26. "Cal State Student Arrested for Playing Video Games," *NBCDFW News*, 7 January 2010, http://www.nbcdfw.com/news/tech/Cal-State-Student-Faces-10-Year-Prison-Term-for-Playing-with-Video-Games-52386872.html.
27. In a 2004 court ruling in Spain modchips had been declared legal, a decision that is discussed in a memo entitled "Aberrant Mod Chip Ruling." The memo expresses concerns that such a ruling might be trendsetting and concludes that the transposition of EU directives on copyright law in Spain will be observed carefully. Retrieved from Cablegatesearch.net: http://www.cablegatesearch.net/search.php?q=%22mod+chip%22andqorigin=0andsort=1.
28. "Crackdown on Modchip Sellers," *BBC News*, 2 August 2007, http://news.bbc.co.uk/2/hi/technology/6928177.stm.
29. This is also true for Google and its Android platform marketplace.
30. Wer-Flasht-Wo.com: http://www.wer-flasht-wo.com.

Bibliography

Bastian M., S. Heymann, and M. Jacomy. 2009. "Gephi: An Open Source Software for Exploring and Manipulating Networks." *International AAAI Conference on Weblogs and Social Media*.

Huang, Andrew. 2002. Keeping secrets in hardware: The Microsoft Xbox case study. MIT AI Lab Memo. http://web.mit.edu/bunnie/www/proj/anatak/AIM-2002-008.pdf.

Huang, Andrew. 2003. *Hacking the Xbox: An Introduction to Reverse Engineering.* San Francisco, CA: No Starch Press.

Goldacre, Ben. 2009. "Illegal Downloads and Dodgy Figures." *The Guardian*, 5 June. http://www.guardian.co.uk/commentisfree/2009/jun/05/ben-goldacre-bad-science-music-downloads.

Karaganis, Joe, ed. 2011. "Rethinking Piracy." In Joe Karaganis, ed., *Media Piracy in Emerging Economies*. New York: Social Science Research Council.

Lim, Yee Fen. 2008. "New hope for consumers of digital copyright material in Hong Kong." In Brian Fitzgerald, Fuping Gao, Damien O'Brien, and Sampsung Xiaoxiang Shi, eds., *Copyright Law, Digital Content and the Internet in the Asia-Pacific*. Sidney: Sydney University Press.

Nieborg, David B. 2005. "Am I Mod or Not? – An Analysis of First Person Shooter Modification Culture." Paper presented at Creative Gamers Seminar – Exploring Participatory Culture in Gaming, Hypermedia Laboratory, University of Tampere, Finland. http://www.gamespace.nl/content/DBNieborg2005_CreativeGamers.pdf.

Nieborg, David B., and Shenja van der Graaf. 2008. "The Mod Industries? The Industrial Logic of Non-Market Game Production." *European Journal of Cultural Studies* 11.2: 177-195.

Patry, William. 2009. *Moral Panics and the Copyright Wars*. Oxford: Oxford University Press.

Scacchi, Walter. 2010. "Computer Games, Mods, Modders and the Mod Scene." *First Monday* 15.5, 3 May. http://firstmonday.org/htbin/cgiwrap/bin/ojs/index.php/fm/article/view/2965/2526.

Schäfer, Mirko Tobias. 2011. *Bastard Culture! How User Participation Transforms Cultural Production*. Amsterdam: Amsterdam University Press.

Schulz, Celine, and Stefan Wagner. 2008. "Piracy and Outlaw Community Innovations." *International Journal of Innovation Management* 12.3: 399-418.

Takahashi, Dean. 2006. *The Xbox 360 Uncloaked: The Real Story Behind Microsoft's Next-Generation Video Game Console*. N.p.: Spiderworks.

Toward a Theroy of Media Piracy

6.   On the Political Economy of Copy Protection

Stefan Meretz

Why does copy protection exist? What is been protected against whom? The spontaneous answers to these simple questions refer to the prevailing forms of thinking in commodity society: The "intellectual property" just has to be protected against theft, just like everybody locks their door in order to prevent the television set from be carried away by "TV pirates."

Aside from the fact that locking the door isn't common everywhere in the world, the analogy to the material world is inadequate too. The analogy is created arbitrarily; it is an ideological form. The digital copy does not affect the original; it does not take anything away, but adds something to the world. In many Asian societies, a copy is something noble to strive for. The copyist imitates the master; she wants to perfect the imitation, and then to surpass the master to become a master herself. This understanding of accumulating human knowledge is completely lacking in Western societies. On the other hand, the Western ideological form of a "pirate copy" is simply incomprehensible in many Asian countries. But also in the West, the everyday reasoning of the "smartphone generation" can hardly comprehend that somebody should lose something if a private copy is made for personal pleasure.

The ideology of "intellectual property" and "pirate copies" had become fragile in the West and has never been completely established elsewhere. Is it possible to trace back this ideology to the political/economic constitution of bourgeois society? This will be tried below. In order to start, we first have to determine the meaning of what is called a "copy." This will be done by a conceptual logical-historical reconstruction of its emergence in capitalism. The goal is not to give a historical account, but to develop a conceptual mapping of consecutive logical steps of development. Afterward the gained concepts of copying are investigated in respect of their economic form, which then makes it possible to clarify the concept and meaning of "copy protection."

Let us start with the copy. What is a copy? A copy is the result of a reproduction, the realization of something conceived, or the replication of something already produced. The English language makes this ambiguity obvious: "copy" does not only mean "duplicate," but also "instance." Now we will need some conceptual clarifications. So far, mainly the digital copy was mentioned, but forms of *physical* and *analogous* as well as of *digital* reproductions should be distinguished. Additionally, both the aspects of *product* and *production process* have to be considered.

The Physical Copy

The emulation or imitation of a physical product is deemed to be *plagiarism* if the different authorship is not unveiled but the work is presented as original, and it is deemed to be *counterfeit* if the authorship is claimed to be identical to the original author and the copy is claimed to be genuine. However, the imitation never fully corresponds with the copied object, original and copy always exhibit material differences. Hence, not the item itself is reproduced, but mainly the idea or purpose is copied by approaching the original physique through imitation as closely as possible.

Imitation requires knowledge about the production process, because otherwise the copyist cannot realize the copy. A copy is always both process and result. The side of the process is about the production know-how, while the side of the result is about the product's purpose. Plagiarism and counterfeit were outlawed long ago, while *open copying* (imitation without a false authorship claim) has only been delegitimized with the emergence of the commodity society. What is conceived as an acceptable or a condemnable copy is the result of societal struggles and cannot be justified independently. Today, "me-too" products are permitted if they represent some properties of an "original," but not all of them. Generics as agent-identical drugs are illegal during the patent lock period, while effectively equal analogous compounds with slight variations in agent composition are allowed. Imitation cheese is equally legal, though its origin as a copy from an original cheese model has to be veiled, because otherwise the fake cheese could hardly be successfully sold.

Historically, immediate physical copying occurs in the period of pre-capitalist handcrafted production of artifacts as well as in the period of manufacture production during early capitalism. The intended purpose of the product – what it is good for – is completely concentrated in the producing persons who have the production know-how. Manufacture differs from handcrafted production by the formal subordination of labor under capital, which acquires the produced commodities and thereby the surplus value, while craftsmen still self-determine their labor and valorize their products themselves.

The societal meaning is objectified within the product as *realized purpose* whereas the production know-how as *intended purpose* remains volatile since it almost – except for symbolic representations like drafts, plans, models – does not undergo material fixations. This fundamentally changes with industrial revolution. Copies as results of inaccurate manual reproduction processes have such different individual physical qualities that the resulting items have to be viewed as being unique. Thus, also in this respect immediate physical copying always leads to individual products, quasi material originals. Only the purpose is duplicated with each new realization.

Copying and Copy Protection in the Materiality Realm

The craftsmen's copy as the repetitive making of the same product was implicitly limited by the knowledge about the production process possessed by the craftsmen, which cannot be readily revealed by simply looking at the final product. However, this more or less large knowledge advantage could eventually be leveled by other manual copyists catching up. Thus guilds and granted privileges acted to provide "copy protection."

As the industrial revolution lead to more and more tools and process knowledge being transferred "into" machinery, materialized knowledge became increasingly important. The hand-copied product could not compete with the industrial product, because handcrafting was too time-consuming. Now, the interest of copyists turned toward the copy machinery itself. The machinery, i.e., its design and functional principles, has to be kept secret, since it represents an essential part of the copying know-how in an objectified form. Often copyists of machine-embodied copying know-how were – as "late adaptors" – able to avoid faults of the original machines by copying them in an improved manner. German companies have been experts in this field by catching up and finally outpacing technological advances of English producers – until they themselves learned how to defend their advance against other copying desires using governmental support. The essential mean for doing so become the *patent*, the state-secured limited monopoly guarantee of valorization.

Economically, material mass copies are normal commodities. Realized in separate private production processes, they are exchanged on markets for money, thus gaining societal validity and generality. Markets act as indirections mediating and generalizing private work. The measure of mediation is not utility but value, which is the societal average effort to produce the commodity. Thereby markets as mediators of private work enforce the split-up of use value (abstracted utility) and value (abstracted labor). The commodities gain societal generality by their labor abstraction.

The Analogous Copy

Capitalist mass production starts with industrialization. While the hand-crafted copy was unique due to different qualities of each reproduced item, the mass product is structurally uniform due to the objectified craftsmen operations "in" a machine. The template for the singular crafted reproduction does not come from a material role model, but from the objectified algorithmic production logic.

The intended purpose which is to be objectified is no longer the living empirical know-how of the craftsman, but it is implemented "in" a machine in the form of engineer-dissected and resynthesized knowledge. Now, the copy is the repeated application of a machine-objectified algorithmic definition of the product. The knowledge of the intended purpose has migrated from the human being into the machine and can now be applied as analogous, material mass copy. Mass products as analogous copies are multiple repeated carriers of always the same intended purposes, which finally enter commodity circulation as both use value and abstract value. What is copied here is the intended purpose, not the incarnated product. Despite uniformity the single copies are not identical, but they are only analogous. Each single product remains an "individual" with its own "biography" of use.

Mass production is a precondition for the development of *materially neutral* products. While with materially bound products, their physical qualities immediately shape utility and societal meaning, materially neutral products are those where the physical shape is only relevant as *carrier*, but does not constitute utility and societal meaning itself. This applies especially to knowledge products. Analogous copies are not only related to materially bound mass products, but also to basically materially neutral content on physical carriers. Now, product purpose and meaning are no longer determined by the physical quality of the carrier, but only by the carried content.

The text of a book may be released as a hardcover or a paperback and it may show different aesthetic qualities, but the text itself is normally not affected by these different shapes. The same applies to music or film using different media for recording. Since nonmaterial content and physical carrier are separated, plagiarism may be recognizable by content, whereas a counterfeit is not detectable without further ado. Thus, the notion of a pirated edition had to be created before outlawing the reprinting of well-selling books in the early modern era, because no exclusive exploitation right existed at that time. Also citation as a socially legitimate form of reproduction arose in this context. While at first author credits were not obligatory (e.g., in musical citations), today giving credit is a legally established obligation (for texts) or the use has to be explicitly allowed or licensed (for music, e.g., via collecting societies).

The content transferred to a separate carrier can be relevant for the production process itself. Hence, algorithmic production know-how can be separated from its mechanical form. Early examples are Jacquard looms, where the production logic exists in form of punch cards separated from the machine, which can be changed according to the intended purpose. The machine generates its process steps by direct mechanical reading of the card holes. The weaving pattern as part of the intended purpose has now moved to an external representation.

The punch cards of the Jacquard loom are materially dependent. They can be made of cardboard or another material (e.g., wood or plastic), but their physical constitution must suffice the machine-reading mechanics. Here, the neutrality of matter is related to the content, to the algorithmic production know-how, which has emancipated itself from the machine. The machine no longer represents a specific intended purpose, but rather is neutral. Anybody who wants to copy the production know-how does not need to rebuild the entire machine, but only the punch cards. But these reproductions have to fit to the machine they are made for, which limits the material choice and predetermines the minimal quality of the analogous card copy, in order to work with a machine identical in construction. The automatic loom is therefore still a specialized machine, so only the spectrum of products (weaving patterns) is extended. The limited material neutrality – neutral in relation to purpose, but not in relation to the production process – will only be overcome in the digital age.

Analogous Copy and Copy Protection

After the execution machine has been separated from the knowledge carrier, the interest of the copyist turns toward both aspects. Since the execution machine is a specialized machine of the analogous age – needing a material-specific knowledge carrier, in order to operate as a complete machine – machine and carrier isolated from each other are inoperable. However, provided the execution machine is available (e.g., acquired as means of production), the knowledge carrier – representing the productive logic – shifts into the copyist's focus. If suitable punch cards of the Jacquard loom can be copied and raw material is available, then nothing prevents the production of the latest fashionable fabrics. The creator of the new pattern will be duped and eventually ruined. Here, modern copyright law and its derivatives (utility models, trademarks, etc.) have to intervene. However, first copyright law has to be transformed from a traditional right based on privileges to an exploitation right.

With the separation of the information carrier from the execution machine, the production of information carriers itself is commodified, whereas the production of physical carriers becomes a subaltern moment of the represented information. The labor and material effort required to produce analogous sound carriers is small compared to the effort it takes to create and record the sound itself. Since the execution machine is a special machine, which only functions together with the specific carrier, and since the analogous information carrier cannot be reproduced in the same quality as the original without a great effort (i.e., copies of analogous sound carriers are of minor quality compared to the master), there is a technically immanent barrier preventing unlimited copying. This technical limitation together with copyright provide an effective hindrance, therefore explicit technical copy protection is yet not an issue.

Economically, the information carriers do not essentially differ from conventional mass commodities. They can become fully fledged commodities if execution machines (e.g., players for analogous sound carriers) are sufficiently widespread. Again, there is a material interconnection between carrier and carried content, although production costs become minimal and highly scalable. While each carrier represents an "individual," the informational content is of a general nature. The content appears on each single product and can be potentially transferred to another type of carrier as long as a special execution machine also exists for the new carrier (e.g., from the analogous record to the analogous tape).

Since the production costs of additional information carriers are small compared to the initial effort for producing the content, producers get an ideal mean to realize extra surplus value. An extra surplus value can be gained if it is possible to reduce the cost for the commodities to a level below the societal average. This explains why the culture industry strives for generating "hits" by creating a uniform mass taste.

The Digital Copy

The coupling between carrier medium and content, which had already become loose, dissolves completely with the digital copy. Now, the focus is exclusively on the reproduction of content, while the carrier medium becomes neutral in regard to the content (as earlier the production know-how in regard to the machine). With analogous copies, the quality of the carrier material was still reflected in the quality of the product, so that an identical reproduction was difficult or even impossible. A copy (nearly) always implied a quality loss of the carried content. In case of digital copies, previously and newly made products are *identical*. There is no longer a substantial distinction between "original" and "copy," but only a social one: Who has copied what from whom? Due to the separation from a distinct material carrier – it only has to be *any* carrier – in the realm of the digital *all* copies are *originals* and vice versa.

The second important characteristic of the digital sphere is the decoupling of the reproduction process from the material effort. Note that decoupling does not mean that there is *no* effort. Indeed, the input of material, energy, and labor is vanishingly small *at the moment* of reproduction, however, establishing the infrastructural *conditions* requires an significant amount of material, energy, and labor. Compared to the production of material goods, the effort has completely shifted toward the infrastructure.

Before, the process description emancipated itself from production process, now it emancipated itself from the carrier material. The triplet of digital algorithmic description, carrier of the digital representation of the described object, and a process machine executing the algorithmic description is always there. In this regard, there is no difference between producing steel or playing music. Digitality means universality, thus complete content neutrality: Every content can be coded if a code executing machine exists. What a missing executing machine implies becomes obvious when one desperately searches for a slot for an "ancient" floppy disk. Archiving has become an important problem in the digital age.

The universality of the code corresponds to the universality of the executing machine, the computer. In manufacturing, the universal computer is accompanied by the universal process machine, e.g., a production robot. Temporarily there has been the idea of a totally digitized and automated production (called computer-integrated manufacturing [CIM]). But this was an illusion, since automated processes cannot implement something genuinely new or unknown (including disturbances, see Baukrowitz 2006, 102-104).

Digital Copy and Copy Protection

The separation of the external information and knowledge carrier from the execution machine was a huge developmental step. Compared to this big step, the change from the analogous to the digital representational form seems to be less important. However, the consequences have been much more profound. The analogous form of representation sticks to a distinct material manifestation, which is able to map continuous transitions. Be it the groove shape of a record, the degree of magnetization of a tape, or the pattern for the production of trousers – continuous scales are always described in a physical form. The measuring accuracy limits the precision of the analogous mapping.

With the transition to the digital form, these limitations (and some more) have been overcome. The material dependence of the carrier disappears, and is replaced by an immaterial carrier. The mapping precision is potentially unlimited, because by extending the digital numeric representation limits can be arbitrarily shifted to an extremely big or extremely small scale. In short: the digital form is a universal representation form. The universal digital form is complemented by an equally universal execution machine, or better: a *mediation machine*, which is no longer defined for a specific intended purpose and which can supply nearly any execution machine with adequate control signals. The computer has risen to a universal mediator of the societal infrastructure: Internet, production, consumer goods, services.

With the digital form, the creation of a copy became drastically easier and more cost efficient. Binary codes can be arbitrarily combined, and binary combinations create new meanings, purposes, and applications. From the moment of its creation, each digital invention is only a mouse click away from global distribution through copying. Copying is no longer an extraordinary event, but the core of the digital movement pattern of the binary code. The general digital infrastructure is based on the copy. Stopping this movement would imply switching off the infrastructure and shutting down the society.

Economically, the digital copy perpetuates a tendency which began with the analogous copy. The main effort in commodity production is directly related to the content, while due to the digital form the distribution has moved into the general digital infrastructure. The universality of the digital form contradicts the social form as a proprietary commodity. A precondition for being a commodity is the scarcity of the good. Contrary to the assumption of classical economics, scarcity is not a natural property of the good, but the result of the social form of its production as a commodity (Meretz

2007, 68f). However, the singularity and limitation of a material good can easily be used to practically arrange scarcity – e.g., by preventing access to commodities, reducing their production, organizing delivery restrictions, destroying goods, etc.

Arranging scarcity is not possible with digital informational goods without additional measures. Usage and scarcity are contradictory. Usage means copying, the commodity form implies prevention of coping. In terms of valorization, "good copies" have to be separated from "bad copies." This separation can only succeed if producers of content – who want to press their contents into the commodity form – can control and manipulate the digital good as well as the digital infrastructure. This target was and is pursued. Two technological approaches have evolved.

The first approach was (and is) the digital copy protection of the product, thus connecting the usage of the digital information with the availability of a key, which is distributed over other channels (e.g., as imprint on a DVD cover). However, as the keys can be easily digitized and distributed over the same general infrastructure, this is bound to happen on a massive scale. If such keys do not originate as *leaks* directly from the source, they can be decoded by cracking, or the source code can be manipulated to accept any key. Every "protection" in the medium of the digital can also be discovered, bypassed, or levered out in this medium. It is only a question of skills and effort, thus of time, until new digital locking mechanisms are made useless. The tortoise often catches up with the hare in the first meters.

The second technical approach is to control not only the digital good, but also the execution machine. This is the basic idea of digital rights management (DRM), which has largely failed. DRM combines an encrypted product with a virtual execution machine, which alone is able to "play" the encrypted product. Many DRM systems only exist as software, however, the real goal is to combine DRM software with DRM hardware. An individual key is deposited inside a DRM chip which can be read by the content controllers (cf. Meretz 2007, 74). With isolated devices like set-top boxes, DVD players, game consoles, e-book readers, etc., a certain degree of durable digital control can be maintained. What DRM in e-book readers implies suddenly became obvious in 2009 when Amazon remotely deleted legally purchased texts of Orwell's *1984* and *Animal Farm* from their costumers' readers – including their personal notes (see Stallman 1997).

The DRM approach reveals the irresolvable contradiction of capital. On one hand, the digital infrastructure is the ideal medium for the distribution of informational products, because it is freely accessible. Openness and neutrality are essential conditions. On the other hand, these are exactly the two conditions which facilitate the activities against the commodity form, showing a whole spectrum from "piracy" (illegal copying) to the creation of free cultural and informational goods. DRM is the attempt to build private subnets into the public network, which can be controlled only by private exploiters. A complete control, however, would require the enclosure of the private subnets. But such an enclosure is very complex and difficult to achieve, because all virtual "transition points" to the general public network have to be controlled. Additionally, it would stall the very innovations which are the precondition for new exploitable products. This contradiction between openness and control must turn out in the favor of openness, because otherwise the basis of valorization will be strangled. The simple rule of this rivalry is: Who is more open, prevails (cf. Bauwens 2007).

But there is an exception to every rule. With Microsoft's almost complete control of desktop operating systems, there exists a special situation. The company could reach a monopoly when the general digital infrastructure was still very weak, which it defended until today with crude tricks. Microsoft can afford not to be open, but first break-ins into its dominance have been successful. The company had to replace their old proprietary document format with a new open version (so called OOXML), in order to achieve an ISO certification. The Open Document Format (ODF), which is used by OpenOffice and LibreOffice, had achieved this status before OOXML. Moreover, Microsoft had massively to intervene to push the national standardization bodies to accept its proposal, since the submitted and then approved draft (6,000 pages!) actually contradicts the idea of transparency. Additionally, Microsoft had to waive numerous OOXML-related patents.

Technical obstructions as measures to prevent digital copies do only have a chance of success if they are accompanied by *legal hedging* (for details, cf. Nuss 2006, 67). Grassmuck writes (2006, 168):

DRM is intended as a self-help of the industry.... DRM promises that the entertainment industry can create scarcity – which is the condition for their market and which so far is secured by law – by themselves. Technicians never made a secret of the fact that DRM cannot work. But only when it could no longer be denied that every single newly introduced DRM system is cracked within a very short time, the exploiters had to realize: the answers from the machine, the technical self-help measures apart from the state, are ineffective without the laws and the power monopoly of the state.

Prohibiting the circumvention of DRM became therefore the central demand of the content industry, which was included in the World Intellectual Property Organization (WIPO) treaty on copyrights in 1996. With the Digital Millennium Copyright Act (DMCA) of 1998, the USA transferred the provisions into national law; the EU followed in 2001 with a corresponding directive. Germany implemented the EU guidelines in 2003 and 2008, including the circumvention prohibition for DRM. The legal private copy was mostly eliminated (Weißenborn 2009).

Struggle for the Commodity Form

The development from the material copy via the analogous to the digital copy reflects the double algorithmic revolution in the development of the productive forces of capitalism. The *immediate physical copy* falls into the period of handcrafted production in the manufacture of beginning capitalism. The *analogous copy* falls into the period when the tools and production know-how of the craftsmen were transferred into machines, including the algorithmic integration of single processes into the integrated production flows of the Fordist-Taylorist total process. Finally, the *digital copy* falls into the period of the separation of the flexible process machine from the digital algorithmic universal computer in post-Fordist production (cf. also Meretz 2003).

Initially, the copy was related to a physically embodied purpose, then to a content narrowly coupled with a physical carrier, and finally to the digital representation of content on an arbitrary carrier. Today, the three elements are produced separately: content, carrier, and digital representation. It is obvious that the carrier is insignificant in this relationship and the digital representation is a vanishing moment. The existence of an execution machine is always necessary. If an execution machine is available – chemical factory, automotive plant, music player, police force – then the content represents the final "product": the drug, the car, the song, the computer surveillance. The execution machine is less and less a single machine for specific purposes, but it is increasingly integrated into a general infrastructure, where the universal representation is the digital form and the universal mode of processing is copying.

For capitalism, whose basis is the exploitation of living labor, a fundamental contradiction emerges: The same medium, the general infrastructure, is the place and the means of *production*, *distribution*, and *consumption*. For *production,* the digital medium has to be enclosed and made exclusive, in order to guarantee the private form of production. Using physical separation of devices, data, and knowledge from the general infrastructure by technical (firewalls, virtually closed networks) and organizational (nondisclosure agreement) means, the public shall remain excluded. At the same time, the public sphere is always present: in scientific cooperation, by using the general infrastructure, during the exchange with customers, when using the customers' knowledge to optimize products, and finally cumulating with user-generated product innovation via "crowdsourcing." Patent and copyright are legal means to cope with the contradiction of private and public aspects of production in a way that enables valorization. However, the share of general preconditions of production is steadily increasing. Every private dissociation repels potential innovators. Only openness can prevail. The strategy is: Release some parts of your private production (knowledge, patents, devices, labor, code, documents, etc.) to the general infrastructure and thereby win innovative power, trust, and knowledge. Only those who are open can exploit the general infrastructure for private gain.

The *distribution* depends on the openness of the digital infrastructure as a "free market." At the same time, each of the private market participants wants to control "their" market share in two directions: On one hand, competitors shall be kept distant; the other hand, products in the hands of users shall be kept private. For a long time, the implementation of their own proprietary functions as "standard" was the dominant path for the first goal (see the struggle on a high-definition video disc format where Blu-ray prevailed), while DRM was the preferred means for the second goal. In the field of online services, the user should originally be kept in "own" networks separated from competitors, while the new tendency supports those who open their interfaces, support cooperation, and also grant at least partial access to their data. The "free network market" needs net neutrality, but service providers are interested in the specific valorization of separated services with a defined transmission quality. Here again, the fight is between openness and privatization, which is essentially a struggle for the commodity form and exploitation.

With *consumption,* the same contradiction is clearly visible. Copy protection and copy control are used with the goal of technically preventing that an essentially general good becomes indeed socially generalized. However, encapsulated devices are "digital islands" that are less interoperable than those with open specifications and open access. New forms of digital control are conceived, e.g., with games. Through the coupling of purchased games with an online connection, new billing models become possible.

Corresponding tendencies of transferring functions into the general network for easier valorization can be observed in the realm of software application under the label "Software as a Service" (SaaS). But each new enclosure on the side of proprietary exploiters provokes new innovations by creators of open and free products.

While the free software movement was a reaction against the proprietary expropriations of software, the free design movement expresses the productive appropriation endeavor in the realm of hardware. Hardware is largely software in the broadest sense: conception, drafting, design, implementation. With digital consumer goods, mainly in the cultural sector, the trend toward prosumeristic appropriation of goods for the creation of derivative new goods (known as remix) becomes particularly clear – followed by an enormous diversification of mass taste. Here in particular, the big cultural corporations have waived the digital control with DRM, because within competition the private can only prevail if it becomes general. The uncontrolled proliferation is grudgingly accepted and combated at the same time, in order to rescue valorization. Digital cultural goods does no longer fit into the commodity form. Thus, Ernst Lohoff (2007) came to the result that digital information goods are not commodities at all.

Conclusion

The copy was and is characteristic for the societal production of all means for life – in every society. The developmental-logical reconstruction has shown that the shape of the copy changes in capitalism from the immediate-physical copy via the analogous to the digital copy. During this development, elements have been separated from each other, which previously existed together as human knowledge and competence (possibly embedded in physical artifacts). This division enabled a separated development to a previously unknown extent, until on the basis of the digital form the reintegration into a potentially global, general digitally based infrastructure has begun. Copy protection, copy control, and fighting "piracy" now only express the necessity to keep production and valorization within the private capitalist form. Objectively and socially, restriction of further general digital integration does not make any sense. The next historical step to be done will be to adapt the societal form to the effective general availability of products, which means to abrogate the private form of production and appropriation in capitalism.

Bibliography

Baukrowitz, Andrea. 2006. "Informatisierung und Reorganisation. Zur Rolle der IT jenseits der Automatisierung." In Andrea Baukrowitz et al., eds., *Informatisierung der Arbeit – Gesellschaft im Umbruch*. Berlin: Edition Sigma, 98-115.

Bauwens, Michel. 2007. "How the Law of Asymmetric Competition Should Affect Innovation Policy." P2P Foundation wiki, 10 August. http://blog.p2pfoundation.net/how-the-law-of-asymmetric-competition-should-affect-innovation-policy/2007/08/10.

Grassmuck, Volker. 2006. "Wissenskontrolle durch DRM: von Überfluss zu Mangel." In: J. Hofmann, ed., *Wissen und Eigentum. Geschichte, Recht und Ökonomie stoffloser Güter*. Bonn: Bundeszentrale für politische Bildung, 164-186.

Helfrich, Silke. 2009. "Wem gehört die Welt? Zur Wiederentdeckung der Gemeingüter." Heinrich Böll Stiftung website, 9 March. http://www.boell.de/de/navigation/wirtschaft-soziales-6315.html.

Lohoff, Ernst. 2007. "Der Wert des Wissens. Grundlagen einer Politischen Ökonomie des Informationskapitalismus." *krisis – Beiträge zur Kritik der Warengesellschaft* 31: 13-51.

Meretz, Stefan. 2003. "Zur Theorie des Informationskapitalismus. Teil 2: Produktive und unproduktive Arbeit." *Streifzüge* 2: 41-46.

Meretz, Stefan. 2007. "Der Kampf um die Warenform. Wie Knappheit bei Universalgütern hergestellt wird." *krisis – Beiträge zur Kritik der Warengesellschaft* 31: 52-89.

Nuss, Sabine. 2006. *Copyright and Copyriot. Aneignungskonflikte um geistiges Eigentum im informationellen Kapitalismus*. Münster: Westfälisches Dampfboot.

Stallman, Richard. 1997. "The Right to Read." *Communications of the ACM* 40.2 (February). http://www.gnu.org/philosophy/right-to-read.html.

Weißenborn, Stefan Robert. 2009. "Kopierschutz und Privatkopie. Die Grenzen der Freiheit." *Der Speigel*, 28 September. http://www.spiegel.de/netzwelt/netzpolitik/kopierschutz-und-privatkopie-die-grenzen-der-freiheit-a-651278.html.

Credits

Special thanks to Christian Siefkes for translation support.

License

Creative Commons Attribution-ShareAlike 3.0 Unported (CC BY-SA 3.0). The text may be copied and/or modified freely as long as you attribute the original author and source and keep the license requirements intact.

7. Paradoxes of Property

Piracy and Sharing in Information Capitalism

Jonathan Paul Marshall and Francesca da Rimini

Introduction

All societies both suffer and benefit from levels of what is perceived as disorder, and the guiding principles of the society may be contradictory, or paradoxical, in that their ordering systems create disorder. Our aim in this text is explore the disorders and vagaries of property that seem essential to its continuance, construction, and destruction, and then demonstrate how these paradoxes play out in the information economy in particular within the domain of peer-to-peer (P2P) file sharing. We do not wish to reduce these paradoxes and contradictions to a temporary error or to a future ordered synthesis, but to take them as they are in all their splintered fury. Much contemporary social action stems from these incoherencies, and the disputes, displays of power, and innovations which circle around them. In the P2P field the disorder generated by the order of property provides opportunities for new productive and adaptive social and technical forms of life to emerge.

By contrasting order and disorder we are not implying the necessary existence of a binary distinction between the two, or that those definitions of order and disorder will not change depending on the social position of the definers. Disorder is not always and everywhere the same. It resists definition, which adds to its effects.

The Incoherence of Property: Property and Imagination

Eighteenth-century British philosopher David Hume argued that private property is both essential for social order, and imaginary: "[D]isputes may not only arise concerning the real existence of property and possession, but also concerning their extent; and these disputes are often susceptible of no decision, or can be decided by no other faculty than the imagination" (1888, 507).

Hume argues that property and its boundaries are constructed via metaphors which do not so much reflect "reality" as they express the proper-ties of the mind and social habit, and this causes problems with drawing ownership boundaries around property. He illustrates this by a story of two Grecian colonies who heard of an abandoned city. Arriving at the same time, their official messengers began a race and, as one was slower than the other, he "launch'd his spear at the gates of the city, and was so fortunate as to fix it there before the arrival of his companion. This produc'd a dispute betwixt the two colonies, which of them was the proprietor of the empty city; and this dispute still subsists among philosophers" (1888, 507-508).

The dispute is impossible to settle rationally because it depends upon claims made to the imagination about the attachment of the messengers to their cities, whether the race was to the gates or the wall, whether the spear forms better or equal contact to the hand, and whether, if the spear had not held in the gates, the claim would still count. For Hume, property is built from metaphor; it becomes a concretizing rhetoric in action. There is no a priori to property, any example can be disputed, even though property is vital for social order.

More conventionally, John Stuart Mill held that what a person owns as property depends on their own labor: "The foundation of the whole is the right of producers to what they themselves have produced" (Mill, 1852, 218). This implies that unequal distributions of property come about either because of a "just" agreement, or because people give up the products of their labor, in exchange for survival. By acknowledging the existence of appropriation by force and the difficulties of drawing a boundary line around people's collaborative labor Mill recognizes difficulties with his formulation, but he largely puts these difficulties aside (ibid., 219-245). Further complications arise when different groups do not agree about what activities and types of labor are valuable, and thus have different imaginings of the "just" distribution of property. Property becomes political, and a matter of relative power. Disputes over imaginings may end up being resolved by force. As Adam Smith wrote: "Civil government, so far as it is instituted for the security of property, is in reality instituted for the defence of the rich against the poor, or of those who have some property against those who have none at all" (1979, II: 715).

Nineteenth-century anarchist Pierre Joseph Proudhon pointed out that property is intrinsically theft (n.d., 37-39); not only because property is often appropriated from others by force, but also because something becomes property only if someone else can steal it. Property and theft give birth to each other. We can here instance the Marxist argument that capitalist systems of property were indirectly promoted when English aristocrats dispossessed peasants of their traditional land and commons, thieving it to make parks or to grow wool, and forcing a newly pauperized class into the cities where they became cheap wage labor (Linebaugh and Rediker 2000). Through this use of enclosure, aristocrats eventually undermined the feudal relationship with the peasantry, which was the basis of their power (Federici 2004).

Another example, this time unsuccessful, of how property/theft works through the appropriation of "common rights" occurred when the Bechtel Corporation in Bolivia, backed by the World Bank, attempted to criminalize the capture of rainwater by alleging that all water was its private property. Its claims were eventually abandoned due to public protest (Chatterjee 2003; ENS 2006). Similar laws exist in the US state of Colorado, where almost all water, even rain, is "owned" by people who have bought rights to the waterways (Ingold 2009). Hence, "[p]reventing that water from reaching a river – and thus, its rights holder – is akin to stealing" (ibid.). "If you try to collect rainwater, well, that water really belongs to someone else," said Doug Kemper, executive director of the Colorado Water Congress. "We get into a very detailed accounting on every little drop" (Riccardi 2009). Similarly, in 1995, the US Congress turned the resource of unused broadcasting frequencies into property, giving those frequencies to media corporations free of charge in perpetuity, thus initiating what Republican politician Bob Dole called "a giant corporate welfare program" (Barnes 2006, 19).

Cultural expression is also increasingly bounded. Before 1976, US copyright could last for a maximum of 56 years. The Copyright Act of 1976 extended that to the life of the author plus 50 years. The Copyright Term Extension Act of 1998 extended that to life plus 70 years, or 75 years in total for "corporate authorship." The US Congress's "multibillion dollar allocation decision... ensured that virtually no creative works would enter the public domain over the following two decades" (Tehranian 2007, 540). More recently, the United States government (in alliance with the entertainment industry) attempted to "bully" Spain into adopting extreme anti-piracy measures, as part of a project of "harmonization" which "continuously ratchet[s] up copyright protection, one country at a time" (Hinze 2010; Anderson 2010). "Property" held in common is being reduced, sometimes by stealth, supporting Adam Smith's already mentioned claim that government exists to extend the reach of the property claims of those who already have.

"Normal Exchange"

A more anthropological way of conceiving property, connects property to what we will call "normal exchange."[1] In this view humans, throughout their existence as a species, have primarily lived in hunter-gatherer, or slash-and-burn agricultural societies, where massively inequitable accumulation is rendered socially unlikely by mechanisms that prevent people from accumulating too much status or property. In these societies, property implies obligation. If your kin demand property from you, and you refuse, then you will be ostracized as a "thief" – a person who does not acknowledge others. As well, in these societies, most goods rot and thus cannot be accumulated. If goods rot slowly, then accumulation is limited by what can be carried. Hence a limit to accumulation arises, and it becomes strategically better to give goods away to make, or reinforce, relationships and culture, and to build obligation, status, or self-identity.

As a result, property is nearly always in circulation. While these societies may have hierarchy (especially a gender and age hierarchy), what members can take or have at the expense of others is limited, while in more hierarchical societies *some* people can violate this balance and accumulate property, without yielding it on demand, or giving it away in exchange and feasting. If we note Proudhon's paradox that what enables society might also destroy it, and that the harm and abuse resulting from property cannot be dissevered from the good, this accumulation might be positive, as it allows people some independence from the group. Yet this anthropological view implies that we can expect that attempts to extend individual or corporate property at the expense of others, or at the expense of cultural expression, will meet resistance, and the hierarchical boundaries between theft and property will be contested.

To summarize: Property is imagined, and it arises out of a social-historical network of coproduction, creation, distribution, conception, and relations of power. It is difficult to extract bordered property from this network and impossible to give it a single cause without an act of socially legitimated "theft," backed by some others, which extracts it from its messy origins. Property has no eternal essence and no boundaries: it is a network, or process, involving the whole of social action. Things are constantly becoming property and escaping being property, amid conflict and decay. As Proudhon claims, "property is impossible" (n.d., 157-218).

Property, Copying, and Culture: Property and Identity

Because property is so implicated in the imagination it can become a way that we imagine ourselves and our potencies.[2] We use property, words, and ideas as tools to express ourselves and participate in social life. Property can give the rewards of, or help establish, class and status, which is why theft or loss might be so powerful; loss can represent a diminishment of personal existence. In some societies there may be no "you" outside of the display or exchange of property. Renunciation is not commonly available in information capitalism as, within its framework, it is primarily newly owned "things" that promise fulfillment in a never-ending cycle of desire, display, and consumption.

The role of property in constituting identity in information capitalism leads the consumer to conflicts. On the one hand, mass consumption provides something to share and discuss; experiences and items in common with others, in what may otherwise be a fractured life. However, in so doing, it also renders you the same as everyone else and thus undermines your valued "individuality." In this set up, there is always the need for *recognized* distinction, although this does not include the distinction which arises from *not* having property; that is simply recognized as failure.

When others buy or take the almost identical property, then you are threatened as they are effectively stealing your distinction and hence your "identity." This can lead to a spiral of ever more intently keeping up with the new, and thus taking the risk of embracing something which does not become recognized, which is just "trash." In that sense, identity becomes fashion, and people will try and embrace the latest as soon as it arrives *and* has a reasonable chance of being accepted and, like other forms of acquiring and producing culture, this often involves copying. Copying may be hindered if brand names (of clothing, cosmetics, hi-tech gadgets, etc.) become a mark of authenticity or wealth or adequacy. However, in some groups the ability to thieve, or rip off, the latest, may be taken as evidence of identity factors of skill, status, or having high-tech marketability. Even so, the thief, pirate, or counterfeiter will have to risk delaying long enough for it to be recognizable that he or she got it first; too soon and it's worth nothing.

Copying and transformation are vital to imagination and hence property. Without copying there is no potential transformation, and no combining images and ideas into new images and ideas. As philosopher and religious scholar René Girard says: "There is nothing, or next to nothing, in human behaviour that is not learned, and all learning is based on imitation. If human beings suddenly ceased imitating, all forms of culture would vanish" (1987, 7). Girard argues that imitation is ambivalent as, while we learn through emulation, if two people reach for the same thing, or the student supersedes the teacher, conflict easily arises. Consequently societies tend to be ambivalent about imitation, recognizing also that it is a source of magical attack and vulnerability, as with the "voodoo doll." Modern Western societies tend to officially regard overzealous imitation as bad, with originality marking creativity, but it has not always been so.

Ambiguity and Poetics of Theft

Even under hierarchy we can point to ambivalences about theft. Some thieving becomes the basis of legally legitimate property, but there can also be sympathy when someone steals to feed their family, or when a Robin Hood-type hero takes from those who have more than they need or who deprive others. In fairy stories, stealing from a giant is particularly acceptable, perhaps because folk tales originate with people facing their giant masters. Hence, the "good thief" is an archetype we cannot ignore, however much it aggravates those with property.

What counts as bad piracy depends on the current politics. Pirates like Francis Drake and Walter Raleigh were much praised in Elizabethan England. They received state sponsorship in reaction to the Spanish theft of gold and silver from South America; and the pirated gold was more productively used in Britain than in Spain. Piracy was an important part of the American Revolution, promoting attacks on the Royal Navy by melding patriotism with commercial gain (Patton 2008). After Independence the US thrived on pirated goods and intellectual property (Ben-Atar 2004); there was no protection given to the books of foreigners manufactured outside the US until 1986 (Choate 2005, 41). Hollywood was founded in an attempt to escape Edison's patents by shifting the site of film production to the other side of the continent (Lessig 2005, 53-54). Today, rising powers such as China also maintain a lax attitude to protecting foreigners' intellectual property for the sake of their own economic development. The imaginings used to establish boundaries between property and theft are disputed and depend on relations of power and capability. Nevertheless, we should not forget that many pirates have gained profit out of murder, terror, and slavery.

There is, then, a piracy of the relatively weak and of the relatively strong. Piracy of the relatively weak occurs when markets are restricted, or the equity of "normal exchange" is violated; whether by "corrupt" class structures, or through what appears to be artificial restriction of goods. Such piracy is often a reaction to perceived illegitimate and excessive profits, or occurs when people revert to hunter-gatherer modes of exchange and control, seizing back property they do not believe belongs exclusively to another. Piracy further occurs when the labor and risk involved in theft are minimal in comparison to the profit or enhanced opportunities.

Piracy is ambiguous, and imagining file sharing as "piracy," and situating it within an exciting and sometimes approved good-thief activity, might have diminished the legitimacy of corporate prosecution. Nowadays, corporations tend to metaphorize file sharing as a "criminal" activity hurting not only admired "celebrity stars" but also the economy, while file sharers still use the metaphor of "pirate" as with The Pirate Bay and the various parliamentary pirate parties.

Intellectual Property in the Information Society

As we have argued, copying, sharing, transforming, elaborating, commenting, building, and innovation are embedded within cultural production. Sociologist Maurizio Lazzarato argues that in the information society commodity property is constituted "in forms *that are immediately* collective," existing "only in the form of networks and flows" (1996, italics in original). Furthermore, the foundations of this property is blurred as "the activity that produces the 'cultural content' of the commodity... involves activities... not normally recognized as 'work' [such as] defining and fixing cultural and artistic standards, fashions, tastes, consumer norms, and, more strategically, public opinion" (ibid.).

Similarly Rasmus Fleischer (musician and founder of the Swedish anti-copyright think tank Piratbyrån) and Palle Torsson (artist and Piratbyrån associate) argue, sharing "is not optional but inscribed in the technique we use every day" (Fleischer and Torsson 2005). However, while information capitalism demands free circulation of information to allow the production of "new" ideas and cultural works, it simultaneously must stop ideas from circulating freely so as to profit from them. This produces incoherency. The more ideas are copyrighted, the less a person can imagine freely without trespassing on another's property rights. Paradoxically, for example, by putting a financial cost on sampling in music, fewer samples are likely to be used in a new song, making it more derivative of its sources and thus less original.

Culture has become restricted by property rights, while at the same time, the skills and tools necessary for successful information/cultural labor are not confined to the working day, as in industrial capitalism, but spill out into cultural and personal life in general. Retaining familiarity with current culture can be vital for a worker's employment, future creativity, and social self-identity. Similarly, capitalists gridlocked by patents (cf. Heller 2008), might even welcome sharing if they were not dependent upon such enclosures and boundaries for profit.

P2P file-sharing systems illustrate the ambiguities of sharing, theft, and cultural value (as appropriation, identity, and creativity) in information society. Although it is often treated as piratical, file sharing can be a legitimate gifting of public domain material or of a person's own work. This "normal exchange" was the way ideas leading to the construction of the Internet were developed, and led Tim Berners-Lee to develop and gift HTML and the graphical interface system of the World Wide Web to the world (Berners-Lee 1999). It is part of what made the early web so attractive to nonspecialist users. However, almost from its outset some wanted to "commercialize the Internet" and make it corporate, rather than common, property, eventually spawning the "venture capitalist's paradise" of Web 2.0 in which mass users provide the creative labor and content which has generated stratospheric profits for an elite in a piracy of the strong (Kleiner 2010, 15). While users might provide the property voluntarily, it is doubtful that they have formally given permission for profit to be seized from their labor or even comprehended that their labor is being monetized for the benefit of others.

In general, files available via P2P sites are usually "cultural products" which are owned by content industry bodies who have either financed their production or been assigned the copyrights. Comments on P2P forums reveal that many P2P users dispute the legal and social assumption that content owners have greater rights than either the original (often exploited) creators or those who desire to participate freely in cultural exchange. This "injustice" is partially remedied by "piracy."

Information piracy is also tied to modes of consumption, becoming easier with the high bandwidth that enables online gaming, video streaming, and legitimate downloads. Thus piracy is caught up in the very process of providing new ways for people to consume. Internet Service Providers (ISPs) may find file sharing a profitable driver of the generous download plans they offer customers. Attempting to prevent piracy to defend someone else's profit cuts into their own income. Hence many ISPs resist the attempts of the media businesses to use the state to enforce media-favorable ownership rules, to constrain the activities of their customers, sometimes proposing solutions to the "problem" that allow them to carry on business as usual (see, for example, iiNet 2011; Lasar 2011).

Peer-to-peer (P2P): Property, Culture, Metaphor, and Control

P2P

P2P refers to the suite of software programs, protocols, and social practices that enable this form of online digital exchange. The P2P phenomenon depends on "normal exchange"; free software conventions, volunteer labor, and a collective desire for access to cultural materials unfettered by hardware and software locks, copyright restrictions, and other forms of enclosure.

P2P also disrupts itself in many ways. Instead of a "network society" P2P fosters a "swarm society" with some unusual features and vulnerabilities. Swarms form temporarily and disintegrate without forming ongoing networks, and people cultivate anonymity. Members display they are there, but do not know on whom they depend. Contact is contingent on the exchange, but may become more stable in the forums attached to particular sites.

As a result, file sharing seems affected by the "tragedy of the commons" argument, that free systems collapse because some people take advantage of them when the means of social control is not strong enough to prevent this. People might take files but not make them available, because they have inadequate storage space, bandwidth, or interest. Such people may be scorned, but the relationships are not strong enough to alter behavior, although many semi-private and private sites insist upon fair download/ upload ratios and suspend privileges of noncompliant members. Nevertheless, the majority of file sharers use public trackers with no such controls, and therefore sociality among P2P participants tends to be relatively weak, and liable to fracture.

Such conflict and incoherence is also implied by Cox, Collins, and Drinkwater's (2010) study comparing the attitudes of Finnish file sharers who uploaded original copies of files ("first-seeders") with those who either downloaded them and continued to seed ("seeders"), and those who did not reseed ("leechers"). They discovered that leechers were much more likely to believe that "legal blame" should fall exclusively "upon the shoulders of seeders." In contrast, first-seeders and seeders believed that "no individual or group should be legally liable for file-sharing activity." As leeching would be impossible without the labor and risks undertaken by first-seeders, it may seem surprising that "leechers" would be so harsh on them, yet this common attitude evidences the fractured ties among members of ephemeral swarms.

P2P is also parasitic on other systems for its survival and the survival of its users. As Andersson (2006) writes, this peer labor "is dependent on already established prosperity; it is a form of 'free' labor which one can afford, given that one has got the required material setup as well as the time, skill, and intellectual capacities." P2P may also undermine the payment of those who use it to produce culture, by making their, or other, work available for free, thus undermining users' prosperity and ability to participate.

P2P has also birthed a burgeoning field of "anti-piracy enterprise," as Ramon Lobato and Julian Thomas (2011, 610) point out. These enterprises are diverse, including developers of digital rights management (DRM) technologies like Audible Magic, Internet traffic analysis firms like Sandvine, and cease-and-desist notice senders MediaSentry and DtecNet (ibid., 8, 10, 13). These organizations all ostensibly seek to "prevent, measure, transform, and otherwise derive revenue from copyright infringement" (ibid., 4). However, as their business models depend upon the continuance of piracy, total prevention would equate with their commercial failure.

This leads to ongoing manufacture of alarm, diversification of their client base, and development of technologies which "monetize, rather than merely obstruct, infringement," a method followed by both Google and YouTube (ibid., 10).

P2P also faces problems around the failure of indexing and ongoing sabotage via promulgation of broken files or the insertion of viruses into files. Companies such as Anti-Piracy LLC, Overpeer, Nuke Pirates, C-Right, and Media Defender specialize in such digital "spoofing" and "spoiling," aiming to drive "would-be pirates" to legal services (Lobato and Thomas 2011, 613). As a result, irritation, disruption, and paranoia become a magnified part of swarm sociality.

Sometimes file-sharing platforms vanish due to legal challenges arising because the software is *too* attractive – as was the case with the early centralized file-sharing system Napster. However, Napster's legal (and later commercial) failure encouraged further inventiveness by hackers and users. In this case leading to the development of the BitTorrent protocol enabling fully distributed file-sharing systems which share bandwidth and file chunks among a network of participants, none of whom know which chunks they are transmitting at any one moment (Bridy 2011). These files are linked by indices (or "torrents") stored on computer servers such as the Swedish initiative The Pirate Bay (TPB).

Significantly, TPB does not store any of the artifact data, only the metadata (keys) to locate it elsewhere.[3] As each peer receives a packet of data onto their own computer, this data is available to be automatically seeded to any other peer connected to the same swarm; in effect downloaders must become uploaders to continue the exchange, at least until they have acquired a complete copy of the file.

Nevertheless, far from retreating from disputes over property by claiming innocent neutrality TPB has taken a "strategic" position in the global "copyfight" (Andersson 2009). The "politicization" of file sharing in Sweden, as exemplified by people's participation in the advocacy organization

Piratbyrån and the political party Piratpartiet, has been directly attributed to the criminalization of the activity by the media industry. Under this pressure, the Swedish "cyberpirate" metamorphosed into a "political partisan," and their discourse expanded from that of "law and copyright," to broader questions of "politics and participatory culture" (Dahlberg 2011, 273).

The Pirate Bay

The Pirate Bay (TPB) was launched in November 2003. In 2008 The Pirate Bay's four founders were charged with copyright infringement offences. The ensuing trial found them guilty, and imposed punitive fines (of about US$3.6 million) and a year's jail time for each. On appeal, jail terms were reduced but the fines increased. Three of the defendants subsequently signaled their intention to appeal to the Supreme Court, and in October 2011 Sweden's Prosecutor General recommended that this final appeal be denied because problems in The Pirate Bay case were "so complex" the country's highest court "might not be the appropriate venue to tackle them" (Enigmax 2011); an unusual argument about the capacity of the courts. The case concluded on 1 February 2012 when the Supreme Court refused to hear the appeal motion, and consequently the founders' existing jail sentences and fines are final (Anderson 2012). However, this outcome does not appear to affect the site's capacity to continue operating as normal, as according to its blog it moved to the.SE domain, thereby giving some breathing space from the legal reach of the "United States of Arrogance" (The Pirate Bay 2012). Moreover, it appears that TPB was sold some years earlier (in mysterious circumstances), and so is no longer under the control of the founders (Anderson 2009).

Meanwhile TPB continues to flourish as the world's largest public torrent tracker. According to the statistics on the site's front page in December 2011, TPB hosts "32,119,444 peers (22,961,788 seeders + 9,157,656 leechers) in 4,053,530 torrents" (The Pirate Bay 2011b). It was also ranked as the 86th most popular website in the world by Alexa Internet (2011) in mid-August 2011.

Popular support for TPB is shown by the Piratpartiet (Pirate Party), a political party which arose in late 2005 from the public support given a petition protesting against a proposed change in Swedish copyright laws which would criminalize downloading (Miegel and Olsson 2008, 208-209). The party's announced core vision is "Shared culture," "Free knowledge," and "Protection of privacy" aims that have been broadly mirrored by pirate parties formed elsewhere. It claims that:

Terrorists may attack the open society, but only governments can abolish it. The Pirate Party wants to prevent that from happening…. The official aim of the copyright system has always been to find a balance in order to promote culture being created and spread. Today that balance has been completely lost, to a point where the copyright laws severely restrict the very thing they are supposed to promote. The Pirate Party wants to restore the balance in the copyright legislation. All noncommercial copying and use should be completely free. File sharing and P2P networking should be encouraged rather than criminalized. Culture and knowledge are good things, that increase in value the more they are shared. (Piratpartiet n.d., 1)

The party is thus in favor of "normal cultural exchange" as defined earlier.

In 2009 the Piratpartiet won two seats in the EU parliament (Schofield 2009). This signaled that the contest over knowledge and property was no longer a fringe matter, nor a subject to be framed only by corporate financial interests. Piratpartiet's precedent-setting success, not only in the European Parliament but in the wider sphere of public discourse, is in part due to the party's deep interconnections with other localized "strategic, politicised entities" such as the "propaganda institute, think-tank and alternative news agency" Piratbyrån (the Pirate Bureau) and TPB (Andersson 2010, 196).

As well as restricting circulation of ideas, copyright can also be used to suppress discussion about property. One company not only threatened The Pirate Bay for violating the copyright of their clients but also threatened the TPB with copyright suits if they made the contents of that threatening e-mail public (Jgela1 2005). Undeterred, TPB continued to publish a cache of such documents, and their own replies, on their website, declaring that "0 torrents has been removed, and 0 torrents will ever be removed" (The Pirate Bay 2011a). A TPB response to DreamWorks in 2004 is typical of their approach:

As you may or may not be aware, Sweden is not a state in the United States of America. Sweden is a country in northern Europe. Unless you figured it out by now, US law does not apply here. For your information, no Swedish law is being violated…. It is the opinion of us and our lawyers that you are morons, and that you should please go sodomize yourself with retractable batons (ibid.).

Such "caustic, sarcastic" letters might even help convince the court that TPB demonstrated enough "subjective intent" to be held liable for copyright infringement (Carrier 2010, 12), again foregrounding the role of imagination in the construction of property and theft.

During the course of The Pirate Bay trial, metaphors were used to define and bound property. The core defense argument was that The Pirate Bay was a search engine like Google and thus subject to the same protections as Google. Defense lawyers claimed that in providing a service, which could be used both legally and illegally, TPB was not breaking the law, any more than manufacturers of cars which could break speed limits were breaking the law. They referred to "safe harbor" protections entrenched in laws around the world, arguing that:

> EU directive 2000/31/EC says that he who provides an information service is not responsible for the information that is being transferred. In order to be responsible, the service provider must initiate the transfer. But the admins of The Pirate Bay don't initiate transfers. It's the users that do and they are physically identifiable people. They call themselves names like King Kong.... According to legal procedure, the accusations must be against an individual and there must be a close tie between the perpetrators of a crime and those who are assisting. (Enigmax 2009)

The prosecution argued that The Pirate Bay assisted the commission of a crime and that, according to Sweden's Supreme Court, a person holding the jacket of someone committing battery can be held responsible for the battery. It was alleged that The Pirate Bay was gaining income from criminal activities via advertising and that it was negatively affecting industry. The court rejected the defense's argument saying that the defendants knew the site was being used for illegal activities and they did nothing to prevent it; they were found to be accessories, to a crime that was not proven (Lewan 2009). As said previously, both sides appealed the result. As Hume implies, whether we accept the argument of prosecution or defense depends to a large extent on preexisting alliance or on whether we are prepared to accept the metaphors describing The Pirate Bay as an innocent search engine, as a mugger, or as holding the coat of a mugger.

Other metaphors came into play. Malin Littorin-Ferm, organizer of pro-Pirate Bay protests, said, "we young people have a whole platform on the Internet, where we have all our social contacts – it is there that we live. The state is trying to control the Internet and, by extension, our private lives" (UPI 2009). This if anything shows the ways that private and public have changed and how that affects contests over property. The argument of the protesters again depends upon us seeing people's activities at The Pirate

Bay as a routine and essential part of social-cultural life. From a different everyday perspective, Paul McCartney, whose music returned over 300 results on a recent TPB search, said "If you get on a bus you've got to pay. And I think it's fair, you should pay your ticket" (McKenzie and Cochrane 2009). His metaphor "forgets" that some places do have free buses.

The vagueness of boundaries of violation arose when one of the prosecuting organizations demanded that ISPs not connect to The Pirate Bay. A lawyer for Telia Sonara, a communications company, responded: "In part, this is not a legally binding decision, but above all, this is a judgment against Pirate Bay and nothing that effects any service provider. We will not take any action [to block] the contents if we are not compelled to do so." And the managing director of another company said: "We will not censor sites for our customers; that is not our job" (TT 2009).

Debates over the correct imagining of intellectual property and the trial continued on public websites showing this is not just a matter for academics, lawyers, or copyright holders, it is an imagining or seeking of metaphors and comparisons that goes on wherever people are concerned about property relations. Rather than seeing these as logical arguments, let us see them instead as metaphors of property showing how the foundations can never be settled.

One person wrote: "This is like prosecuting the postal service, there is a great deal of criminal activity via the post, however, are they on trial here? They are a medium of communication, nothing else, it is not up to the Post Office nor service providers to police IPR [intellectual property rights] infringements!" Others complained that industry was not taking advantage of the new technology and the court's decision was (metaphorically) like legislating to preserve steam trains at the expense of other transport. Another compared P2P to walking into your local supermarket and shoplifting DVDs. Others objected to this metaphor because of the difference between scarce and infinite resources, or because if a friend gave you a copy of a DVD almost nobody would think that was theft. One person wondered if movies should be able to make as much money as they sometimes do in a world with real poverty. In response another said that pirating could destroy small film producers, who made almost no money (Comments on TT 2009). Others argued that while the cost of manufacture of CDs had decreased the price had not, so corporations thieved from the public, and that P2P was like listening to a radio station (Comments on Landes 2009a). Others continued arguments that the corporations were supporting dead technology, that the "major labels could have charged for P2P transfers for the last decade. Instead, they demonised the technology, tried to bully their customers unsuccessfully and left all that money on the table. But that ship has sailed."

The losses corporations were claiming from piracy were compared to speculation or fortune-telling, and it was alleged that mainstream companies destroyed local cultural production and thus should receive no sympathy (Comments on Landes 2009b). This diversity of metaphor and comparison shows that property is not a thing in itself and the difficulties of getting a uniform view of what it is.

Failed Control

Industry-commissioned P2P traffic figures show that attempts to curb mass file sharing by bringing civil and criminal actions against entities and users have failed. The *Technical Report: An Estimate of Infringing Use of the Internet* by anti-counterfeiting and piracy company Envisional estimated that 23.76% of global Internet traffic was "infringing" (Envisional 2011, 2). Moreover, it estimated that BitTorrent traffic accounted for 17.9% of all Internet traffic, two-thirds of which was deemed to be "non-pornographic copyrighted content shared illegitimately" (ibid.). At any time over 8 million people could be exchanging files using the BitTorrent protocol, out of a pool of 100 million regular users worldwide (ibid., 4).

If these figures are more or less accurate then social norms are not changing in response to legal action and spectacular trials, demonstrating Hume's proposition that property belongs to the realm of the imagination. Millions of otherwise relatively law-abiding people are regularly downloading cultural content, implying that they do not imagine their acts as criminal, or reasonably disapproved of. Instead, they imagine cultural artifacts as the property of no one, or of everyone, as in "normal exchange." Moreover, the experience of being in a swarm, especially one associated with a widely used public tracker such as TPB, can assuage an individual's apprehensiveness about personal risk. As regular TorrentFreak commenter Violatoro (Ernesto 2011) noted, "Like wildebeest crossing the river only a few will be taken down and eaten by the crocodiles. Doing the same in small groups leads to a much higher percentage of death so the larger your swarm the better."

Faced with this disobedient multitude, and difficulties with different laws in different countries, powerful industry/state alliances have attempted to preserve *and extend* capitalist profit and property by intensifying copyright legislation in national jurisdictions around the world, developing multilateral treaties to expand copyrights, and decrease fair and previously normal usages. This is an example of "piracy of the strong." Signatories to the most powerful of these treaties, the Anti-Counterfeiting Trade Agreement (ACTA), must agree to change existing sovereign law to comply with ACTA's "harmonization" goals.

Although ACTA's early drafts were kept private, leaks inevitably occurred. Consequently the final draft was considerably watered down due to highly organized lobbying by groups such as La Quadrature du Net (2010) and Knowledge Ecology International (2011), and the growing involvement of pirate political parties. Responding to the transnational piracy of the strong we have a transnational "piracy of the weak" who combine their understanding of contemporary social desires and cultural mores with cooperative, agile use of networks, metaphor, and creative expressions to fight what they deem to be corporate theft. Organization provokes counterorganization to disorder it, and vice versa.

Even when passed, attempts to create obedient consumers are unstable. For instance, Hadopi, the French government agency charged with administering the country's anti-file-sharing laws, struggled with the sheer amount of digital property "crime." In July 2011 it reported it was unable to keep up with the 8 million complaints it had received from the Internet security company MediaSentry; processing only 470,000 initial warning e-mails, 20,000 second notices, and 10 third-strike notifications which require a judge to approve a temporary Internet suspension and/or fine (Lee 2011). Enforcement was being overwhelmed by the theft the new legislation manufactures.

Conclusion

Although property can form, or contribute, a basis for social order it has no logical or inevitable basis in itself. We have suggested that throughout most of human evolution, property has been circulated, not accumulated, and exists to build relationships, be consumed, gain status, and make culture. Class structures arise when these "normal" human modes of exchange are circumvented. Accumulated "private" property, although bringing some security, potentially clashes with "normal exchange" and is a product of a history of appropriation and competing imaginings. Property emerges out of a web of relationships and prior production, appropriation and distribution and, as a result, property ownership always has boundary problems. Extracting it from this web becomes political; a matter of imaginal representation, metaphor, rhetoric, and the use of power. Theft is itself ambivalent, with the common idea of the good thief, taking property from those who either do not need it or who are unworthy of it. The "good" pirate can also be a means of prosperity recognized by the state. In this chapter we distinguished between the piracy of the relatively weak and the relatively strong. The strong tend to legitimate themselves in law and attempt to prevent piracy of the weak. What counts as legitimate property and what as theft is a matter of metaphor, opinion, and power.

At the moment, in information capitalism, corporations attempt to resolve the ambiguities around property by restricting the use of ideas and symbols through police, courts, fines, political pressure, implicit violence, and imprisonment. They also seek to extend their property "rights" even further into the realm of ideas, culture and self-expression, thus thieving more and more from culture generally. What was once partially common becomes limited. This "piracy of the strong" generates social disruption, as sharing, copying, and transformation are vital imaginative, creative, and relationship-building processes. Culture and cultural "advancement" cannot exist without them. People and corporations need to communicate, borrow, and "steal" to make culture and property, therefore turning all information into property cuts people off from normal cultural and commercial production, and thus they have an incentive to rebel. Extension of property is theft, and manufactures theft. Manufacture of theft threatens more property, even though without some ownership of property the people thieving could not survive on their own artistic and cultural labor and productions. Thus the system is unstable.

In The Pirate Bay trial, the comments on the trial, and in the actions of the Piratpartiet we can see the playout of different types of power (political, national, legal, corporate) and the irresolvable metaphors which are used to justify theft and property, and the vagueness bordering those two categories. Metaphorically, there may be *huge* or *no* difference between P2P and listening to a radio or a friend's CDs and then deciding what to buy. P2P can attack social fundamentals, while attacking P2P can also be an attack on social fundamentals. Attempting to suppress P2P can be an attempt by people who made money out of a technology, to halt a new technology of cultural exchange and production that threatens that ability, through institutions which express the power of those old relationships, or it can be an attempt to preserve order and allow cultural producers to survive. The questions of what is theft and what is property, revolve around the question of whether culture and ideas should be shared, rented, or restricted.

It is, however, difficult to resist theft of any kind and rebellion is not easy. The piracy of the weak is enabled by the very mechanisms which attempt to distribute culture as property, and regulate theft by the weak. P2P occurs because of the network of relationships established by the information economy, and may not survive without them. As well, the social forms that develop around P2P are swarm-like, and gain little internal social or moral coherence and organization. These movements also seem parasitic on a successful information property regime (i.e., one which supports producers, and provides the money which allows the swarm to live), so they undermine what they need to survive. Perhaps moving offline and forming organizations like the Piratpartiet allows the possibility of sustained impact.

French anarchists Comité Invisible (the Invisible Committee) have proposed that radical social restructuring could be generated via a web of self-organized experimental communes which would not "occupy"' the territory but become the territory, as "[e]very practice brings a territory into existence" (Invisible Committee 2009, 108). Such a movement would abandon identity politics and pursue what we have implied is the variable visibility of the swarm; turning a socially enforced anonymity to advantage, through "conspiracy, nocturnal or faceless actions, creating an invulnerable position of attack" (Invisible Committee 2009, 113). This could be happening spontaneously in P2P activities, but there is no widespread revolutionary purity, and the problems with property, and P2P's dependence on information capitalism, cannot be resolved easily. These problems arise from the inevitable incoherencies generated by property and social life, and upon which social life and property depend.

We live with uncertainty and mess, with no ultimate coherence, only struggle: only the paradox that property and theft are interconnected, and attempts to regulate property in the information society can undermine the very social functions of the property that allow it to operate. Attempts to give coherence are just comforting illusions whose failure becomes almost instantly apparent by the countermeasures which spring up.

At the moment capitalist information society is saved by the inertia of wealth and power, and the fact that not everything is information. The irreducible basics of water, food, power, shelter, and clothing still have to be bought, grown, or extracted from the earth – and this may become more precarious as environments degrade. On this parasitic basis, all other aspects of information property, both "piratical" and "legitimate," depend – and without recognizing this dependence they can all face destruction.

Notes

1. The writing on "traditional" economics and its politics is enormous. General texts include: Mauss 1997; Sahlins 1974; Clastres 1989; Wilk and Cligget 2007.
2. Basic writings on this subject include: Douglas 1996; Bourdieu 1985; Bauman 2007.
3. In February 2012 TPB shifted from indexing torrents to providing "magnet" links, a system which provides users with a "decentralized way" of requesting a file rather than using a "centralized torrent server to connect the user with another peer" (Geuss 2012). The shift was made for "survival" reasons, as the smaller magnet files significantly reduce server space, allowing "copies of The Pirate Bay site" to be made more easily should anti-piracy laws shut it down without warning.

Bibliography

Alexa Internet. 2011. "About the Pirate Bay." Alexa.com, mid-August. http://www.alexa.com/siteinfo/thepiratebay.org.

Anderson, Nate. 2009. "Reservella: The Shadowy Company behind the Pirate Bay" *Ars Technica*, 12 October. http://arstechnica.com/tech-policy/2009/10/who-owns-the-pirate-bay-part-ii/.

Anderson, Nate. 2010. "How WikiLeaks Killed Spain's Anti-P2P Law." *Ars Technica*, 22 December. http://arstechnica.com/tech-policy/2010/12/how-wikileaks-killed-spains-anti-p2p-law/.

Anderson, Nate. 2012. "'What We Do Is Good': Pirate Bay Lashes out as Swedish Lawsuit Finally Ends." *Ars Technica*, 1 February. http://arstechnica.com/tech-policy/2012/02/what-we-do-is-good-pirate-bay-lashes-out-as-swedish-lawsuit-finally-ends/.

Andersson, Jonas. 2006. "The Pirate Bay and the Ethos of Sharing." In A. Hadzi et al., eds., *Deptford.TV Diaries*. London: Openmute Publishing. http://homepages.gold.ac.uk/j-andersson/The_Pirate_Bay_and_the_ethos_of_sharing.pdf

Andersson, Jonas. 2009. "For the Good of the Net: The Pirate Bay as a Strategic Sovereign." *Culture Machine* 10: 64-108.

Andersson, Jonas. 2010. "Peer-to-Peer-Based File-Sharing beyond the Dichotomy of 'Downloading Is Theft' vs. 'Information Wants to Be Free': How Swedish File-Sharers Motivate Their Action." Goldsmiths College, University of London.

Barnes, Peter. 2006. *Capitalism 3.0: A Guide to Reclaiming the Commons*. San Francisco: Berrett-Koehler.

Bauman, Zygmunt. 2007. *Consuming Life*. Oxford: Polity.

Ben-Atar, Doron S. 2004. *Trade Secrets: Intellectual Piracy and the Origins of American Industrial Power*. New Haven, CT: Yale University Press.

Berners-Lee, Tim. 1999. *Weaving the Web: the Past, Present and Future of the World Wide Web by Its Inventor*. London: Orion.

Bourdieu, Pierre. 1985. *Distinction: A Social Critique of the Judgement of Taste*. London: Routledge.

Bridy, Annemarie. 2011. "Is Online Copyright Enforcement Scalable?" *Vanderbilt Journal of Entertainment and Technology Law* 13.4: 695-737.

Carrier, Michael A. 2010. "The Pirate Bay, Grokster, and Google." *Journal of Intellectual Property Rights* 17: 7-17.

Chatterjee, Pratap. 2003. "Bechtel's Water Wars." *CorpWatch*, 1 May. http://www.corpwatch.org/article.php?id=6670.

Choate, Pat. 2005. *Hot Property: The Stealing of Ideas in an Age of Globalization*. New York: Alfred A. Knopf.

Clastres, Pierre. 1989. *Society against the State: Essays in Political Anthropology*. New York: Zone.

Cox, Joe, Alan Collins, and Stephen Drinkwater. 2010. "Seeders, Leechers and Social Norms: Evidence from the Market for Illicit Digital Downloading." *Information Economics and Policy* 22.4: 299-305.

Dahlberg, Leif. 2011. "Pirates, Partisans, and Politico-Juridical Space." *Law and Literature* 23.2: 262-281.

Douglas, Mary. 1996. *Thought Styles*. Thousand Oaks, CA: Sage.

Enigmax. 2009. "Day 3 – The Pirate Bay's 'King Kong' Defense." *TorrentFreak*, 18 February. http://torrentfreak.com/g-defense-090218/.

Enigmax. 2011. "Pirate Bay Founders "Should Be Denied" Supreme Court Hearing." *TorrentFreak*, 26 October. http://torrentfreak.com/pirate-bay-founders-should-be-denied-supreme-court-hearing-111026/.

ENS. 2006. "Bechtel Drops $50 Million Claim to Settle Bolivian Water Dispute." *Environmental News Service*, January 19. http://www.ens-newswire.com/ens/jan2006/2006-01-19-04.asp.

Envisional. 2011. *Technical Report: An Estimate of Infringing Use of the Internet*. Cambridge: Envisional Ltd. http://documents.envisional.com/docs/Envisional-Internet_Usage-Jan2011.pdf.

Ernesto. 2011. "I Know What You Downloaded on BitTorrent...." *TorrentFreak*, 10 December. http://torrentfreak.com/i-know-what-you-downloaded-on-bittorrent-111210.

Federici, Silvia. 2004. *Caliban and the Witch: Women, the Body and Primitive Accumulation*. New York: Autonomedia.

Fleischer, Rasmus, and Palle Torsson. 2005. "The Grey Commons – Strategic Considerations in the Copyfight." Transcript of lecture given at 22C3, Berlin, December. http://web.archive.org/web/20090115214142/http://publication.nodel.org/The-Grey-Commons.

Geuss, Megan. 2012. "Magnet Links Become the Official Currency of Pirate Bay." *Ars Technica*, 29 February. http://arstechnica.com/business/2012/02/what-torrent-pirate-bay-officially-makes-magnet-links-the/.

Girard, René. 1987. *Things Hidden Since the Foundation of the World*. London: Athlone Press.

Heller, Michael. 2008. *Gridlock Economy: How Too Much Ownership Wrecks Markets, Stops Innovation and Costs Lives*. New York: Perseus.

Hinze, Gwen. 2010. "Not-So-Gentle Persuasion: US Bullies Spain into Proposed Website Blocking Law." Electronic Frontier Foundation website, 17 December. https://www.eff.org/deeplinks/2010/12/not-so-gentle-persuasion-us-bullies-spain-proposed.

Hume, David. 1888. *Treatise of Human Nature*. Oxford: Oxford University Press.

iiNet. 2011. "Encouraging Legitimate Use of Online Content: An iiNet View." Press release, iiNet, 15 March. http://www.iinet.net.au/about/mediacentre/releases/20110315-iinet-framework.html.

Ingold, John. 2009. "Water Bills Back Saving on Rainy Days." *Denver Post*, 10 February. http://www.denverpost.com/news/ci_11667341.

Invisible Committee, The. 2009. *The Coming Insurrection* Los Angeles, CA: Semiotext(e).

Jgela1. 2005. "Re: WHITE STRIPES/Pirate Bay – Torrents." http://static.thepiratebay.org/whitestripes_mail.txt.

Kleiner, Dmytri. 2010. *The Telekommunist Manifesto*. Amsterdam: Institute of Network Cultures.

Knowledge Ecology International. 2011. "The Anti-Counterfeiting Trade Agreement (ACTA)." http://keionline.org/acta

La Quadrature du Net. 2010. "ACTA: Updated Analysis of the Final Version." http://www.laquadrature.net/en/acta-updated-analysis-of-the-final-version.

Landes, David. 2009a. "Showbiz Lawyers Push to Have Pirates Gagged." *TheLocal: Sweden's News in English*, 19 May. http://www.thelocal.se/19544/20090519/.

Landes, David. 2009b. "Showbiz Reps Appeal for More Pirate Bay Loot." *TheLocal: Sweden's News in English*, 20 May. http://www.thelocal.se/19572/20090520.

Lasar, Mathew. 2011. "Aussie ISPs to Trial Notifying Suspected Infringers of Suspected Misdeeds." *Ars Technica*, 28 November. http://arstechnica.com/tech-policy/2011/11/aussie-isps-to-trial-notifying-suspected-infringers-of-suspected-misdeeds/.

Lazzarato, Maurizio. 1996. "Immaterial Labor," trans. P. Colilli and E. Emory. http://www.generation-online.org/c/fcimmateriallabour3.htm.

Lee, Timothy B. 2011. "French Copyright Cops: We're Swamped with 'Three Strikes' Complaints." *Ars Technica*, 15 July. http://arstechnica.com/tech-policy/2011/07/french-agency-were-swamped-with-three-strikes-complaints/.

Lessig, Lawrence. 2005. *Free Culture*. Harmondsworth: Penguin.

Lewan, Mats. 2009. "Sorting out the Pirate Bay Verdict." *CNet News*, 21 April. http://news.cnet.com/8301-1023_3-10224201-93.html.

Linebaugh, Peter, and Marcus Rediker. 2000. *The Many-Headed Hydra: Sailors, Slaves, Commoners, and the Hidden History of the Revolutionary Atlantic*. Boston: Beacon Press.

Lobato, Ramon, and Julian Thomas. 2012. "The Business of Anti-Piracy: New Zones of Enterprise in the Copyright Wars." *International Journal of Communication* 6: 606-625.

Mauss, Marcel. 1997. *The Gift: The Form and Reason for Exchange in Archaic Societies*. Foreword by Mary Douglas. London: Routledge.

McKenzie, Greg, and Greg Cochrane. 2009. "Paul McCartney: Pirate Bay Verdict 'Fair.'" *BBC Newsbeat* 20 April. http://news.bbc.co.uk/newsbeat/hi/music/newsid_8007000/8007950.stm.

Miegel, Fredrik, and Tobias Olsson. 2008. "From Pirates to Politicians: The Story of the Swedish File Sharers Who Became a Political Party." In N. Carpentier et al., eds., *Democracy, Journalism and Technology: New Developments in an Enlarged Europe*. Tartu: Tartu University Press. http://www.researchingcommunication.eu/reco_book4.pdf.

Mill, John S. 1987. *Principles of Political Economy with Some of Their Applications to Social Philosophy*. Fairfield: Augustus M. Kelley. Reprint of 1852 edition.

Patton, Robert H. 2008. *Patriot Pirates: The Privateer War for Freedom and Fortune in the American Revolution*. New York: Pantheon.

Pirate Bay, The. 2008. "25 Million" Blog. http://thepiratebay.org/blog/138.

Pirate Bay, The. 2011a. "Legal Threats against The Pirate Bay." http://thepiratebay.org/legal.

Pirate Bay, The. 2011b. "The Pirate Bay." http://thepiratebay.org.

Pirate Bay, The. 2012. "New TPB Investigation Leaked." http://thepiratebay.se/blog/209.

Piratpartiet. N.d. "International – English – The Pirate Party." http://www.piratpartiet.se/international/english.

Proudhon, Pierre-Joseph. N.d. *What Is Property?*, trans. Benjamin Tucker. London: William Reeves.

Riccardi, Nicholas. 2009. "Who Owns Colorado's Rainwater?" *Los Angeles Times*, 18 March. http://articles.latimes.com/2009/mar/18/nation/na-contested-rainwater18.

Sahlins, Marshall. 1974. *Stone Age Economics*. London: Tavistock.

Schofield, Jack. 2009. "Sweden's Pirate Party Wins EU seat." *The Guardian Technology Blog*, 8 June. http://www.guardian.co.uk/technology/blog/2009/jun/08/elections-pirate-party-sweden.

Smith, Adam. 1979. *Wealth of Nations*. Glasgow ed. Oxford: Oxford University Press.

Tehranian, John. 2007. "Infringement Nation: Copyright Reform and the Law/Norm Gap." *Utah Law Review* 2007: 537-550. http://papers.ssrn.com/sol3/papers.cfm?abstract_id=1029151.

TT. 2009. "ISPs Refuse to Shut Down Pirate Bay." *TheLocal: Sweden's News in English*, 18 April. http://www.thelocal.se/18940/20090418/.

UPI. 2009. "Pirate Bay Sentences Prompt Protests." *UPI Entertainment News*, 19 April. http://www.upi.com/Entertainment_News/2009/04/19/Pirate-Bay-sentences-prompt-protests/UPI-15441240156999/.

Wilk, Richard R., and Cligget, Lisa C. 2007. *Economies and Cultures: Foundations of Economic Anthropology*. New York: Westview.

8.   Reproducibility, Copy, Simulation

Key Concepts of Media Theory and Their Limits

Jens Schröter

The broad field of 20th-century media theory debate is hardly something which lends itself to succinct summarizing. One striking fact, however, especially in the context of a reader on the subject of *piracy*, is that "reproducibility" is a recurring theme. What is seen as a distinguishing feature of technical media (since the emergence of photography and film, and in particular of the new media) is that the content they store can easily be reproduced. And what is more, their content is designed to be reproducible; it seems as though the very difference between original and copy is becoming obsolete. This has been described by various theorists with varying emphasis as a specific feature and an objective of media development: Part 1 of this text will briefly present a few relevant positions. The mere existence, however, of terms such as "piracy" (cf. Yar 2005) or "pirated copy," and of campaigns against "copyright pirates," shows that reproducibility is not a phenomenon which is welcomed unreservedly. Reproducibility clashes with the economic imperative of scarcity, and sometimes with legal regulations. Thus judicial, technical, and didactic procedures work together to prevent unauthorized reproduction – this is outlined briefly in Part 2. Part 3 offers a short conclusion.

I

The obvious association evoked by the term "reproducibility" is Walter Benjamin's well-known text "The Work of Art in the Age of Its Mechanical Reproduction," first published in French in 1936. It should be noted that Benjamin, thinking to diagnose a whole epoch, describes an "*age* of technological reproducibility" (as the better translation would be), one which, however, initially refers mainly to the work of art. He does stress that the work of art has always been manually reproducible, but: "Technological reproduction of the work of art is something else, something that has been practiced intermittently through history, at widely separated intervals though with growing intensity" (Benjamin 2008, 3). Thus it seems that reproducibility has at least intensified in the modern period.

According to Benjamin, the result of this intensification is *firstly* "the most profound changes" in the impact of "traditional artworks" (Benjamin 2008, 5). Reproduction detaches the artwork from tradition and makes it "come closer to whatever situation the person apprehending it is in" (Benjamin 2008, 7); the exhibition value supplants the cult value. *Secondly,* he underlines this diagnosis by pointing to the emergence of art forms – photography and cinema – which are already structurally designed to be reproducible: "From a photographic plate, for instance, many prints can be made; the question of the genuine print has no meaning. *However, the instant the criterion of genuineness in art production failed, the entire social function of art underwent an upheaval*" (Benjamin 2008, 12; emphasis in original).

Benjamin's suggestion has been taken up repeatedly in recent debates on the subject. Rosalind Krauss, for example, wrote: "The structural change effected by photography's material base is that it is a medium of direct copies, where there exist multiples *without* an original." She takes this as evidence of a "totally new function of art" (Krauss 2001, 1002; emphasis in the original), arguing that the art of modernity cannot be understood without this recourse to photography as a multiple without an original (and the art of so-called postmodernity still less). She thus regarded the appropriative art forms of the 1980s, which worked closely with the strategy of the copy, as particularly important. She pointed to the work of artists such as Sherrie Levine, who had, for example, photographed the photos of Walker Evans and presented them as her own work.

But Benjamin had already noted that "its significance [i.e., that of re-producibility – *J. S.*] points beyond the realm of art" (2008, 7). And indeed: even without explicit recourse to Benjamin, comparable diagnoses were made elsewhere. Günther Anders, for example, had remarked on television reporting in his 1956 text "The World as Phantom and as Matrix": "When the event in its reproduced form is socially more important than the original event, this original must be shaped with a view to being reproduced: in other words, the event becomes merely a master matrix, or a mold for casting its own reproduction" (Anders 1956, 20). Again, reproduction seems to be the signature of an epoch, replacing the "original," whatever that might be, and/or cancelling out the difference between original and reproduction. Admittedly, Anders was referring to television rather than to photography and film, and his attitude toward this change was marked by much greater cultural pessimism than Benjamin's.

Another similar but more affirmative diagnosis is found in the work of Jean Baudrillard, beginning in the mid-1970s. Very briefly: he formulates – partly with reference to Benjamin – a history of simulacra. His argument is that "Western" societies, after a phase of imitation in the Renaissance and a phase of industrial production of identical objects, entered the era of "hyperreal simulation" at some point (he does not specify when) in the 20th century (cf. Baudrillard 1993, esp. 70-76; on Benjamin cf. e.g., 55-57). By "simulation" – insofar as it is possible to determine this precisely in his sometimes confusing texts – Baudrillard does not mean (or only means in a metaphorical sense) the construction of performative models in computer simulation, which has become increasingly important, particularly in the military, technology, and science, since 1945 (cf. Schröter 2004a). Instead his main contention, rather like Anders (cf. Kramer 1998 on Baudrillard and Anders), is that reproduction has already secured a conclusive victory over the real, and that original and copy can therefore no longer be distinguished. If I understand correctly, he seems to argue that nowadays, no substantial depth of reference can be assumed to exist behind chains of signifiers pointing exclusively at other signifiers – political attitudes, for example, are becoming interchangeable lifestyle accessories. In any case Kramer summarizes (cf. 1998, 259) that "simulation thus levels out the differences between original and copy, between the real and its reproduction, and in the end eradicates all references to the referent."

Whatever one may think about individual aspects of this strident diagnosis, Baudrillard's texts were extensively discussed the 1980s and early 1990s. It is probably no coincidence that a series of further publications on related issues followed in the 1990s and early 2000s. To name just two of these: *Culture of the Copy* is the title of a 1996 book by Hillel Schwartz. In 2004 a book entitled *OriginalKopie. Praktiken des Sekundären* (OriginalCopy: Practices of the secondary) was published in Cologne at the research center for "Media and Cultural Communication," describing diverse forms and processes of reproduction (cf. Fehrmann et al. 2004). We can see, even beyond the question of originality and its relationship to the copy in art, an increasingly firm diagnosis that we live in an "age of technological reproducibility," a "culture of the copy," even the "era of simulation." And this diagnosis does seem plausible. Just a few examples, deliberately taken from a wide range of spheres:

1. *Science*: The sciences relevant for modernity are based on an epistemology of experiment (however problematic this may be), in which the reality of a theory can only be confirmed if an effect is reproducible. Baudrillard (1993, 73) wrote: "The very definition of the real is *that of which it is possible to provide an equivalent reproduction.*" In this sense, reality depends on its reproducibility.

2. *Material production*: The industrial manufacturing of goods surrounds
    us with an abundance of largely identical copies, e.g., of chairs. These
    obviously follow a reproducible prototype. Andy Warhol gave a well-
    known, ironic commentary on this development with endless series of
    Campbell's soup cans and Brillo boxes.

3. *Production of signs*: Reproducible photography covers the world with
    identical-looking photos. Then of course we all use photocopiers to dupli-
    cate written documents or pictures, a development Benjamin could not
    have foreseen. And finally, the emergence of digital media really seems
    to have brought about the collapse of the difference between original and
    copy. Digital data is, on a basal level, just a sequence of zeros and ones, and
    if one simply copies this sequence (or if a computer does), the resulting file
    is *exactly* the same as the original. Unlike analog processes, copying no
    longer causes a loss in quality, distancing the copy from the original. The
    difference becomes obsolete. Indeed the argument initially seems more
    convincing for digital data than for photography (the focus of Benjamin's
    and subsequently Krauss's theses); most photographic procedures, after
    all, still distinguish between an original negative and the positive prints.

This, then, is the grand narrative recounted by certain representatives of
media theory: *We are entering an "age of reproducibility" in which everything
and everyone will soon be able to be reproduced – and the difference between
original and copy will thereby collapse.* Thus, for example, Geoffrey Batchen
also claims that "we are entering a time when it will no longer be possible to
tell any original from its simulations" (2000, 10). Cinema and television are full
of corresponding phantasms, particularly in the case of science fiction. There
are the fantasies of genetic reproduction, suggesting that we will soon be able
to create identical clones of dinosaurs, humans, etc. Or phantasms of virtual
simulation, in which future computers will be able to reproduce the world
in its materiality – just think of the "holodeck" from the popular American
television series *Star Trek: The Next Generation,* or of course the film *The Matrix*
(cf. Schröter 2004b, 152-276). The simulations shown here are (almost) as real
as reality; the difference between original and copy becomes meaningless.

II

Having followed this idea to its final, phantasmagoric climax, a critical commentary on this grand narrative is pertinent, and several points of departure
offer themselves here. From a historical point of view, for example, we can

ask whether culture has not always been based on the reproducibility of linguistic signs; thus reproducibility is not exclusively correlating with technical or new media. One should also draw attention to the historical contingency of reproducibility as an attribute of certain technical media: photography, for example, is not reproducible "in itself"; there have also been nonreproducible photographic processes (daguerreotype, Polaroid, etc.).

The thesis that we live in an age of technological reproducibility, can be criticized from another angle, too, one leading up to the central theme of the present volume. The thesis is: *The expansion of reproducibility – regardless of whether the principle has always existed or not – into an increasingly broad range of subject areas inevitably entails the emergence of strategies of nonreproducibility.* The description of modernity as an age of ever increasing reproducibility is not false, but one-sided. Especially if, like Anders or Baudrillard, one takes this as evidence that the difference between original and copy is imploding – or has imploded.

For it is obvious that this difference still exists on an everyday level, despite the expansion of analog and digital technical media. Therefore, the reproduction of, e.g., *money, secret documents, and identity documents* is prohibited for all but certain institutions. Otherwise the criteria for their "authenticity" – and this means nothing less than their operability – would be nullified. These types of document function on the basis of a distinction between original and copy – a copied banknote is no longer a banknote. Of course, there is a history of "unauthorized reproduction,"[1] as it is explicitly called in the relevant guidelines in the European Central Bank, and the counterfeiting of coins, for example, has long attracted severe penalties (cf. Voigtlaender 1976). There are legal regulations against certain forms of reproducibility – regulations which find expression in pejorative terms such as "pirated copy" or "piracy."

But the legal penalty always comes *after the fact*. When it comes to the currency system, the damage must be prevented in advance, since large-scale counterfeiting would lead to inflation and could even bring about an economic collapse. Because of these dangers, increasing efforts were made in the 20th century to delegate the legal prohibition to technical – and sometimes legally protected – processes, simply to cope with the increase in reproducibility. One way in which reproducibility has increased is the spread of photocopiers since the 1960s.

Parallel to this increase, new types of nonreproducible markings have been devised, or old techniques such as the watermark (cf. Gerstengarbe et al. 2010) have been resurrected – watermarks are also found on banknotes. But such technical processes as watermarks only work if the subjects concerned – i.e., all of us – know how to decipher the marks denoting authenticity – hence the mass distribution of information about physical and attentional techniques which help to detect forgeries. The German police advice website (polizei-beratung.de) gives information on a holographic "special patch" on the lower-right-hand side of the €50 note: "On the right of the front of the note is a special patch. If you move the banknote, then depending on the angle of viewing either the value of the note or the architectural motif depicted on the note appears in changing colors as a hologram."[2] So one is supposed to learn how to move the banknote, and what to pay attention to in order to be able to distinguish genuine from fake, original from copy. The hologram added to the banknote, which changes its appearance in the light and which cannot be photocopied – e.g., with a modern color copier – helps achieve this.

To support this aim the website provides a Java applet with the name "Euro-Blüten-Trainer" ("fake euro trainer," sometimes translated as "funny money advisor") (Fig. 8.1). Here, applying comparative visual analysis in a way Heinrich Wölfflin would surely never have imagined, one can learn to recognize the crucial security markings on banknotes. "Train your gaze to 'incorruptible inspector' standard." Similar training software with corresponding short films can be found on the website of the German Federal Bank.

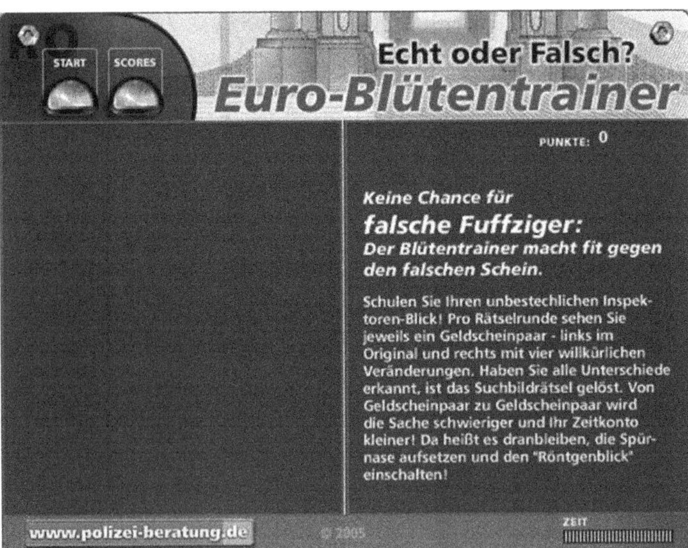

Fig. 8.1: Euro-Blüten-Trainer ("funny money advisor"), screenshot (Source: http://bluetentrainer. polizei-beratung.de/blueten_euro/trainer_d.html, 04.11.2009)

This didactic endeavor also includes film and poster campaigns such as "Copyright pirates are criminals" (Fig. 8.2). These and similar disciplinary paratexts are important since – and this brings us back to the legal side – there are severe penalties (prison sentences of up to five years) for even unknowingly passing on counterfeit money. These paratexts interpellate all of us, alerting us to our duty of learning the physical and attentional techniques which will help us recognize legally protected technical effects that signal the criminal offence of unauthorized reproduction of money or documents.

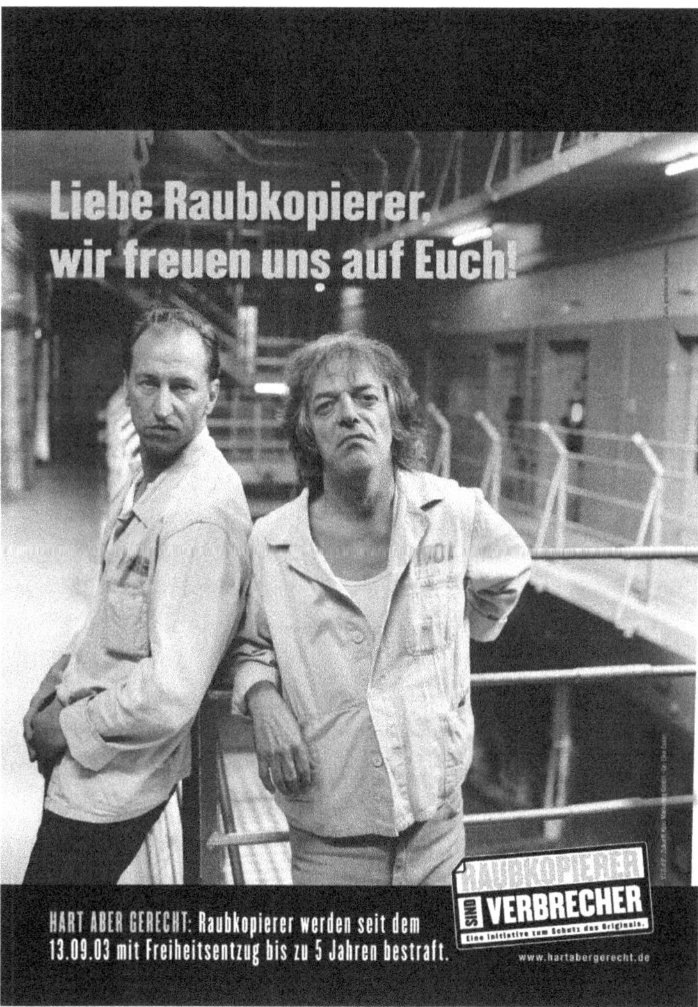

Fig. 8.2: "Raubkopierer sind Verbrecher" (Copyright pirates are criminals)

For this reason, counterfeiters try to distribute their fake notes in chaotic, hectic situations where there is too little time and/or light for a thorough examination. In summary: the aim is to prevent unauthorized reproduction with a heterogeneous combination of three components:

1. Legal threats and the institutional conditions which allow them to function: the legal-institutional complex.
2. Technical effects which cannot be reproduced by the general public (e.g., holograms).
3. Physical or attentional techniques focused on the special effects provided by the technical processes at (2), in order to recognize the differences between authorized and unauthorized reproduction defined according to (1).

This heterogeneous configuration, designed to stabilize what one might call the *reproductive difference* between original and copy, appears in a wide variety of areas. I will outline just a few of these:

1. In the area of *material commodities,* there is *product counterfeiting.* At the beginning of 2009, a group of secondary school students from Lübeck went on a fatal drinking spree in Kemer, on the Mediterranean coast of Turkey, drinking raki laced with methanol. Following this incident the *Süddeutsche Zeitung* reported on problems with the counterfeiting of raki in Turkey, and more precisely on "2005, the year of the raki crisis," in which one incident stands out in particular: "First of all, 500,000 holograms, which were supposed to be attached to bottles to guarantee the authenticity of the liquor, were stolen from a raki distillery in Izmir" (trans. from Strittmatter 2009, 10). Two points can be deduced from this. *Firstly*: even if Baudrillard may be right in thinking that industrial mass production of goods has led to an unprecedented spread of identical series of objects, this does not necessarily nullify the distinction between original and copy (cf. the example of machine construction, see Paul 2010). *Secondly*: holograms are mentioned again here, as in the discussion of banknotes above. Holography is one of a number of irreproducible photographic processes, designed to curb reproducibility in conjunction with corresponding legal institutions and physical techniques. An original hologram is easy to recognize, due to its specific visual features, and no copier can copy it in such a way that these features remain intact. The fact that there are small, identical holograms on many banknotes shows that holographs can be reproduced in certain circumstances, but not by the general public. Reproducibility is not something that exists or does not exist; it is present in a graduated and variously distributed state (cf. Schröter 2009).

2. As already mentioned, one of the most important areas in which reproducibility must be contained and reduced is that of documents pertaining to governmental and economic structures. Money and identity documents, etc., must only be duplicated or produced by the appropriate institutions. These documents are generally to be found in wallets. You, dear reader, can understand this easily: you have, in your wallet, *firstly* your identity documents, and *secondly* money or cards with which you can access money. You can easily verify the vital importance of this archive of nonreproducible elements for your economic and political existence, i.e., your existence as a bourgeois and *citoyen*. Go to a bank without a credit card or identity card and try to get money. Try to travel to another country without a passport – it might work, but bad luck if you strike a checkpoint. You can claim that you are creditworthy as often as you want, and cry all you like – no one will believe you unless you can present a real credit card or a real passport. You would be considered highly suspicious if you dared to present a photocopy of your passport (or your credit card). You are only "yourself" by virtue of your *original* documents.

A clear difference does emerge here, though: in the case of money, you have to be able to recognize e.g., a fake €50 note, i.e., you have to learn to distinguish it from other €50 notes. But you come across a lot of €50 notes, i.e., you have to learn to tell *genuine copies* from *fake copies*. With your ID card, the situation is somewhat different. It is only allocated to you, and of course it would make no sense to distribute numerous copies of it. I can scarcely use a copy of someone else's ID card to prove my identity, however good the copy may be. Here the nonreproducibility of the ID card is connected to the prototype of my signature and face. My signature and the photo of my face connect me and my identity document *indexically* (this also applies to biometric data).[3] *My face and my signature have to match the face and signature on the document – and vice versa.* Thus the prototype has to be reproduced, but it is fixed on a document which is rigorously protected against unauthorized production, by having security features which cannot readily be reproduced.

This shows that it is not a matter of playing reproducibility and nonreproducibility off against each other, but of observing their actual configurations, historically, culturally, even situationally. This essay is just a preliminary attempt to chart this difficult terrain. The ID card, which I cannot validly produce myself, assigns my face, and therefore my body, to my name. And this ID card can only be allocated to the specific, i.e., addressable person, by the approved governmental body. *A person can be defined as a living body + an identity document.*[4] Much the same can be said for staff ID cards, company ID cards, or military ID cards. Access to certain institutions or resources can only be obtained through such processes of identification; this is why "identity theft" (cf. Hoofnagle 2007) is now a key crime in the areas of espionage, industrial espionage, illegal immigration, and emigration.

While every banknote in a series shows the same reference, e.g., €50, the singular reference is the difference between ID cards. The issue with ID cards is therefore to distinguish a *fake* from a *genuine* original. Strictly speaking, every banknote is also an original, since it has a singular number, but here the question is always whether a given banknote is a valid copy of its prototype. Besides, as users in practice we do not really have any opportunity to check whether the number is correct – e.g., by visiting a bank. Hence we can and generally must disregard this singularity and differentiate, in the case of banknotes, between *fake* and *genuine* copies. This strange expression may cause discomfort – perhaps it would be better to say "authorized" and "unauthorized" copies – but from the point of view of the authorizing bodies this is the same as the difference between genuine and fake.

3. In the *art system*, of course, the distinction between original and copy is still maintained. This is particularly evident in the "vintage print" in photography, a practice which would undoubtedly have seemed very peculiar to Walter Benjamin, and would probably also strike Rosalind Krauss as odd. The first print made from the negative by the photographer is valued higher than every subsequent reproduction, and there are always conflicts about the secure documentation of these processes. It is, furthermore, standard practice today for photographers to make just a few prints of their photos – sometimes even destroying the negative after producing the prints – to ensure that only a small number of copies are in circulation. Thus even the works of Appropriation Art which Krauss valued so highly have now become expensive originals.

4. In the *digital* field, too – and especially here – the reproductive difference is continually being reconstructed. Precisely *because* a loss-free reproduction could theoretically diminish the difference between original and copy (if one disregards the frequent need to compress data, thus entailing losses, cf. Salomon 2008), the frantic efforts to rebuild this distinction are redoubled. In the digital realm, increased reproducibility seems liable to break down the object's nature as a commodity and thus the very condition which makes an economy possible. A digital commodity – software, a film, music – can be reproduced any number of times. This has a huge negative impact on its commercializability if the digital commodity is reproduced by users rather than producers. But the problem is even more fundamental: whether I hand over a piece of software for money or for free, I always keep a

copy. No exchange takes place, and thus the object's nature as a commodity seems questionable (cf. Grassmuck 2004).[5] Again: strict laws and their institutions of enforcement, complicated technical processes – think of digital rights management[6] or copy protection systems for DVDs and audio CDs (cf., for example, Wöhner 2005) – and physical and attentional techniques are supposed to prevent the technical potential of digital technologies from becoming usable, because this potential is not compatible with the economic principles which are currently in place.

III

Reproducibility presents a fundamental threat to the existing governmental and economic structures of modern societies; I believe Benjamin saw this much correctly, albeit in a different way.[7] Hence the emergence of dramatic terms such as piracy (cf. Yar 2005). To combat these threats, a heterogeneous ensemble of (a) special technological processes (such as holography), (b) legal regulations, and (c) attentional techniques is constructed. I call this the "heterogeneous ensemble of reproductive difference." It is intended to stabilize the differences between genuine and fake originals, and between genuine and fake copies. The heterogeneous ensemble of reproductive difference is a mode of – to borrow Foucault's use of the term (1981, 58) – "rarefaction," without which neither the circulation of money, nor personal identity, nor the circulation of goods can be maintained. Such rarefactions seem, depending on the individual practice or subsystem, to be a more or less urgent necessity. It is nonsense to claim that the difference between original and copy is now obsolete. Whole industries have sprung up which earn their money by preventing copies and thus stabilizing originals.

Some of the media theories with which this text began tend to consider the potential of technologies in an abstract way, separate from their social context, and thus to draw overstated and one-sided conclusions about their effects. The reproducibility of some forms of photography, for example, leads them to announce an "age" in which reproducibility conquers all. But the age of technological reproducibility is also the age of technical nonreproducibility. There seem to be social structures or imperatives which are more powerful than changes in media technology, but which nonetheless have to respond to these changes (cf. Winston 1998, 1-18). In other words, our use of the term *piracy* today is the effect of a conflict between technological and societal structures or entities. It remains to be seen how this struggle will end.

Notes

1. EZB/2003/4, http://www.ecb.int/ecb/legal/pdf/l_07820030325de00160019.
    pdf, [25.03.2003], 04.11.2009.
2. http://www.polizei-beratung.de/attension_ressources/downloads/infotex-
    te/Falschgeldkriminalitaet.doc, 04.11.2009.
3. The indexicality of the signature is also demonstrated by the fact that, e.g.,
    an erasable pencil is not "acceptable for use on official documents" since
    the mark can be deleted or changed. (http://de.wikipedia.org/wiki/Doku-
    mentenechtheit, 08.06.2011). A particularly strange phenomenon, which we
    cannot go into here, is the so-called "facsimile signature stamp," i.e., a stamp
    which imitates a handwritten signature as closely as possible.
4. It is not customary to possess ID cards in every country or culture, though –
    this should be made the subject of a comparative cultural study on the pro-
    duction of identity. In the conditions of modern mass societies, however,
    some sort of mechanisms of identification are generally necessary, cf. the
    very detailed overview at: http://en.wikipedia.org/wiki/Identity_document,
    08.06.2011.
5. See essay by Stefan Meretz in this volume.
6. On DRM see the wealth of information at the website http://waste.infor-
    matik.hu-berlin.de/Grassmuck/drm/, 04.11.2009. On the problem of law
    relating to digital media cf. Boehme-Neßler 2008.
7. Benjamin hoped that reproducibility would encourage socialist transforma-
    tions of society.

Bibliography

Anders, Günther. 1956. "The World as Phantom and as Matrix." *Dissent* 3: 14-24.
Batchen, Geoffrey. 2000. "Ectoplasm: Photography in the Digital Age." In Carol Squiers, ed., *Over Exposed: Essays on Contemporary Photography*. New York: The New Press, 9-23.
Baudrillard, Jean. 1993 [1976]. *Symbolic Exchange and Death*. London: Sage.
Benjamin, Walter. 2008 [1936]. *The Work of Art in the Age of Mechanical Reproduction*. London: Penguin.
Boehme-Neßler, Volker. 2008. *Unscharfes Recht. Überlegungen zur Relativierung des Rechts in der digitalisierten Welt*. Berlin: Duncker and Humblot.
Fehrmann, Gisela, et al., eds. 2004. *OriginalKopie: Praktiken des Sekundären* Köln: Dumont.
Foucault, Michel. 1981 [1970]. "The Order of Discourse." In Robert Young, ed., *Untying the Text: A Post-Structuralist Reader*. Boston: Routledge, 48-78.
Gerstengarbe, Carina, et al. 2010. "Wasserzeichen. Vom 13. Jahrhundert bis zum Digital Water-marking." In Jens Schröter et al., eds., *Kulturen des Kopierschutzes II*. Siegen: universi, 9-62.
Grassmuck, Volker. 2004. *Freie Software: zwischen Privat- und Gemeineigentum*. Bonn: Bundeszentrale für politische Bildung.
Kramer, Wolfgang. 1998. *Technokratie als Entmaterialisierung der Welt: Zur Aktualität der Philosophien von Günther Anders und Jean Baudrillard*. Münster: Waxmann.

Krauss, Rosalind. 2001. "1959, 9 January: The Ministry of Fate." In Denis Hollier, ed., *A New History of French Literature*. Cambridge, MA: Harvard University Press, 1000-1006.

Paul, Holger. 2010. "Hologramme auf die Maschinen. Um sich vor Plagiatoren zu schützen, setzen die deutschen Maschinenbauer vor allem auf technologischen Vorsprung. Das reicht nicht aus, findet ihr Verband." *Frankfurter Allgemeine Zeitung*, 19 January, 20.

Salomon, David. 2008. *A Concise Introduction to Data Compression*. London: Springer.

Schröter, Jens. 2004a. "Computer/Simulation. Kopie ohne Original oder das Original kontrollierende Kopie?" In Gisela Fehrmann et al., eds., *OriginalKopie. Praktiken des Sekundären*. Köln: Dumont, 139-155.

Schröter, Jens. 2004b. *Das Netz und die virtuelle Realität. Zur Selbstprogrammierung der Gesellschaft durch die universelle Maschine*. Bielefeld: Transcript.

Schröter, Jens. 2009. "Das holographische Wissen und die technische Nicht-Reproduzierbarkeit." In Stefan Rieger and Jens Schröter, eds., *Das holographische Wissen*. Berlin: diaphanes, 77-86.

Schwartz, Hillel. 1996. *The Culture of the Copy: Striking Likenesses, Unreasonable Facsimiles*. New York: Zone Books.

Strittmatter, Kai. 2009. "Selbstgebranntes Gift. In der Türkei sterben öfter Menschen, weil sie gepanschten Alkohol trinken – der Tod eines deutschen Schülers ist kein Einzelfall." *Süddeutsche Zeitung*, 3 April, 10.

Voigtlaender, Heinz. 1976. Falschmünzer und Münzfälscher: Geschichte der Geldfälschung aus 2½ Jahrtausenden, Münster/WF: Numismatischer Verlag Dombrowski.

Winston, Brian. 1998. *Media, Technology and Society: A History from the Telegraph to the Internet*. London: Routledge.

Wöhner, Thomas. 2005. "Analyse und Bewertung von Kopierschutzverfahren für Audio-CDs." In Hannes Federrath, ed., *Sicherheit 2005*. Bonn: Gesellschaft für Informatik, 175-188.

Yar, Majid. 2005. "The Global 'Epidemic' of Movie 'Piracy': Crimewave or Social Construction?" *Media, Culture and Society* 27.5: 677-696.

The Aesthetics of Piracy

9.   Degraded Images, Distorted Sounds

Nigerian Video and the Infrastructure of Piracy

Brian Larkin

In Kano, the economic center of northern Nigeria, media piracy is part of the "organizational architecture" of globalization (Sassen 2002), providing the infrastructure that allows media goods to circulate. Infrastructures organize the construction of buildings, the training of personnel, the building of railway lines, and the elaboration of juridicolegal frameworks without which the movement of goods and people cannot occur. But once in place, infrastructures generate possibilities for their own corruption and parasitism. Media piracy is one example of this in operation. It represents the potential of technologies of reproduction – the supple ability to store, reproduce, and retrieve data – when shorn from the legal frameworks that limit their application. It depends heavily on the flow of media from official, highly regulated forms of trade but then develops its own structures of reproduction and distribution external and internal to the state economy.

It is through this generative quality that pirate infrastructure is expressive of a paradigmatic shift in Nigerian economy and capital and represents the extension of a logic of privatization into everyday life. Piracy's negative characteristics are often commented on: its criminality, the erosion of property rights it entails, and its function as a pathology of information processing, parasitically derivative of legal media flows (Chesterman and Lipman 1988; Coombe 1998). As important as these questions are, the structural focus on legal issues tends to obscure the mediating nature of infrastructure itself. In the Nigerian case, this is seen most strikingly in the rise of a new video industry that makes feature-length films directly for domestic video consumption (see Larkin 2000; Haynes 2000; Ukadike 2000; Ukah 2003). This new industry has pioneered new film genres and generated an entirely novel mode of reproduction and distribution that uses the capital, equipment, personnel, and distribution networks of pirate media. These Nigerian videos are a legitimate media form that could not exist without the infrastructure created by its illegitimate double, pirate media.

In recent years, then, there has been a wholesale shift in which many entrepreneurs previously involved in the distribution of pirate material have switched to the reproduction and dissemination of legal media. The mass importation of foreign music and films brought about the capital and professional expertise that facilitated the rise of a local film industry. This wandering over the lines that separate the legal from the nonlegal has been a common experience for urban Africans, who have been progressively disembedded from the infrastructures linking them to the official world economy and instead have poured energy into developing informal networks – equally global – that facilitate traffic in economic and cultural goods outside the established institutions of world trade (Simone 2000, 2001; Bayart, Ellis, and Hibou 1999; Mbembe 2001).

In addition to generating new economic networks, piracy, like all infrastructural modes, has distinct material qualities that influence the media that travel under its regime of reproduction. Piracy imposes particular conditions on the recording, transmission, and retrieval of data. Constant copying erodes data storage, degrading image and sound, overwhelming the signal of media content with the noise produced by the means of reproduction. Pirate videos are marked by blurred images and distorted sound, creating a material screen that filters audiences' engagement with media technologies and their senses of time, speed, space, and contemporaneity. In this way, piracy creates an aesthetic, a set of formal qualities that generates a particular sensorial experience of media marked by poor transmission, interference, and noise. Contemporary scholars of technology returning to the Frankfurt School have stressed that technology's operation on the body is a key factor in producing a sense of shock – the complex training of the human sensorium associated with modern urbanism (Benjamin 1999; Crary 2000; Doane 2002; Hansen 1995, 2000; Kracauer 1995; Schivelbusch 1986). This work is crucial in understanding the phenomenological and cognitive effects of technology when it is working at its optimum. What is less discussed (see Schivelbusch 1986; Virilio 2003) is how technology influences through its failure as much as through its successes. Yet the inability of technologies to perform the operations they were assigned must be subject to the same critical scrutiny as their achievements. Breakdown and failure are, of course, inherent in all technologies, but in societies such as Nigeria, where collapse is often the default state of technological existence, they take on a far greater material and political presence (see also Mbembe and Roitman 1995; Koolhaas et al. 2001).

Rather than elide pirate infrastructure by using it as a window into legal questions of intellectual property, I wish to foreground it. If infrastructures represent attempts to order, regulate, and rationalize society, then breakdowns in their operation, or the rise of provisional and informal infrastructures, highlight the failure of that ordering and the recoding that takes its place. By subjecting the material operation of piracy and its social consequences to scrutiny, it becomes clear that pirate infrastructure is a powerful mediating force that produces new modes of organizing sensory perception, time, space, and economic networks.

Infrastructure

Capitalism, as many thinkers from Marx to Henri Lefebvre and David Harvey have reminded us, is not separable from space but produces the spaces through which it operates. All regimes of capital depend on infrastructures – shipping, trains, fiber optic lines, warehouses – whereby space gets produced and networked. Cities, or social space itself in Lefebvre's (1991) terms, take on real existence through their insertion into networks and pathways of commodity exchange, and it is infrastructure that provides these channels of communication. Infrastructure is the structural condition of the movement of commodities, whether they are waste, energy, or information. It brings diverse places into interaction, connecting some while divorcing others, constantly ranking, connecting, and segmenting spaces and people (Graham and Marvin 1996, 2001; Sassen 2002).

Infrastructures were key to the first modern corporations, which were organized around the continuous circulation of goods, services, and information on a large scale (Mattelart 2000). As such they have been enormously influential by organizing territory, standardizing time, and innovating new forms of economic organization. The rise of new electronic communication has intensified these processes, in turn instituting their own effects on people's sense of time and distance and on their conceptions of the present and simultaneity (Kern 1983; Mattelart 1996; Schivelbusch 1986; Virilio 1997).

The difficulty here is that much of the work on the transformative effects of media on notions of space, time, and perception takes for granted a media system that is smoothly efficient rather than the reality of infrastructural connections that are frequently messy, discontinuous, and poor. Technologies of speed and the infrastructures they create have had a profound impact on countries like Nigeria, but it is painfully obvious to people who live there that they often do not work as they are supposed to. This does not simply reflect national poverty but rather is inherent in the functioning (and the threat of collapse) of all technological systems. What distinguishes poor countries is the systemic nature of these failures, so that infrastructure, or the lack of it, becomes a pressing economic and social issue and a locus of political resentment toward the failures of the state and state elites. At the same time, the creation of successful infrastructures sets in motion other types of flows that operate in the space capital provides and that travel the routes created by these new networks of communication. The organization of one system sets in motion other systems spinning off in different directions.

The Corruption of Infrastructure

Piracy's success lies in its own infrastructural order that preys on the official distribution of globalized media, thus making it part of the corruption of infrastructure. By *corruption* I mean the pirating of a system's mode of communication – the viruses that attach to other kinds of official or recognized movement. Technological infrastructure creates material channels that organize the movement of energy, information, and economic and cultural goods between societies but at the same time creates possibilities for new actions. In Nigeria, this can be seen clearly in the so-called 419 schemes.[1] Sending letters by fax and e-mail, 419 fraudsters claim to be a senior Nigerian official – a bank president, a petroleum minister, a relative of a dictator – and state that they urgently need to transfer a large amount of money out of the country (for an overview see Apter 1999; Hibou 1999). The recipients are told that if they agree to help, they will receive a percentage of the money. In this way, complete strangers are lured into what the FBI has described as the most successful fraud in the history of the world – and one of Nigeria's main foreign currency earners. The 419ers target foreign businesses; they make use of international financial arrangements, such as bank accounts and international money transfers; and they depend on new communication technologies – first fax machines and now e-mail. It is a form of fraud that depends on a certain cosmopolitanism, on the internationalization of finance, and as a form of action it is inconceivable without the technological and financial infrastructure brought by Nigeria's oil boom. The oil monies of the 1970s and 1980s allowed for a deep penetration of corporate capitalism in Nigeria and created the professional and technological networks upon which 419ers prey. It also inaugurated the spectacular corruption that gives 419 letters believability to victims. The fraud pirates the discourses and procedures of capitalism but also requires its own infrastructure of communication. In this way, the very success of any infrastructural flows create possibilities for their own corruption, placing in motion the potential for other sets of relations to occur and creating a ripple effect on movements of people, culture, and religion.

Like 419, piracy operates as a corruption of communications infrastructures that develops its own circuits of distribution using officially organized media. Films made in Hollywood and intended for distribution in an organized, domestic circuit are copied by pirates; sent to Asia or the Middle East, where they are subtitled; recopied in large numbers as videocassettes, video CDs (VCDs are the dominant technology for media storage in much of Asia), or DVDs; and then reshipped mainly within the developing world. In recent years, as Nigeria has become progressively disembedded from the official global economy (with the single exception of its oil industry), it has become ever more integrated into a parallel, unofficial world economy that reorients Nigeria toward new metropoles such as Dubai, Singapore, and Beirut (what AbdouMaliq Simone [2001] more broadly calls the "worlding of African cities." See also Bayart, Ellis, and Hibou 1999; MacGaffey and Banzenguissa-Ganga 2000; Mbembe 2001).

Kofar Wambai is best known for the sale of thread used in the elaborate embroidery of the long Hausa gown, the *babban riga*. Whole tracts of the market are suffused in the bright colors of thread hanging from the stall doorways, but in one section is lane after lane of small shops specializing in the reproduction and wholesale distribution of audio- and videocassettes: Indian, Sudanese, Western, and Hausa music; Islamic preaching; and Indian, Western, and Hausa videocassettes.

Cassette sellers at Kofar Wambai are represented by the Kano Cassette Sellers Recording and Co-operative Society Ltd. (Kungiyar Gawa Kai Ta Masu Sayar Da Kaset Da Dauka Ta Jihar Kano), a society whose headquarters is at Kofar Wambai but whose members spill out far beyond the confines of the market. The success of Kano's cassette-reproduction industry is grounded in three developments: First, in 1981, the Motion Picture Association of America (MPAA) suspended the distribution of Hollywood films to Nigeria. This was in response to the seizure of MPAA assets by the Nigerian government in an attempt to indigenize the control of Nigerian companies. Second, the oil boom of the late 1970s boosted consumption, allowing for the mass dissemination of cassette-based technologies. Finally, the longstanding position of Kano at the apex of wide-ranging transnational trading networks facilitated the quick exploitation of these possibilities and the forging of a distribution network that stretches over northern Nigeria and beyond. The subsequent rise of piracy means that far from disappearing, Hollywood films have become available at a speed and volume as never before.

The everyday practice of piracy in Kano was based around the mass distribution of the two most popular drama forms, Indian and Hollywood films, and the reproduction of televised Hausa dramas and Islamic religious cassettes. Nearly all of those who might be described as pirates were at the same time involved in the duplication and sale of legitimate media, and the organization that emerged made Kano the regional distribution center for electronic media in northern Nigeria and the wider Hausaphone area (which covers parts of Chad, Cameroon, Benin, Ghana, and the Sudan). The system is this: the main dealers are based at centers in Kano like the Kofar Wambai market. They then sell to distributors in other northern cities, who in turn supply smaller urban and rural dealers, who supply itinerant peddlers. The system is based on a complex balance of credit and trust; and although it depends, in part, on piracy, it has evolved into a highly organized, extensive distribution system for audio- and videocassettes. The success of this new form of distribution has not been lost on the government, which – though critical of piracy – has used cassette distribution as a way of spreading political messages.[2] As Alhaji Musa Na Sale, president of the cassette-sellers association, told me, if something is popular, "even the nomads will hear it." The decentralized nature of this distribution system means that neither the government nor the association knows exactly how many people are tied to the industry, especially given its massive expansion with the rise of Hausa video films.

Hausa distributors have had to rely on Lebanese and Indian traders for access to foreign videos that were coming from the Persian Gulf. In the 1990s, these videos often had the distributor's name superimposed on the tape itself: for example, Excellence Kano for Hollywood films and Al-Mansoor, Dubai, for Indian ones. Hollywood films were imported to Kano directly from the Middle East or transported north from Lagos. Because of the great popularity of Indian films among the Hausa (Larkin 1997, 2003), Kano was and is the main clearinghouse for Indian films. This traffic is controlled by two primary distributors, both based in Kano. For many years the trade was routed through Dubai, and it was common to watch Indian films with advertisements scrolling across the bottom of the screen announcing "Al Mansoor's video" followed by a long list of his many shops in Dubai, Abu Dhabi, and other parts of the gulf, along with their telephone, telex, and fax numbers. These videos often found their way to the Kano television station, CTV, where announcements for Al Mansoor's many video shops sometimes obliterated the Arabic and English subtitles at the bottom of the screen.

With the recent emergence of video CDs, the routes of the market for Indian film have changed considerably. According to one Indian distributor, the market is now oriented toward Pakistan, where VCD plants make high-quality dubs of Indian films. Master copies are shipped via DHL to

Kano, where they are then transferred to tape and sold in bulk to Hausa distributors. I was told the gap between a film's release in India and its appearance in Kano could be as little as seven days.[3] American films are pirated through similar networks. They are copied illegally in the United States and shipped to Dubai or Beirut, often arriving in Nigeria while they are still on first-run release in the United States. One Jean-Claude Van Damme film I watched had Chinese subtitles superimposed over Arabic ones, providing a visible inscription of the routes of media piracy. Frequently US videos contain a message scrolling across the bottom of the film every few minutes stating: "Demo tape only. Not for rental or sale. If you have rented or purchased this cassette call 1-800 NO COPYS (1-800-662-6787).[4] Federal law provides severe civil and criminal penalties for unauthorized duplication or distribution."

Kofar Wambai is the apex of a formal, highly ordered system of reproduction and distribution for media goods in northern Nigeria and is one example of the ways in which media piracy generates new infrastructures of the parallel economy in Nigeria. It is part of a much larger process whereby the Nigerian economy has split between a traditional official economy oriented toward legal participation in the international division of labor and an unofficial economy, each one with its own infrastructures and networks, sometimes overlapping, sometimes opposed.

Piracy

Piracy is an ambivalent phenomenon in countries like Nigeria. It is widely feared by indigenous film- and music makers as destructive of the small profits they make by way of intellectual property. It has had disastrous effects on indigenous music makers and contributes substantially to the erosion of the industry as a whole. Yet at the same time, many of these same people consume pirate media both privately and professionally. Piracy has made available to Nigerians a vast array of world media at a speed they could never imagine, hooking them up to the accelerated circuit of global media flows. Where cinema screens were once filled with outdated films from the United States or India, pirate media means that Nigerian audiences can watch films contemporaneously with audiences in New York or Bombay. Instead of being marginalized by official distribution networks, Nigerian consumers can now participate in the immediacy of an international consumer culture – but only through the mediating capacity of piracy.

Piracy is part of a so-called shadow (second, marginal, informal, black) economy existing in varying degrees beyond the law. It produces profits, but not for corporations, and provides no revenue for the state.[5] The second economy is untaxed and unmonitored and enjoys all of the benefits and precariousness of this location. Until recently, media infrastructures in Nigeria, from the construction of radio diffusion networks to the building of television stations, have usually been state controlled and organized around the fundamental logic of providing publicity for the state – indeed, of representing its progressivist, developmentalist logic (Larkin 2000). Piracy, by contrast, is based in unofficial, decentralized networks, and Nigerian video represents the migration of these networks into the mainstream.

The rise of privatized media represents not so much an erosion of state power but a larger movement in which the shadow economy has reconfigured the state itself. According to US State Department figures, Nigeria is the largest market for pirate goods in Africa, and one estimate suggests that up to 70% of current Nigerian GDP is derived from the shadow economy, making it, in percentage terms, the largest such economy in the world, matched only by Thailand (see Schneider 2000; Simone 1998; Bayart, Ellis, and Hibou 1999; Mbembe 2001; Apter 1999). Figures such as these are always provisional and, like many statistics about Nigeria, often simulacral, being not so much a numerical reference to the actual state of affairs in Nigeria but rather a mimicking of rationalist representations of economies that are measurable. But in Nigeria, the second economy has grown to such a scale that no one really knows how to represent it. No one is sure how large the GDP is; no one can calculate the balance of payments or even the size of Nigeria's population (Bayart, Ellis, and Hibou 1999; Hecht and Simone 1994). Strong forces are at work to make sure that revenue streams from major industries, like oil, are obligingly opaque. Jean-François Bayart, Stephen Ellis, and Béatrice Hibou (1999) have argued that illegal activities in Nigeria (such as fraud, corruption, and the import and export of illegal oil, drugs, and videos) have grown to such a degree that they now form part of the routine operations of the state rather than a pathology outside of it. Nigerians have become famous within Africa and beyond for migrating as workers, importers, exporters, smugglers, drug carriers, and fraudsters. While the federal state continues to take part in the formalized ritual of the official economy, many Nigerians see a widening gap between it and the everyday reality of how Nigeria functions. Piracy is part of this larger reconfiguration of the Nigerian state and economy.

Ravi Sundaram (1999) argues that informal processes in Indian media ecology should be seen as a pirate modernity – a mode of incorporation into the economy that is disorganized, nonideological, and marked by mobility and innovation. This formulation nicely captures the ambivalence of piracy, refusing the simple equation that piracy is an alternative or oppositional modernity (though there are elements of this in people's justification that pirate media goods redress economic inequalities between developed and underdeveloped countries). Piracy is nonideological in that it does not represent a self-conscious political opposition to capitalism – it is not a kind of tactical media (Garcia and Lovink 2001). But it is also worth stressing the high degree of formality that marks this "informal" world. A focus on the mobility, innovation, and provisionality of piracy elides the fact that pirate networks are highly organized and determinative of other sets of relations.

Hausa Video

In the 1990s, distributors who had been involved with the reproduction and distribution of religious, Hollywood, and Indian cassettes began to turn their attention to Nigerian and especially Hausa-language videos. Nigerian videos are narrative, feature-length films produced in English, Hausa, or Yoruba (Haynes 2000; Ukadike 2000; Ukah 2003; see also Meyer 2003 and Wendl 2001).[6] They are not the kind of African movies usually screened at film festivals but rather are oriented toward popular audiences – meaning that their production and financing depends entirely on how well they perform in the marketplace. By 2001, over 3,500 films had passed through the Nigerian film and censorship board – dwarfing by many times the total number of Nigerian feature films. The films are produced in Yoruba, English, and Hausa, with English-language videos – commonly called "Nigerian videos" – receiving the greatest investment and prestige and distribution to Ghana, Kenya, and as far south as South Africa. Hausa-language videos emerged in the mid-1990s, spurred by local drama troupes, disaffected television professionals, and popular Hausa-language authors seeking to make films of their books. In 2001 alone, 200 Hausa videos were released, easily making this one of the most vibrant forms of African media.

Hausa films have distinguished themselves from southern Nigerian videos by deemphasizing story lines about magic and the corruption of urban life, concentrating instead on themes of love. In this they draw heavily on the narrative and visual style of Indian films, especially in their use of spectacular song and dance sequences (Larkin 2000, 2003). The production of such a large number of videos has resulted in a small army of people working in the industry as editors, camera operators, directors, set designers, actors, composers, musicians, singers, and graphic designers as well as those involved in distribution and sales. At least three video magazines modeled after the Indian film magazine *Stardust* are in circulation, and, as with Indian films, there is a substantial local audio market based on the sale of movie sound tracks.[7] Hausa videos, which can sell anywhere from 10,000 to 100,000 copies, have come to dominate audio- and videocassette production, marginalizing – for the moment – foreign film and music distribution. Video rental shops that used to carry a mixture of many different cassettes are now dominated by Hausa films, and the shops themselves, along with video clubs (many of them illegal), have proliferated across the urban landscape.

Alhaji B. K. is the former vice president of the Kano Cassette Sellers Recording and Co-operative Society Ltd. In 1995, Alhaji B. K. specialized in recording religious cassettes that he dubbed in his studio/shop in Kofar Wambai. The explosive market for Hausa video films transformed his business, so that by 2002 it was almost wholly devoted to the reproduction and distribution of Hausa films. His shop now functioned primarily as a place to meet clients traveling to Kano. This transformation is common among most, if not all, distributors. Many still sell Indian and American films, of course; their sales do not seem to have suffered even though their proportion of the market has dropped with the unprecedented popularity of Hausa and Nigerian videos. The shift in businesses like this is indicative that, in the north, Hausa video films have fed off of the networks of piracy much as piracy fed off networks of official media.

As Hausa film exploded in popularity, the style and shape of the video market changed considerably. Hausa videos have come to dominate the market, creating a huge demand that was not there previously.[8] Hausa video film production has become highly organized and regulated, with producers, distributors, and camera operators organized into their own professional associations. An established system of production, postproduction, and distribution has been put into effect: a producer puts up the initial money, finds a writer, director, and actors, and produces the film. Once the film is made, the editing complete, and the covers for the tapes printed, the film enters into a waiting list for release, which ensures that no more than six films come out per month. On the release date, the producer takes the film to one of the distributors in Kano and sells a master copy of the tape and several hundred copies of the jacket for about Nigerian Naira 50 (about US$0.50) each. The film sells for Nigerian Naira 250 (about US$2.50) each. Intellectual property is vested not so much in the tape, which is the prerogative of the distributor, but in the jacket, which is created and controlled by the filmmakers themselves. The jackets for Hausa films – wraparound sleeves in which cassettes are inserted – are the only way to distinguish pirate from legal media. The distributor covers the cost of the dubbing machines and the capital outlay and provides important access to the network of distributors. No money is paid to the producer until the film has been sold. Unsurprisingly, this system has been the source of considerable tension between producers and distributors, as it leaves producers carrying all the risks of failure. On at least one occasion, producers in the Kano State Filmmakers Association got together to threaten to boycott distributors in order to increase the price of the jackets.[9] Some filmmakers do exhibit films at the cinema, and others try to sell to television stations, but the economic heart of the industry is the exploitation of domestic video technology.

Video filmmaking, like many aspects of the informal economy, is a precarious and highly volatile business. The tension between distributors and filmmakers is indicative of a struggle for control over the industry, but both parties remain vulnerable to the leveling out of the market. The early boom period of Hausa and Nigerian videos – when it seemed that anyone could make money in the film industry – has passed. Now filmmakers say they have to work harder for less profit, and this has led to an exodus of key directors from the industry (especially in southern Nigeria and Ghana). The precariousness of the industry in the north also comes from increasing moral criticism of the films themselves, especially the contentious accusation that they are influenced by un-Islamic Indian films. This threat was heightened in 2001 when, following the introduction of sharia law in Kano State, all Hausa filmmaking was banned.

Filmmakers responded to the government's ban by organizing themselves under the Kano State Filmmakers Association, a formal interest group that could negotiate with the government. Because filmmaking was such a new phenomenon, most filmmakers were young (many in their 30s) and lacked ties to senior patrons allied with older forms of trade. Still, the association possessed several ways of exerting pressure on the government. First, magazines such as *Fim* argued that even Islamic states such as Iran had film industries, so that film was not inherently un-Islamic. Tabloids such as *Bidiyo* noted that sharia law was being applied only to filmmakers – there was no question of banning films from India, Hollywood, or southern Nigeria – and threatened to run popular actors and actresses against incumbent politicians. In a meeting with the Ministry of Information of Kano State, the association pointed out that when Zamfara State (the first state in northern Nigeria to turn to sharia law) banned prostitution, they supplied prostitutes with alternative forms of employment and that when they closed down cinema halls, they compensated the owners.[10] By this precedent, they argued, the Kano State government should now be responsible for the welfare of the producers, directors, actors, musicians, composers, writers, editors, and graphic designers employed in the film industry. Since the industry was so large and established, there was no way such compensation would be possible. As a compromise, the filmmakers proposed establishing a censorship board that would certify the Islamic and cultural acceptability of films but allow filmmaking to continue. When the proposal was accepted in March 2001 and the censorship board was put in place, one of its first moves was to ban mixed-sex song sequences in films.

The market for Hausa films has solidified, so that five main distributors now dominate the industry. Cassettes are dubbed in bulk and sold on a wholesale basis through wide-ranging networks forged when Hausa films did not yet exist. Kano, long important as a media center for Indian films and religious cassettes, is now the dominant center for the much larger market for Hausa films. Small distributors travel there from all over northern Nigeria, Chad, Cameroon, and Ghana. Hausa distributors have their own networks that are restricted almost wholly to the Hausa-speaking diaspora.

The roots of all Nigerian film (whether English, Hausa, or Yoruba) in piracy means that the physical quality and look of Nigerian video films has been determined by the formal qualities of pirate infrastructure. Piracy standardized a particular quality of reproduction; both filmmakers and distributors believe that while people like Nigerian videos, they will not pay higher prices for better image or sound quality. Because the new Hausa videos are dubbed using the same machines as pirate films, because they rely on the same blank cassettes and are distributed through the same channels, piracy has created the aesthetic and technical horizons for nonpirate media. It is this question of aesthetics to which I now turn.

The Materiality of Piracy

In his film *Kumar Talkies*, director Pankaj Kumar evokes the role of the cinema in small-town Indian life. In one scene, a group of men talk about going to watch films in the nearby city. The newness of the films there, the high quality of their reproduction, and the experience of movie-going come to stand for a temporal and cultural difference between the town and the city. One man says that he doesn't watch films at home because he never gets to see the entire film. Kumar then cuts to the local cinema owner, who explains that this indeed is the case: in order to save electricity costs, he takes out a few reels from each film, imposing enormous jump cuts on the formal integration, slicing whole chunks of narrative from the audience's view. The big city, not surprisingly, becomes the place where this fracture can be repaired, where films are shown in their entirety, and where audiences do not have to confront their physical and cultural marginality every time they attend the cinema.

I have argued elsewhere (Larkin 1998-1999) that media technologies do not just store time, they represent it. As Stephen Kern (1983) has written, different societies can feel cut off from history or excessively attached to the past – without a future or rushing toward one. Technology, especially the media, often provides the conduit for our experience of being "inside" or "outside" history. The materiality of media creates the physical details and the quotidian sensory uses through which these experiences are formed. In *Kumar Talkies*, the everyday operations of cinema houses provide a sign vehicle and symbol for marginality and provincialism. In postcolonial societies, such as India or Nigeria, this sense is intensified due to the powerful link between technology and colonial rule, where modern technology was part of a civilizing mission of colonial power (Adas 1989; Mrázek 2002; Prakash 1999; Spitulnik 1998-1999).

Breakdown

In Nigeria, the ubiquity of technological breakdown and repair imposes a particular experience of technology and its cultural effects. Contemporary urban theory, perhaps understandably, has been less quick to explore these cultural articulations, focusing instead on the reconfiguration of urban space brought about by new media. Paul Virilio, in a typically contradictory fashion, lobbies fiercely for both sides of the argument. On the one hand, he proclaims with dystopian excess that the immediacy of real-time technologies has fundamentally transformed our ability to understand time and space. Instead of being marked by duration or the unfolding of events in succession, time, he argues, is now exposed instantaneously (Virilio 1997, 2000). Events that take place at a distance are experienced immediately thanks to the telepresence brought about by real-time technologies. Speed here is the crucial dimension (see also Kern 1983). Speed conditions our experience of time, producing temporal compression and allowing us to act at a distance. Cities that used to be organized around entrances and exits – nodes that regulate the exchange of people and goods – have given way to the immaterial interface of information exchange. This is certainly the case in contemporary Nigeria, where a series of technological changes over the last ten years, including the rise of satellite television, the growing penetration of Internet culture, and the belated arrival of mobile phone networks, has created new technological portals through which Nigerians engage with one another and the world beyond.

The difficulty with this side of Virilio is his assumption that the experiential transformations he analyzes presume a stable, smoothly operating technological infrastructure. The transition he identifies is totalizing, penetrating homogeneously and organizing universally. It partakes of a world of fast-operating computers, clear-picture televisions, and constant telecommunication signals. But Virilio (2003) also notes that with the invention of the train came the derailment, and few thinkers have been as insistent as he is that the development of technology is tied to the development of catastrophe. My interest in technological collapse is somewhat different. It is not in extravagant spectacles like collapsing bridges or exploding space shuttles but in the small, ubiquitous experience of breakdown as a condition of technological existence. In Nigeria, cars, televisions, VCRs, buses, and motorbikes are often out of service. Even when they work, electricity supplies are unreliable and beset by power surges that damage consumer equipment. NEPA, the Nigerian Electric Power Authority, is famously known by the epithet "Never Expect Power Always," and phone lines are expensive and difficult to obtain. Poverty and the disorganization of the Nigerian economy mean that consumer technologies such as scooters and cars arrive already used and worn out. After their useful life in Belgium or Holland, cars are exported to Nigeria as "new" secondhand vehicles. After these vehicles arrive in Nigeria, worn parts are repaired, dents are banged out, and paint is resprayed to remake and "tropicalize" them (see Verrips and Meyer 2001). This is, of course, a temporary state of affairs. Other parts expire, secondhand parts break down, while local "innovations" and adjustments designed to make cars, televisions, and VCRs work fail. A cycle of breakdown, repair, and breakdown again is the condition of existence for many technologies in Nigeria. As a consequence, Nigeria employs a vast army of people who specialize in repairing and reconditioning broken technological goods, since the need for repair is frequent and the cost of it cheap (Sundaram 1999; Verrips and Meyer 2001).

Critical work on urbanism has argued that utopian theories of technology and urban transformation deemphasize the fact that entire societies are excluded from the new information infrastructures (what Manuel Castells [1998] terms "technological apartheid"; see also Castells 1996; Graham and Marvin 1996, 2001; Sassen 2002). These arguments recur somewhat in debates over the so-called digital divide and the division of the world into technological haves and have-nots. My difficulty with this move is with the dichotomizing logic it promotes and its assumption that the economic and cultural effects of new technologies are absent from "disconnected" societies. The danger here is that this polemic looks through rather than at the object at hand and fails to examine the structuring effects that technologies and their failures – however dysfunctional – have in everyday life. Virilio's account of the experience of speed in contemporary urbanization is highly relevant to societies such as Nigeria, but perhaps not in the ways he imagines. There is no question, for instance, that new technologies have resulted in profound temporal acceleration for Nigerians. But the poor material infrastructure of Nigeria ensures that as the speed of Nigerian life increases, so too does the gap between actual and potential acceleration, between what technologies can do and what they do do. Thus, even as life speeds up, the experience of technological marginalization intensifies, and the gap between how fast society is moving and how fast it could move becomes a site of considerable political tension.

The poor condition of infrastructure and the ubiquity of breakdown bring about their corollary: repair as a cultural mode of existence for technology. This is a consequence of both poverty and innovation. Breakdown and repair structure the ability of subjects to use and be used by technologies and also these subjects' sense of time and place. The culture of repair rests on the experience of duration in the everyday use of technology. Breakdown creates a temporal experience that has less to do with dizzying, real-time global integration than with waiting for e-mail messages to open, machines to be repaired, or electricity to be restored. In Nigeria, all technologies are variously subject to a constant cycle of breakdown and repair; the promise of technological prosthesis is thwarted by the common experience of technological collapse. Each repair enforces another waiting period, an often frustrating experience of duration brought about by the technology of speed itself. The temporal experience of slowness comes as a consequence of speed-producing technologies, so that speed and acceleration, deceleration and stasis are relative, continually shifting states.

In cassette recorders that have been stringed together to dub audiocassettes in Kano, the covers – intended to protect the cassette while recording – have been ripped off for ease of ejection. Wires hang loosely, sometimes tangled in bunches; many machines have their casings broken, and all are exposed to the harmattan winds that deposit layers of dust on every surface of the city. Piracy depends on material modes of reproduction such as these. The operations of piracy create material effects on the storage and retrieval of data and sensorial effects on notions of space, time, culture, and the body.

In Nigeria, the infrastructure for media, especially pirate media, is often marked by disrepair and noise.

Nigerian dealers in the legal and illegal reproduction of media record data on cheap tapes with low-quality machines. This information is retrieved for the most part through old VCRs, televisions, and cassette players marked by distortion and interference. Watching, say, Hollywood or Indian films on VCRs in Nigeria, where there is no official distribution of nonpirate media, means necessarily watching the dub of a dub of a dub. As the same dealers, using the same equipment and same blank cassettes, dub Hausa video films, the result is that the visual standard for pirate media remains in place. Pirated images have a hallucinogenic quality. Detail is destroyed as realist representation fades into pulsating, pure light. Facial features are smoothed away, colors are broken down into constituent tones, and bodies fade into one another. Reproduction takes its toll, degrading the image by injecting dropouts and bursts of fuzzy noise, breaking down dialogue into muddy, often inaudible sound. This distortion is often heard in the vibrating shrillness of the tape players used by *masu saida kaset*, itinerant cassette hawkers who travel around the city selling eclectic collections of music.

The quality of the tape player used by these cassette sellers is standard in Nigeria. As the seller travels, the cassette player blares out Indian film sound tracks, Islamic preaching, or Hausa songs at such a high volume that the signal degenerates into the pure vibration of the machine. In this, the machine actually mimics the sound of live musical performances in Kano, which often rely on the distorted amplification of microphones, loudspeakers, and portable generators.[11] This distortion affects many media in Nigeria. Film prints, for instance, arrive at the end of long, picaresque journeys that begin in the metropolitan cinematic centers of India or Europe and cross the cinema halls of many countries before reaching the Nigerian circuit. There, they are often shown until they literally fall apart. All are scratched and heavily damaged, full of surprising and lengthy jump cuts where film has stuck in the projector and burned. Although the image and sound of video are poor, Ghanaian video filmmaker Willy Akuffo has warned video makers against a nostalgia for the "quality" of film that forgets how terrible film prints actually were. As a former projectionist, he had to deal with repairing burned film and refixing previous repairs that the prints had accumulated on their journey to Africa.[12] Likewise, the quality of video projection, with its low-resolution, ghostly images, can be highly variable depending on the age and condition of the equipment. In the poorer cinemas that converted to video in the mid-1990s, there were terrible problems with tracking and inaudible sound. The projected image often filled only a portion of the cinema screen or would be distorted into an hourglass shape. At other times, the corners of the image vibrated as if the screen were a photograph peeling off.[13]

The infrastructure of reproduction, like most contemporary infrastructures in Nigeria, is marked by cheapness, faulty operation, and constant repair. "All data flows," the media theorist Friedrich Kittler (1999, 14) reminds us, "must pass through the bottleneck of the signifier," and in so doing they are vulnerable to being "engulfed by the noise of the real." The "real" here is precisely the fuzziness of cinematic images or the hissing of tape recorders – the noise produced by the medium of transmission itself as it encodes and disseminates data across space and time. Yuri Tsivian (1994) has termed this effect the "semiotics of interference" and has analyzed the operation of early Russian cinema, arguing that the physical conditions of media exhibition – scratches on the film and noise and vibrations from projectors – became part of the "message" of films themselves.[14] For Nigerians, the costs of consuming and producing world media require operating on the margins of technology. Distortion on an audio tape, like dropouts on a video or a slow connection to the Internet, are the material conditions of existence for media. While media infrastructure creates the reality of being ever more connected to a globalized world, it does so by emphasizing Nigerians' marginalization at the same time. Electricity blackouts, snowy television images, difficulties getting international phone lines, and distorted loudspeakers on cassette players all create a technological veil of semiotic distortion for Nigerians.

Some of this distortion is taken for granted, rendered invisible to people by its ubiquity. It is clear, for instance, that many of the most popular transnational media forms, such as sports, action films, wrestling, and Indian films, are highly visual and thus capable of overcoming both linguistic differences and audio degradation. But this degradation is rarely commented on. Instead, what these films evoke is the fantasy of other countries where deficiencies in infrastructure are believed not to exist. For many northern Nigerians, Saudi Arabia is a place where electricity always flows, where roads have no potholes, and where hospitals are of the highest quality – just as everyone in Europe and America is thought to own televisions and mobile phones.[15] These fantasies represent implicit and sometimes explicit critiques of the failures of the Nigerian state to provide basic infrastructures for everyday life. The breakdown of infrastructure provides a conduit for critiques of the state and of the corruption and ethnic favoritism of political elites (Verrips and Meyer 2001).

Conclusion

In his exhaustive study of the rise of print, the historian Adrian Johns (1998) argues that piracy, rather than being an aberration of an "original" mode of text production, is central to the way print operates and spreads over time and space. The qualities we now associate with print – its fixity, guarantee of authorship, and commodity form – were not inherent in the technology but the result of a social compact, the institution of a technological order of reality. Johns is instructive in reminding us that, in many parts of the world, media piracy is not a pathology of the circulation of media forms but its prerequisite. In many places, piracy is the only means by which certain media – usually foreign – are available. And in countries like Nigeria, the technological constraints that fuel pirate media provide the industrial template through which other, nonpirate media are reproduced, disseminated, and consumed.

Piracy and the wider infrastructure of reproduction it has generated reveal the organization of contemporary Nigerian society. They show how the parallel economy has migrated onto center stage, overlapping and interpenetrating with the official economy, mixing legal and illegal regimes, uniting social actors, and organizing common networks. This infrastructure creates its own modes of spatiality, linking Nigeria into new economic and social networks. Piracy means that Nigerian media production and circulation no longer depend on the intervention of the state (colonial or postcolonial) but are captured by the logic of privatization and gradually extend over differing areas of social experience. Sundaram (1999, 61), writing about everyday electronic culture in India – self-trained programmers who build computers and servers by cobbling together secondhand computer parts – refers to this as "recycled modernity," one that is "everyday in its imaginary, pirate in its practice, and mobile in its innovation." Rem Koolhaas (Koolhaas et al. 2001) has recently explored a similar phenomenon in the collapse of traffic systems in Lagos, a city overwhelmed by an increase in cars and a lack of roads. There, jams and bottlenecks force detours through "nonflow" areas, spreading traffic off the planned grids and expanding the motorable space of the city. As cars back up for longer periods of time, they create markets for hawkers. Over time the markets get formalized, roadside mosques are marked out to service the workers, and new infrastructures emerge to paper over the inefficiencies of the old (see also Mbembe and Roitman 1995; Simone 2001; Verrips and Meyer 2001).

The infrastructure of reproduction created by piracy generates material and sensorial effects on both media and their consumers. Cheap tape recorders, old televisions, blurred videos that are the copy of a copy of a copy – these are the material distortions endemic to the reproduction of media goods in situations of poverty and illegality, and they shape the ways these media take on cultural value and act on individuals and groups. The dialectic of technological breakdown and repair imposes its own cultural experience of modernity, an alternative speeding up and stasis, and a world where gaps in space and time are continually annihilated and reinforced.

Notes

1. 419 refers to the section of the Nigerian criminal code that deals with cases of fraud. Criminals who engage in this type of crime are known as 419ers (Apter 1999).
2. After the Maitatsine riots of 1981, the Nigerian government circulated a video of the mass arrest of followers of the millenarian leader Maitatsine as a warning to other followers. Musa Na Sale, one of the most prominent cassette dealers working with traditional Hausa singers, said that he would meet with singers and *malams* (religious leaders whose teachings were sold on cassette) to instruct them as to "what the government needs to talk about and what the government doesn't want."
3. This could be true, but there is likely an element of boastfulness to this claim. In 1993 when distribution was still by cassette, I was told that films could arrive in Kano as little as seven days after their release in India. In 2002, I was told by the same distributor (but a different person) that the reason for the shift to VCDs was to increase speed and quality and that the problem with videos was that they could take up to a month or more to be received from Dubai.
4. This is now a number for information about new drugs.
5. Although, as Jonathan Haynes pointed out to me, governments do collect revenue through taxes on blank cassettes.
6. Ghana is the only other country in West Africa to have developed its own video film industry. Over time, there has been a cross-pollination between Ghanaian and Nigerian English-language videos, so that similar themes, genres, and cultural styles crop up in both.
7. Two of these magazines, *Mujallar Fim* and *Mujallar Bidiyo*, can be accessed online at www.kanoonline.com.
8. This trend is confirmed by Indian film distributors who told me their sales remained constant during the rise of Hausa films and that sales currently remained strong. Certainly, Indian films remain hugely popular among Hausa filmmakers and continue to provide a source of inspiration, technical ideas, and narrative themes for Hausa films.

9.   I was told on a number of occasions that many people in the video industry
      – distributors, editors, jacket designers, musicians, and actors – can make
      more money than producers, though many actors complain that they do
      not get paid until after the producer receives money from the distributor.
10.   Ironically, perhaps, when filmmakers from Kano traveled to Zamfara to
      shoot a film, they were invited to the governor's mansion to meet Zamfara's
      first lady – a huge fan of Hausa video.
11.   Christopher Waterman (1990) points out that distortion by amplifiers
      became such an accepted part of live performance that musicians would in-
      tentionally destroy new loudspeakers to achieve the desired buzzing sound.
      I thank Andrew Apter for reminding me of this.
12.   Birgit Meyer reminded me that Akuffo described this problem with poor
      film prints at a workshop organized by the International Study Commission
      of Media, Religion, and Culture (19-27 May 2000, Accra, Ghana).
13.   Yet despite these problems, cassettes remain the more popular medium in
      northern Nigeria. In January 2002, when I asked Hausa video filmmakers
      why they had not switched to video CDs to distribute their movies, they
      pointed out that the technology was not yet widely available in the north, in
      part because damage to a VCD could ruin the entire disc, while damage to a
      tape created only passing moments of fuzziness.
14.   James Ferguson (1999) makes an interesting but different argument on the
      role of "noise" in globalization. Ferguson focuses on the traffic in cultural
      meanings, arguing that cities are culturally "noisy" in that all sorts of forms
      of cultural flows clash and are available to urban dwellers. But Ferguson's
      central question concerns "which of the bits floating in the swirl of events
      does any given social actor bear" (1999, 208).
15.   Writing about the cosmopolitan sexual relations between Hausa *'yan daudu*
      (men who act like women) and men in Saudi Arabia, Rudolf Gaudio (1996)
      argues that when these *'yan daudu* return from Saudi Arabia, they parade
      their sophistication and cultural savoir faire – part of which involves raving
      "about the creature comforts that Saudi Arabia [has] to offer: telephones,
      air conditioning, a constant supply of electricity and running water. *'Ba abin
      da babu'* they would say, 'there's nothing that isn't there.'" See also O'Brien
      1999.

Bibliography

Adas, Michael. 1989. Machines as the Measure of Men: Science, Technology, and Ideologies of
      Western Dominance. Ithaca, NY: Cornell University Press.
Apter, Andrew. 1999. "IBB = 419: Nigerian democracy and the politics of illusion." In John L.
      Comaroff and Jean Comaroff, eds., *Civil Society and the Political Imagination in Africa: Critical
      Perspectives*. Chicago: University of Chicago Press.

Bayart, Jean-François, Stephen Ellis, and Béatrice Hibou. 1999. *The Criminalization of the State in Africa*. Bloomington: Indiana University Press.

Benjamin, Walter. 1999. *The Arcades Project*. Cambridge, MA: Harvard University Press.

Callaway, Barbara. 1987. *Muslim Hausa Women in Nigeria: Tradition and Change*. Syracuse, NY: Syracuse University Press.

Castells, Manuel. 1996. *The Information Age: Economy, Society and Culture, Vol. 1: The Rise of the Network Society*. Oxford: Blackwell.

Castells, Manuel. 1998. *The Information Age: Economy, Society and Culture, Vol. 3: End of Millennium*. Oxford: Blackwell.

Chesterman, John, and Andy Lipman. 1988. *The Electronic Pirates: DIY Crimes of the Century*. London: Routledge.

Coombe, Rosemary J. 1998. *The Cultural Life of Intellectual Properties: Authorship, Appropriation, and the Law*. Durham, NC: Duke University Press.

Crary, Jonathan. 2000. *Suspensions of Perception: Attention, Spectacle, and Modern Culture*. Cambridge, MA: MIT Press.

Doane, Mary Ann. 2002. *The Emergence of Cinematic Time: Modernity, Contingency, the Archive*. Cambridge, MA: Harvard University Press.

Ferguson, James. 1999. *Expectations of Modernity: Myths and Meanings of Urban Life on the Zambian Copperbelt*. Berkeley: University of California Press.

Garcia, David, and Geert Lovink. 2001. "The ABC of Tactical Media." In *The Public Domain: Sarai Reader 01*. Delhi: Sarai, the New Media Initiative.

Gaudio, Rudolf. 1996. "Men Who Talk Like Women: Language, Gender, and Sexuality in Hausa Muslim Society." Ph.D. diss., Stanford University.

Graham, Stephen, and Simon Marvin. 1996. *Telecommunications and the City: Electronic Spaces, Urban Places*. London: Routledge.

Graham, Stephen, and Simon Marvin. 2001. *Splintering Urbanism: Networked Infrastructures, Technological Mobilities and the Urban Condition*. London: Routledge.

Hansen, Karen Tranberg. 2000. *Salaula: The World of Secondhand Clothing and Zambia*. Chicago: University of Chicago Press.

Hansen, Miriam. 1995. "America, Paris, the Alps: Kracauer (and Benjamin) on Cinema and Modernity." In Leo Charney and Vanessa R. Schwartz, eds., *Cinema and the Invention of Modern Life*. Berkeley: University of California Press.

Hansen, Miriam. 2000. "The Mass Production of the Senses: Classical Cinema as Vernacular Modernism." In Christine Gledhill and Linda Williams, eds., *Reinventing Film Studies*. London: Arnold.

Haynes, Jonathan, ed. 2000. *Nigerian Video Films*. Africa Series no. 73. Athens: Ohio University Center for International Studies.

Hecht, David, and A. M. Simone. 1994. *Invisible Governance: The Art of African Micro-politics*. Brooklyn, NY: Autonomedia.

Hibou, Béatrice. 1999. "The 'Social Capital' of the State as an Agent of Deception, or the Ruses of Economic Intelligence." In Jean-François Bayart, Stephen Ellis, and Béatrice Hibou, eds., *The Criminalization of the State in Africa*. Bloomington: Indiana University Press.

Johns, Adrian. 1998. *The Nature of the Book: Print and Knowledge in the Making*. Chicago: University of Chicago Press.

Kern, Stephen. 1983. *The Culture of Time and Space: 1880-1918*. Cambridge, MA: Harvard University Press.

Kittler, Friedrich. 1999. *Gramophone, Film, Typewriter*. Stanford, CA: Stanford University Press.

Koolhaas, Rem, Stefano Boeri, Sanford Kwinter, Nadia Tazi, and Hans Ulrich Obrist. 2001. *Mutations*. Bordeaux: Arc en rêve centre d'architecture.

Kracauer, Siegfried. 1995. *The Mass Ornament: Weimar Essays*, trans. Thomas Y. Levin. Cambridge, MA: Harvard University Press.

Larkin, Brian. 1997. "Indian Films and Nigerian Lovers: Media and the Creation of Parallel Modernities." *Africa* 67.3: 406-440.

Larkin, Brian. 1998-1999. "Introduction" (to Media Technologies and the Design for Modern Living: A Symposium). *Visual Anthropology Review* 14.2: 11-13.

Larkin, Brian. 2000. "Hausa Dramas and the Rise of Video Culture in Nigeria." In Jonathan Haynes, ed., *Nigerian Video Films*. Africa Series no. 73. Athens: Ohio University Center for International Studies.

Larkin, Brian. 2003. "Itineraries of Indian Cinema: African Videos, Bollywood, and Global Media." In Ella Shohat and Robert Stam, eds., *Multiculturalism, Postcoloniality, and Transnational Media*. New Brunswick, NJ: Rutgers University Press.

Lefebvre, Henri. 1991. *The Production of Space*. Cambridge, MA: Blackwell.

Lombardi, Gerald S. 1999. "Computer Networks, Social Networks, and the Future of Brazil." PhD diss., New York University.

MacGaffey, Janet, and Rémy Bazenguissa-Ganga. 2000. *Congo-Paris: Transnational Traders on the Margins of the Law*. Bloomington: Indiana University Press.

Mattelart, Armand. 1996. *The Invention of Communication*, trans. Susan Emanuel. Minneapolis: University of Minnesota Press.

Mattelart, Armand. 2000. *Networking the World, 1794-2000*, trans. Liz Carey-Libbrecht and James Cohen. Minneapolis: University of Minnesota Press.

Mbembe, Achille. 2001. *On the Postcolony*. Berkeley: University of California Press.

Mbembe, Achille, and Janet Roitman. 1995. "Figures of the Subject in Times of Crisis." *Public Culture* 7: 323-352.

Meyer, Birgit. 2003. "Ghanaian Popular Cinema and the Magic in and of Film." In Peter Pels and Birgit Meyer, eds., *Magic and Modernity: Interfaces of Revelation and Concealment*. Stanford, CA: Stanford University Press.

Mrázek, Rudolf. 2002. *Engineers of Happy Land: Technology and Nationalism in a Colony*. Princeton, NJ: Princeton University Press.

Na Sale, Musa. 1995. Interview by the author. Kano, July.

O'Brien, Susan. 1999. "Pilgrimage, Power, and Identity: The Role of the *Hajj* in the Lives of Nigerian Hausa *Bori* Adepts." *Africa Today* 46.3/4: 11-40.

Prakash, Gyan. 1999. Another Reason: Science and the Imagination of Modern India. Princeton, NJ: Princeton University Press.

Sassen, Saskia, ed. 2002. *Global Networks, Linked Cities*. New York: Routledge.

Schivelbusch, Wolfgang. 1986. *The Railway Journey: The Industrialization of Time and Space in the Nineteenth Century*. Berkeley: University of California Press.

Schneider, Friedrich. 2000. "Dimensions of the Shadow Economy." *Independent Review* 5.1: 81-91.

Simone, AbdouMaliq. 1998. "Urban Social Fields in Africa." *Social Text* 16: 71-90.

Simone, AbdouMaliq. 2000. "Going South: African Immigrants in Johannesburg." In Sarah Nuttall and Cheryl-Ann Michael, eds., *Senses of Culture: South African Culture Studies*. Oxford: Oxford University Press.

Simone, AbdouMaliq. 2001. "On the Worlding of African Cities." *African Studies Review* 44.2: 15-41.

Spitulnik, Debra. 1998-1999. "Mediated Modernities: Encounters with the Electronic in Zambia." *Visual Anthropology Review* 14.2: 63-83.

Sundaram, Ravi. 1999. "Recycling Modernity: Pirate Electronic Cultures in India." *Third Text* 47: 59-65.

Tsivian, Yuri. 1994. *Early Cinema in Russia and Its Cultural Reception*. London: Routledge.

Ukadike, N. Frank. 2000. "Images of the 'Reel' Thing: African Video-films and the Emergence of a New Cultural Art." *Social Identities* 6: 243-261.

Ukah, Asonzeh F.-K. 2003. "Advertising God: Nigerian Christian Video-films and the Power of Consumer Culture." *Journal of Religion in Africa* 33: 203-231.

Verrips, Jojada, and Birgit Meyer. 2001. "Kwaku's Car: The Struggles and Stories of a Ghanaian Long-Distance Taxi Driver." In Daniel Miller, ed. *Car Cultures*. Oxford: Berg.

Virilio, Paul. 1997. *Open Sky*. London: Verso.

Virilio, Paul. 2000. *The Information Bomb*. London: Verso.

Virilio, Paul. 2003. *Unknown Quantity*. London: Thames & Hudson.

Waterman, Christopher Alan. 1990. *Jùjú: A Social History and Ethnography of an African Popular Music*. Chicago: University of Chicago Press.

Wendl, Tobias. 2001. "Visions of Modernity in Ghana: Mami Wata Shrines, Photo Studios, and Horror Films." *Visual Anthropology* 14: 269-292.

10. Slashings and Subtitles

Romanian Media Piracy, Censorship, and Translation

Tessa Dwyer and Ioana Uricaru

Friday nights in Romania under the communist regime (which came to an end in December 1989), friends and family would gather in front of their television sets trying to guess what they were actually watching. Telephone calls would be made, film reference and theory books consulted. Such detective skills were required due to the government's censorship tactics which included screening foreign films (both on television and in cinemas) with their titles altered beyond recognition, credit sequences removed, entire scenes eliminated and dialogue ideologically "cleansed" through the subtitling process.[1] Coauthor and Romanian national Ioana Uricaru recalls that "God" was invariably translated as *Cel-de-Sus* or "the one above" and "church" as *edificiu* or "edifice."[2] Sometimes films playing in cinemas would differ dramatically at the beginning and end of their run, as elements requiring excision came to the attention of officials.[3]

Subtitling was the translation method associated with government media channels. As such, it was considered official, professional, and proper – both "ideologically correct" and the industry standard. With subtitles, interference of the "original" is kept at a minimum.[4] As lines of text superimposed onto the film image, subtitles neither erase nor noisily intrude upon the foreign soundtrack. Consequently, they are often viewed as a clean technique that respects the source material by enabling it to remain intact. However, in Romania, the identification of subtitling with "quality" translation was compromised by its close link to adjacent practices of content deletion and paraphrasing for the sake of ideological alteration. The role that subtitling played in making meaning palatable for the "party line" meant that this technique was, concurrently, subject to suspicion and distrust, especially by those (extremely numerous) audience members who understood foreign languages and were able to fact-check official versions.

In the following discussion, we note how translation can function both in the service and subversion of censorship, and how both roles are complicated by contradictory notions of quality and authenticity. We begin by pitting Romania's official, government-sanctioned translation methods against the unofficial, amateur, and alternative practices that typify piracy operations. We then proceed to unpack and expand notions of media piracy to include niche, expert, and online modes of engagement. Further, by focusing on Romanian piracy operations involving the translation of banned foreign-language films and television programs, we seek to engage with the unintentional, excess productivity of censorship revealed through its secondary by-products. Both censorship and translation are themselves commonly positioned as second-order modes – occurring *after*, or *in opposition to*, the primary process of production. From this perspective, both are seen as somewhat improper and prone to misuse, troubling and exceeding notions of authenticity and originality. Thus, the three keywords structuring this discussion – piracy, censorship, and translation – all represent discourses mired, to varying degrees, in negativity.

Even in the case of translation, which might seem the most benign of the three, an acknowledgment of its "badness" lingers as expressed in the common popular saying *Traduttore, traditore* (translator, traitor) – an Italian phrase also adopted in Romanian. By thinking through their interrelation, we wish to reevaluate this secondary status in order to engage more productively with the differences and inequalities of national, minority, and subcultural reception contexts.

In particular, we take issue with the supposed errors and failures of pirated translation, demonstrating how in certain geopolitical circumstances, such limitations can achieve legitimacy, ultimately signaling a certain uncensored authenticity. Here we glimpse how second-order discourses are excessive and untoward precisely because they call into question notions of first-ness. In communist Romania, pirated foreign-language media complicated notions of originality, directing attention toward the primacy of the viewing *context* as much as that of the source *text*. The translations that proliferated within this environment need to be considered beyond the parameters of "quality" alone. Finally, it is our contention that the rubric of language difference and translation enables us to glimpse some of the subtleties of censorship, directing attention toward the everyday rather than the extreme. Variances in the audiovisual translation techniques that accompany both censorship and piracy operations provide a largely unexamined angle from which to view and interrogate the politics of film exhibition, distribution, and reception.

Censored Subtitles

Within multimedia/audiovisual streams of translation studies,[5] countries are commonly identified as belonging to either the dubbing or subtitling camp. A mid-1990s report by Josephine Dries of the European Institute for the Media indicates that Romania falls heavily on the subtitling side. According to her findings, Romania subtitles *all* foreign film imports and 90% of foreign television programs (Dries 1994-1995, 36). In Uricaru's experience this is not the case. She confirms that even before 1989, occasional special interest television programs were officially translated using single voice-over commentary. For instance, she recalls voice-over accompanying a documentary series entitled *Teleenciclopedia* and some episodic children's television animations.[6] Additionally, however, simultaneous translations were performed live at many of the Bucharest Cinematheque film screenings [7] while voice-over and on-the-spot interpreting dominated the county's piracy operations, thus suggesting the manner in which official data and media channels present only one side of the picture.

Interestingly, in contemporary, post-totalitarian Romania there have been repeated attempts to introduce professional dubbing. The first television program entirely dubbed by professional voice actors was the Mexican telenovela *Mirada de Mujer* (The gaze of a woman) (Antonio Serrano, TV Azteca, 1997-1998) first aired on Romania's PRO TV in 1997,[8] while the first theatrically distributed film to undergo such treatment was *Babe* (Chris Noonan, 1995). These isolated experiments in dubbing were then followed by a long hiatus and it is only recently, from around 2006 onward, that there has been a revival of this phenomenon. US animation companies such as Walt Disney and DreamWorks now require and oversee the dubbing of feature films such as *Cars* (John Lasseter and Joe Ranft, 2006) and *Shrek the Third* (Chris Miller and Raman Hui, 2007) using popular local actors as voice talent.[9] The move to use "star dubbers" originated as a domestic marketing tactic for English-language audiences and has now been adopted in most export contexts, bringing new layers of meaning and local flavor to the translation experience.[10]

Certainly, however, on an official level, Romania remains a proudly subtitling nation. This method of translation is identified with cosmopolitanism, an awareness of foreign languages and cultures, and high levels of education and literacy.[11] In this way, subtitling has become ingrained in the national psyche and is equated with quality, "art," and authenticity, in much the same way as it is in many English-speaking countries such as Australia, Canada, the US, and the UK. Romanians are particularly proud of their unique status as one of only a handful of subtitling nations in the whole of Europe.[12] Indeed, as Dries reports, even Eastern European countries tend to prefer dubbing, despite the fact that, here "one would expect countries to choose subtitling, being a cheaper, less complex and faster way of language conversion." Thus, Romania presents a curious anomaly, as despite being one of the largest Eastern European countries, with around 23 million inhabitants, it favors subtitling while many of its smaller regional neighbors such as the Czech Republic, Slovakia, Bulgaria, and Hungary opt, in large part, for dubbing (Dries 1994-1995, 36).

Romanian spectators, on the other hand, have a fondness for the practice of double-spectatorship: they enjoy performing simultaneous comparisons between the "original" soundtrack and the subtitles. Dubs are thus considered inferior to subtitled or, for that matter, untranslated versions. Even in the case of young children, subtitles are seen to bring educational and social benefits by exposing children to foreign-language programming from an early age. Many parents consider reading and explaining subtitles to their children as an opportunity for family bonding and learning. In 2007, when Cartoon Network Romania decided to start dubbing their programming, parents and children alike revolted, declaring they would refuse to watch the station's content. A petition started by middle school students and signed online by more than 25,000 requested the government to intervene in order to stop the "devastating effect" that dubbing is having on children's foreign language abilities.[13] Interestingly, when polled about the circumstances in which they think dubbing *is* acceptable, Romanians express a leniency toward (perceived) marginal discourses such as documentary-style programming based on the relay of supposedly "pure" information (such as Discovery Channel or Animal Planet programs) and low-grade genres (such as B-series action films and pornography).

This national bias toward subtitling would seem, however, to have undermined the logic of censorship and in particular, appears at odds with the communist government's efforts to mask the identity of foreign films and programs by removing credit and title sequences. With subtitling, the foreign-language soundtrack is not erased or dubbed over, but remains intact and audible, thus potentially exposing efforts to cut, edit, and manipulate a film's dialogue.

Romania's most famous pre-1989 pirate translator (and employee of Televiziunea Romana)[14] Irina Margareta Nistor, wonders at the ill fit between subtitling – which enables "original" meanings to remain *en face* with their (mis)translation[15] – and government censorship practices, concluding that here, economic interests would seem to have prevailed over and above the ideological (Mihalcea 2006). She concedes nevertheless that subtitling did accommodate the unpredictable, changeable nature of the censor's agenda, by allowing for speedy, last minute alterations (Nistor 2008). Ironically, low-quality dubbing in the form of single-voice commentary, constituted the cheapest and fastest way to translate *pirated* videos, and with the voice of the translator covering up most of the original dialogue, it was close to impossible to consult the original for authenticity.

Subversive Dubs

By the mid-1980s (the approximate period when VCR technology and VHS tapes entered the country) Romania had been ruled by a Marxist totalitarian regime for almost 40 years.[16] The Romanian population showed an amazing creativity in circumventing the apparently immutable conditions of the political status quo. Firstly, ways were found to bypass censorship bans.[17] People who had the opportunity to travel abroad (usually because of their work status – as crew members on commercial ships, for example) or who had connections with foreign nationals (such as international students studying in Romania), managed to smuggle various illicit cultural products into the country. Old issues of *Time, Newsweek, Paris Match* or even mail-order clothing and furniture catalogs became objects of desire as symbols of the Western world. By 1987, a major new element had been introduced: the VCR/VHS. Although largely an urban phenomenon, the presence of VCRs in many Romanian households had a huge impact on the whole population.

A veritable underground economy developed around these devices. People who owned VCRs would organize viewing nights, usually in the living room of their apartment. Those invited would pay a fee (about four times the price of admission for a regular cinema ticket) and spend the entire night watching six or seven films in a row. Discounted admission was offered to anyone who provided a tape for viewing. In a matter of months the market had diversified. Certain hosts offered specific genres and programs – such as comedy, thrillers, or adult movies. Others specialized in distribution (procuring and selling/renting videotapes) or exhibition (providing the venue, VCR, and television set). Competition brought about a differentiation in prices depending on the quality and number of films shown. Even new jobs were created: translators, audio-dubbers, and technicians able to troubleshoot the equipment. A veritable, spontaneously organized, underground entertainment industry flourished.

The black-market translation of films was usually made with a single voice-over recorded on the videotape's second channel of audio. Since the translation was typically done in a rush and without prior viewing (Nistor 2008), the voice-over was more an approximate rendition of the dialogue than a faithful translation. Usually, it was read with little attempt to act the lines and would sometimes merely summarize a scene's dialogue in the passive voice. The foreign soundtrack remained faintly audible (although unintelligible) in the background. The numerous layers of language difference evident in these tapes testify to the complicated, circuitous nature of global piracy routes. For instance, a Hollywood film pirated from German television, would initially be dubbed in German with a Romanian voice-over then added on top.

However, dubbing (or, to be accurate, voice-over commentary) was not the only translation method supported by piracy. The most sought-after and luxurious translations were those performed live by one of the spectators, on the rare occasion when a "clean" or first-hand dub made straight from an untranslated "original" was available. Ironically, those tapes that bore a copyright infringement warning at their start were extremely valuable – the warning itself became a measure of quality, signifying that the dub had been made with little to no tampering. The live translator would often be called upon to repeat the performance for further viewings, sometimes up to 50, thus recalling the film interpreting traditions that proliferated in the silent and early sound eras, and that flourished in Japan and Korea where skilled performers developed highly polished, entertaining routines, and received higher billing than film stars.[18]

These underground experiences of media and translation enabled via piracy bear certain similarities to what Miriam Hansen describes as "primitive" spectatorship, following Noël Burch's delineation of this concept.[19] For Hansen, it is the "emphasis on exhibition" that distinguishes early cinema from the classical model (1991, 42): "Early exhibition still claimed the singularity of a *live performance*, even though the films themselves were circulated on a national and international scale" (ibid., 43). In Romania's newly developing group viewing contexts, audiences interacted with each other and the film during screenings – providing commentary and expressing emotions and opinions. Exhibitors were responsible for selecting the evening's program, usually proposing a number of titles from which the audience could choose. Some films were provided by audience members and viewer recommendations were common. Often spectators would test a film by watching the first 5 to 15 minutes and then decide whether to continue watching, fast-forwarding over "boring" parts or replaying selected scenes. Furthermore, the insertion of translation and commentary at strategic points in the flow of the story recalls the role of intertitles in silent film. For Hansen, such "locally and culturally specific acts of reception," open up a "margin of participation and unpredictability" (ibid., 43).

She continues that it is in this margin that "the cinema could assume the function of an alternative public sphere for particular social groups" (ibid.,

43-44). The resurgence of early spectatorship practices in 1980s Romania, during a situation of cultural crisis, supports this argument, along with her claims regarding the audience's complex relationship with the spectacle and intricate mechanisms of pleasure and desire, which industry and/or ideologically driven regulation attempts to tame and normalize. In Romania, the economic structure instituted via piracy produced major social implications, creating a truly oppositional public arena. Film spectatorship (via the living-room television) became a significant means of contact with the "outside" world.

If, as Hansen suggests, "the reciprocity between film on the screen and the spectator's stream of associations becomes the measure of a particular film's use for an alternative public sphere" (1991, 13), then those films accessed through pirated VHS tapes definitely helped shape the Romanian people's resistance to the political status quo by offering at least the glimpse of a desirable alternative. Notions of power and status, community and leadership were all affected in a manner that had not been foreseen by the government. Access to VCRs or VHS tapes became a status symbol that could translate directly into either economic or social power.

One's status within the community might significantly improve, for instance, by inviting people to watch films for free, throwing a video-watching birthday party or managing to procure a hard-to-find, recently released title.[20] In a society that was rigidly organized and allowed little room for personal initiative or individuality, the new evaluation system introduced through piracy and pirated translation effected major social changes.

***

It is symptomatic that the aesthetic or production values of pirated films did not always warrant the appreciation they received: people would watch hours of low-quality American television or B-grade action movies and, during the same evening, sit religiously through their personal fourth or fifth screening of *One Flew over the Cuckoo's Nest* (Miloš Forman, 1975) or *Amadeus* (Miloš Forman, 1984) – two of the hit movies of the period. Additionally, the audio and picture quality of bootlegged material was usually substandard. Muffled soundtracks with missing channels, unpleasant-sounding voice-overs, and images with bleeding contours and altered colors, were the norm. Likewise, the accuracy of the translations left much to be desired. For instance, in the extremely popular mini-series *Jesus of Nazareth* (Franco Zeffirelli, 1977), the ancient Jewish council or court known as the "Sanhedrin" was rather nonsensically translated as "Saint

Hadrian" because of the similar English pronunciation of the two items. The sometimes amusing results of mistranslation led to the circulation of jokes and urban legends, such as the anecdote (possibly accurate, but as yet unconfirmed) about the translation of *The Deer Hunter* (Michael Cimino, 1978) as *Draga Vinatorule* or "Beloved Hunter," indicating the popularity and public awareness of these underground exhibition and translation practices.

Such errors, however, ultimately proved of little consequence. More important was the fact that alternatives to official media offerings existed at all. The small community of underground translators included people who were working concurrently for Televiziunea Romana or the State Film Department Centrala Romania Film. The presence of their names at the end of officially subtitled films reinforced their aura: government employees by day, superhero-translators by night. With their faces never seen but their voices haunting the collective unconscious, these translators came as close to stardom as was possible.

In this context, the "bad" translation and degraded sound and picture typical of pirate media came to signify a different kind of quality: that of uncensored content. The misunderstandings, transformations, and obscurations that occurred were relatively unimportant. What mattered was the underground viewing context itself. The artisan quality, whiff of the clandestine, social interaction, and vague connotation of resistance, were as much a part of the signifying experience as the content itself. Thus the failures and limitations of pirate media did not so much undermine the experience as enhance it, acting as signifiers of the "authentic" – as distinct from the censored, subtitled offerings of the communist regime. In this sense, the secondary, supplementary nature of the piracy industry marks it as an oppositional discourse – not just in terms of ideology and legality, but also in regard to its reevaluation of apparently positive, primary terms such as "quality," "professional," and "correct." As a sideline or by-product of censorship, piracy assumes a new legitimacy, providing modes of access and empowerment for disenfranchised subjects. Here, the deleterious, viral image of the pirate proliferated by global media corporations (with current DVD warnings sporting huge fines for individuals and corporations) is somewhat undone.[21]

Niche Piracy

The Romanian piracy context is interesting in relation to fan activities which provide yet another take on the notion of quality, revealing its inherent instability. As discussed, in communist Romania the technical and translational quality of bootlegged videotapes was typically poor. However, piracy is also often associated with a particular niche form of expert, highly specialized activity. Here, we refer to the various subcultural or fan networks that focus on the translation of foreign-language media. Such activities usually involve (either directly or indirectly) illegal procurement, exhibition, and distribution of media products, utilizing file-sharing technologies and Internet communities.

One such group that is particularly prominent in the US and other parts of the world is that of anime subculture consisting of fans of Japanese-produced animation largely intended for the Japanese market.[22] Anime fan culture currently revolves around issues of translation with fansubbing (subtitling "by fans for fans")[23] occupying a central position. As access has improved since the inception of such groups in the 1970s and 1980s when commercial distribution was particularly rare and unreliable, the issue of translation has now surfaced as a primary locus of activity. Although "at one time fansubs were virtually the only way that fans could watch (and understand) anime" (Hatcher 2005, 519),[24] these days, fans look to online communities and networks to provide either speed translations (some groups specialize in producing translations within 24 hours of a program's first airing or release) or "quality" *otaku*-style translations that accommodate fan sensibilities (Hatcher 2005, 528-530).[25]

Fansubbing is usually done at home by amateur translators on amateur computer equipment. The process is time-consuming, cost-intensive and usually a collective enterprise (Jenkins 2006). Once a "raw" or untranslated version of a show is obtained either legally or illegally through "ripping" or peer-to-peer networks,[26] it then goes through three to four rounds of translation and editing as it is time-stamped, matched (so that subtitles appear at the correct intervals), typeset, encoded to create a single video file and distributed through a variety of Internet channels such as P2P services, BitTorrent, IRC, and newsgroups (Hatcher 2005, 521-523). As such, fansubs are highly prized items, despite their typically degenerated video quality (Cubbison 2005, 48). Indeed, fansubbing practices and distribution have emerged as the cornerstones of the anime fan community – providing the only means of *trusted* access to source material. Complicated honor systems, rules of conduct, quality measures, and codes of ethics have developed which tend mostly to champion subtitling over dubbing.[27]

This subtitling ethos reveals certain contradictions. Firstly, fansubbing is seen to ensure quality, ironically, because of its very *low quality*. Indeed, it is the home-based nature of fansubbing that differentiates it from commercial translation practices enabling priorities other than profitability to surface. Fansubbers or fansubbing syndicates are able to pour countless hours into their practice, pool their knowledge base in order to provide in-depth cultural referencing and, most importantly, are free to experiment. Fansubbing is hailed for its creativity and inventiveness in regards to language use and formatting, as well as its technical innovation (Hatcher 2005, 529).[28]

Characters might speak with differently colored subtitles, for instance, or with different font styles in order to indicate a particular aspect of their personality.[29] Subtitle size and spacing are made particularly malleable, enabling word definitions to be inserted in small type on the screen or at fleeting interstices only legible through the VCR or DVD pause function (Nornes 2007, 182-183). Moreover, fan subtitles are not restricted to the bottom edge of the screen but are able to roam freely across the frame (Nornes 2007, 183, fig. 25). Translated lines of nonspoken text (such as signs and newspaper headlines), for instance, are sometimes "made to move on the screen to seamlessly match the image" (Hatcher 2005, 522). Fansubbing can also foreground issues of *un*translatability. Character names, honorifics, slang and culturally obscure terms are often left untranslated, sometimes accompanied by detailed explanatory notes (Nornes 2007, 182). This tendency, according to Abé Mark Nornes, highlights and respects the cultural otherness of the source material (Nornes 2007, 184).

The experimental, nonconventional nature of fansubbing is largely due to the fact that these translations are not aimed at a mass audience. Rather, theirs is a proudly niche market.[30] In this context, the very fact of translation does not have to be somehow shrouded over or disavowed in order to ensure accessibility. Rather, translation is an accepted, openly discussed, and avidly guarded aspect of anime fandom. Hence, with fansubbing, translation can be loud and irreverent. Despite these potential advantages, before the advent of DVD technology, fansubs were notorious for their low image quality (Tyler 2007). The best one could hope for, explains anime fan "Tyler L" on the Toonami Digital Arsenal website, was a fourth-generation video copy (Tyler 2007). Thus, even though the technology has not always been of the highest quality, fansubbing has been able to bring an expert *sensibility* to translation practices, inviting distinctions to be made between terms such as "low-quality" and "amateur." Unrestrained by commercial strictures, this type of translation is able to be experimental, nonconformist, messy, and in-depth – not subject, that is, to many of the constraints that professional subtitlers recognize as an integral part of their craft.[31]

In Romania there exists an interesting parallel to anime fansubbing: an online, voluntary, nonprofit group of foreign media translators with the website titrari.ro that sports the tagline "Nr. 1 in Romania – *Cele Mai Bune Titrari*" or "The Best Subtitles." This group mirrors the activities of anime fansubbing networks like Anime-Keep and We Suck Fansubs (Hatcher 2005), yet with one essential difference: they are fansubbers pure and simple in that they are actually fans of subtitling itself, rather than of any particular genre or product. In the recent debate over Cartoon Network Romania's foray into dubbing, for instance, the titrari.ro community sides, predictably, with those who consider subtitling a superior translation method, not to mention an excellent opportunity for children to learn foreign languages (Patronu 2008a). The website was started by four students using their own funds and now includes approximately 70 translators of which around 75% are active. It is strictly noncommercial (providing links and banners for free to "friend" sites only) and according to its administrator and guru (site nickname: Patronu),[32] if anybody tried to buy it or turn it for-profit the entirely voluntary community of translators would cease to offer their services. He states: "This is a project of pure passion for film and desire to assist those who don't have the necessary knowledge of foreign languages. At the end of 2007, we had about 19,000 visitors daily and about 5 million visitors throughout the year. About 1-1.2 million translations are downloaded from our site every month" (Patronu 2008b). He also wrote:

> We have a set of rules so that the translators' labor is respected, and we are well organized – we know who is translating what, so we minimize redundancy. Many times our translations are better and are published in advance of the official TV or theatrical versions, so actually it happened more than once that DVD distributors and TV stations shamelessly plagiarized our translations. (Patronu 2008a)

The site offers free downloads of software necessary for using the Romanian-language subtitles on either a personal computer or a DivX player,[33] and for adding the subtitles to legally purchased DVDs not intended for the Romanian market. Due to DVD region coding regulations, this practice normally also requires some form of "region-hacking" of the DVD player.[34] Brian Hu sees region coding as enforcing "economic and political censorship by denying the option to see alternative films or alternate versions with alternative languages," making it "illegal – or at least difficult – to import unapproved versions" (Hu 2006, 4). He proposes that region coding and new digital technology is "the terrain on which anti-piracy is fought," identifying piracy operations as "fan agency" fighting "the Hollywood behemoth" (Hu 2006, 6).

The *titrari* community takes an active role in improving the quality of translations by running an Internet forum where questions can be asked and versions compared, providing free training for beginner translators and awarding a yearly prize for the best subtitles. When asked whether their work facilitates piracy, the group's administrator points out that this is not their intention (as noted, their subtitles can be used with legally purchased DVDs or as an alternative form of translation) (Patronu 2008). However, the translations they provide can be downloaded via file-sharing technologies and used for the purposes of piracy.[35] What is certain is that this enterprise of huge commercial potential prides itself on the quality of its accurate, detailed, thoughtful work and a disinterested approach that rejects monetary gain, plagiarism, hidden advertisements of any kind, appropriation of another translator's work, and grammatical mistakes – hardly characteristics generally associated with piracy. The titrari.ro community is a fan community of translation *as such*, valuing translation as education, access-provider, community-building activity and symbol of a niche-type ideal of fairness and nonmaterial values.

Quality Control

Inspired in part by the specialized piracy of anime fansubbing, Nornes' *Cinema Babel* constitutes a seminal text, providing one of the first sustained considerations of audiovisual translation from a film studies perspective.[36] In this analysis, Nornes identifies three distinct epochs of media translation that relate both to specific time periods and to attitudes or trends that exist contemporaneously (Nornes 2007, 177). Within this useful, tripartite schema, fansubbing is positioned as exemplifying the "emergent" third epoch characterized by the concept of "abuse." Equal parts reverence and rebellion, for Nornes, abusive translation "does not present a foreign divested of otherness, but strives to translate from and within the place of the other by an inventive approach to language use and a willingness to bend the rules, both linguistic and cinematic" (2007, 179). However, although the term "abusive" brings up radical connotations of a subversive and potentially harmful impropriety, Nornes advocates for a very *particular* type of abuse that is ultimately quality-controlled, remaining responsible foremost to the otherness and unassailable primacy of the "original."[37]

With his unwavering commitment to quality (stemming in part from his practical experience as a translator), Nornes applauds the foreignizing experimentation of much fansubbing, yet presumably would not extend his appreciation to more typical forms of bootlegging featuring rushed, substandard subtitles that aim to replicate the formal and textual invisibility of conventional, commercial translation. In this sense, his theory of abuse disengages with many wholly abusive situations – such as those occurring under, or in response to, censorship.[38] Nornes counterposes the concept of abuse to that of "corruption," which typifies his second (currently dominant) epoch, associated with professionalization (hence regulation and standardization) and the "thorough domestication" of the foreign, whereby translations are made to read as though they were written in the target language (Nornes 2007, 178).[39] The everyday realities of censorship and censored translations, however, begin to stretch and strain these very categories of abuse and corruption.

Censorship is not usually a discourse associated with quality. Rather, in relation to translation, censorship is commonly understood to focus less on execution than purpose. How *well* a censored translation reads usually pales in importance to the ideological purpose it serves. The errors, cuts, and disjunctions apparent in Romania's censored translations were deliberate, not unintentional, and hardly subtle. When credit sequences were removed in order to mask the identity of films which changed noticeably during their run, or when translations included code words (such as "the one above" for "God"), audiences were made well aware that these films had been doctored. Despite the rhetoric of quality, therefore, Romania's official, subtitled broadcasts and screenings of foreign-language films constituted instances of deliberate *mis*translation that foregrounded, rather than attempting to hide, their misrepresentation of the "original."

Censorship heightened the visibility and "in your face" nature of translation, yet it managed nevertheless to uphold (and indeed shape) ideals of professionalism and quality. Here, we witness the manner in which such concepts can function in a repressive sense to maintain and legitimate political and ideological agendas. One of the broader aims of the current research is precisely to consider translation issues beyond the mire of quality control in which they are routinely swamped. By focusing so unrelentingly upon issues of quality, current translation discourse is often unable to effectively engage with the types of practices engendered via actual historical and contemporary conditions of reception – including state-controlled censorship, subversive community responses, and everyday industry regulations.

It is well to remember that even under conditions of corruption or, at the least, officialdom, spectatorship does not always abide by the rules. In communist Romania, audiences created their own modes of engagement with subtitled media, at the translation's expense. Censored subtitling processes effectively created multiple, alternative versions of the text, encouraging forms of double-spectatorship and challenging ideas of originality and authenticity. Firstly, there was the official, censored version imposed through the translation. Then, the "closer-to-original" one surmised by listening to the foreign-language soundtrack. Lastly, by comparing the subtitled and auditory versions, a third was created which exposed the embedded intentions of the censor while conveying the government's political priorities of the day. Under such conditions, Romanian audiences were offered a number of different, competing "originals." Indeed, in relation to domestic media as well, the notion of an "original" was controversial and contested. Self-censorship was a major factor in local productions, as were decoy elements (intended to distract censors) and encoded meanings (intended to circumvent censors).[40] Decoys were easily spotted by the censor and consequently removed. Thus gratified, the idea was that the censor would then not pay close attention to the rest of the text. Coded meanings, on the other hand, testify to the way that censorship practices could backfire, resulting in the explosion of a corresponding creative/productive practice: the use of coded (allegorical) expression.

Characteristics of this phenomenon can also be observed in the works of filmmakers from other communist countries (Tengiz Abuladze in the former Soviet Union being a famous example). Such active interventions into censorship and subtitling were no doubt influenced in part by contemporaneous piracy practices typified by a lack of either quality or control. Despite the errors and pitfalls of their substandard voice-overs or amateur, on-the-spot translations, pirated media offered new, unconventional viewing contexts coupled with access to otherwise unavailable content – fostering forms of community empowerment and subversion. Here, we can talk of the primacy of context over content. With piracy, spectatorship itself was recast as a performative, interactive, undisciplined, by all means improper yet highly entertaining activity. The fact that this type of viewing was similar to that of the early silent film era suggests that there is no "natural" evolution from the primitive to the classical, but rather that either mode of spectatorship can have primacy depending on the circumstances. In 1980s Romania, the two were coexistent.

Romanian audiences living under (and post) communism saw themselves as entitled to free access to media content when crucial for maintaining the dynamic and lively quality of intellectual life. Even if nowadays Romanians are ready to pay for "quality" content exhibited in a fitting manner, they reserve their right to resort to piracy if the offer falls short of expectations

– if content is not delivered in a timely manner for instance (due to the regional marketing policies of global media companies), if it is prohibitively expensive, or if it does not conform to Romanian tastes and standards (such as the preference for subtitling over dubbing). In this sense, the subversive or ideologically beneficial strain underlying some forms of piracy has taught Romanians a healthy instinct when it comes to media content: do not passively accept products (including translations) being imposed upon you; instead, pitch in and improve the content when inspired.

This critical and active attitude toward media has been, we contend, fostered by the censorship-translation-piracy dynamic pre-1989 (supported by the VCR/VHS and later satellite antennae/broadcasting) and is very close to the type of "free culture" mindset described by popular copyright commentator Lawrence Lessig and supported by digital and Internet technologies (Lessig 2004, 8). [41]

Lessig opposes the notion of "free culture" to that of "permission culture," the latter being controlled by legal gatekeepers who serve political and/or financial interests rather than considering the true interests of the public and the creator (Lessig 2004, 30). He decries the US copyright legislation's favoring of record companies, big movie studios, and global media companies (especially in relation to new Internet technologies) without allowing enough room for what he calls "Disney creativity": an artist's freedom to use some previously published material in order to create new content, as well as the consumer's unrestrained access to certain intellectual property (such as music records that are no longer available on the market, which, according to Lessig, should be free to use in file-sharing communities) (Lessig 2004, 69-72). The alternative techniques and varying standards of translation accompanying Romanian piracy and fan operations need to be considered in relation to Lessig's notion of creative "tinkering" – as an unregulated, spontaneous contribution to the text driven by passion and, at times, financial gain (Lessig 2007, 46).

Necessary Failure

As a by-product of global hierarchies of distribution and totalitarian censorship practices, piracy has become associated with translations of translations and dubs of dubs. In Romania circa 1993 (following communism's demise), Uricaru recalls viewing a pirated VHS copy of *Intersection* (Mark Rydell, 1994), which came out in American theatres a few months later. More interestingly, the tape bore commercial breaks and subtitles in a nonidentified language: it seemed to have been pirated from either a Central Asian or Middle Eastern TV station, presumably in a country in which there was no planned theatrical release. Pirated videotapes and DVDs typically involve third-, fourth-, or fifth-generation copies of copies. This exponential amplification of the secondary, allows us to reconsider the necessary failures of translation in a new light. In relation to Romania, the mistranslations common to substandard pirated voice-overs, for instance, testify to a further overriding failure: that of censorship.

Brian Larkin's valuable work on video piracy in Nigeria offers a fascinating reinterpretation of failure within the context of globalization and piracy. He describes how Nigeria's Kano acts as the "main clearinghouse for Indian films" and for American films shipped via Dubai or Beirut "often arriving in Nigeria while they are on first-run release in the United States."[42] These circuitous piracy operations inevitably produce blurred images and distorted sound… marked by poor transmission, interference, and noise. However, in Kano, the cheap tapes and old VCRs, televisions, and cassette players marked by distortion and interference have actually underwritten the emergence of a new local-language, feature-length video industry, known as "Nollywood." This video industry is characterized by what he terms the "aesthetic" of piracy – produced through technological failure as much as success. Specifically, he mentions a "hallucinogenic quality" where "facial features are smoothed away, colors are broken down into constituent tones, and bodies fade into one another."

***

As the example of communist Romania reveals, the failures of pirated media often reach beyond the technological, extending toward the realms of language, cultural difference and translation. As in Nigeria, however, where the blurred, "hallucinogenic" piracy aesthetic has been creatively adopted by a developing local industry, the amateur, improvised or downright shoddy translations common to piracy can function to enhance rather than inhibit the viewing experience. The example of anti-censorship piracy in Romania reveals that even the lowest quality translation (of a translation) can achieve a liberating, subversive authenticity. The shadow economy fostered by piracy in Romania created a new social order signified by the prestige of the VCR and the popular image of the translator-as-superhero. This translation-censorship nexus invites a reevaluation of the secondary and a new framework for translation discourse that is able to move beyond ideals of quality alone. Despite the failures, limitations, and corruptions that tend to dog piracy practices, these operations challenge the stability of the consumer/producer divide while interrogating social and economic inequalities. Such geopolitical contingencies need to be considered in any discussion of contemporary media reception practices – including censorship, anti-censorship, and translation.

Notes

1. Strangely enough, the government's reason for altering film titles was, in many cases, partly to do with its own piracy practices as when Televiziunea Romana would air preview tapes, for instance, instead of legally purchasing films. See Nistor 2008.
2. Other governmental directives, as recalled by Televiziunea Romana translator Irina Margareta Nistor, included the following: "Easter" and "Christmas" were translated as "holidays." all sex scenes were deleted, a kiss wasn't supposed to last more than the count to three, films about elderly characters were not accepted (as they could have been interpreted as an allusion to the ruling couple) and neither were films featuring alcoholism (one of the dictator's sons was a notorious drunk). Scenes featuring abundant food and luxurious dwellings were banned as they would have created an obvious contrast with the indigent everyday life in Romania (Nistor 2008).
3. Cuts were most commonly made in relation to sexually explicit scenes, as party officials curiously maintained a consistent policy of modesty in line with their discouragement of divorce and extramarital affairs (a woman who suspected her husband of cheating could appeal to the local party secretary to "have a talk" with him).
4. Throughout this paper, we place the term "original" in inverted commas in order to indicate its contested status.
5. Key anthologies in this area of translation studies include Gambier and Gottlieb 2001 and Heiss and Bosinelli 1996.
6. *Teleenciclopedia* (TV encyclopedia) was an extremely popular Saturday evening, hour-long show, usually made of three to four segments compiled from foreign-produced educational programming focusing on science, art, and history. The original credits, titles, and production information were not provided during the broadcast and the translation was done through a mixture of subtitling and voice-over dubbing.
7. The Cinematheque was the exhibition program of the Arhiva Nationala de Filme, organizing daily projections of prints in a dedicated screening room that could accommodate about 200 people. Many of the archived foreign films had never had a theatrical release and therefore were not subtitled. A translator, located in the projection booth, would perform a simultaneous, single-voice translation over the microphone.

8.   Translated into Romanian as *Suflet de femeie* (A woman's soul), this tel-
     enovela made the cover of the June 1997 Latin American edition of *Time*
     magazine for revolving around an untraditional older woman/younger
     man couple. It's sequel aired on the television station Acasa, roughly the
     Romanian equivalent of Lifetime television, aimed at female audiences.
     On Acasa's online forum, viewers expressed their disappointment at the
     dubbed translation and their desire to see reruns of the show with the origi-
     nal actors' voices and subtitles (Acasa TV 2008).

9.   These dubbing operations have had mixed results among Romanian audi-
     ences. Some viewers were very surprised to find out in the theater, after
     they had paid for their ticket, that the film had been dubbed. On cinemagia.
     ro (the most popular and best-managed Romanian online forum dedicated
     to movies in all their forms of distribution and exhibition on the Romanian
     market), some participants even suggested that exhibiting the film in a
     dubbed version might lead to increased Internet piracy as audiences would
     prefer to watch these films subtitled or even untranslated. This, despite Dis-
     ney's sustained efforts at preserving the quality of the soundtrack through
     financial and logistical investment in the voice dubbing. It seems that the
     corporate interest – in this case Disney and DreamWorks – is bent on spar-
     ing no expense in order to impose a new form of translation – probably
     counting on the fact that young children who grow up with this form will
     come to prefer it as adults. This is a true "culture war" in which, surprisingly,
     some Romanians would rather not have the media accommodated to their
     native language.

10. DreamWorks's *Shrek* series provides a pertinent example, with the list of
     star dubbers multiplying with each successive sequel. *Shrek* (Andrew Ad-
     amson and Vicky Jenson, 2001) featured voice-acting by Mike Myers, Eddie
     Murphy, and Cameron Diaz. *Shrek 2* (Andrew Adamson, Kelly Asbury and
     Conrad Vernon, 2004) added Julie Andrews, Antonio Banderas, John Cleese,
     Rupert Everett, and Jennifer Saunders to the list, while *Shrek the Third*
     included singer/songwriter Justin Timberlake. In Korea, local actor Song
     Kang-Ho worked on DreamWorks's *Madagascar* (Eric Darnell and Tom
     McGrath, 2005) and, according to one fan, "made people… reconsider the
     film and see it in a new light" (Twitchfilm 2005). For more on this phenome-
     non, see McNamara 2005 and, in relation to Spain, Zabalbeascoa et al. 2001.

11. According to Nistor, the fascination for subtitled foreign media such as
     telenovelas caused an increase in the literacy rate of the Roma people and
     of remote rural groups such as shepherds (Nistor 2008).

12. According to Dries, Romania's commitment to subtitling far exceeds that of
     any other Eastern bloc country. The only other country officially considered
     a "subtitling" nation is Slovenia, which only subtitles 62% of its imported
     television programs (1994-1995, 36, fig. 2). Although Poland subtitles all
     foreign-language cinema, voice-over dubbing is used in relation to televi-
     sion (ibid., 36, fig. 2).

13.   Here we witness the legacy of communism. This petition, in effect, calls for
      a certain form of censorship – requesting (and assuming) that the govern-
      ment has control over private business.

14.   Government owned, operated and, controlled, Televiziunea Romana (with
      two channels) was the only TV broadcast outlet in the country until 1990. In
      January 1985, the second channel (which was only available in and around
      Bucharest) ceased its broadcast, which resumed in May 1990. By 1986,
      programming had been reduced to two hours per day on weekdays (8 to 10
      p.m.) and ten hours on weekends.

15.   The concept of subtitles being "en face" is borrowed from Abé Mark Nornes,
      who writes: "The subtitled moving image is a constellated figure; both the
      original and the translation are simultaneously available, as if they were en
      face" (2007, 186).

16.   The ideology enforced by the Romanian government had a Marxist core,
      with a nationalistic nuance that became more and more poignant after
      1965. In the 1980s, after an initial Stalinist regime (1948 to the early 1960s)
      and a subsequent relaxation period (1965 to the mid-1970s), the totalitarian
      system became tougher than ever. Mass media were highly regulated and
      indeed there was no Romanian independent (nongovernmental) outlet, as
      all media (print, television, radio) were state owned, produced, and distrib-
      uted. Film production was administered by Centrala Romania Film (sub-
      ordinate to the Ministry of Culture), which also handled distribution and
      exhibition, including imports and exports. There were seven film studios
      in total, which included one documentary film studio and one animation
      studio. Directors, producers, writers, and all other creative and professional/
      technical personnel were employees of these studios. Every foot of film shot
      and processed through the lab had to be recovered and accounted for at the
      end of the editing process. With the economy strictly controlled, advertis-
      ing was virtually nonexistent and media productions were evaluated for
      their ideological content and political implications only, not for audience
      appeal or commercial potential.

17.   Physical censorship in Romania was aided by the fact that it shares no
      borders with any Western country, there was no Internet access or satellite
      TV (the first satellite dishes entered Romania as late as 1988) and VCRs were
      extremely rare before 1987 or so. Along with bans on importing cultural
      products, there were strict border and customs controls and limited access
      to subscriptions to foreign publications or other kinds of mail delivery
      services. This type of censorship was complemented by content censorship,
      applied (postproduction) to those cultural products that were made avail-
      able, and self-censorship whereby writers and filmmakers learned how to
      detect potentially objectionable elements in their work and eliminate them
      before submitting the work for release/publication. All publications, pub-
      lishing houses, film studios, and television and radio stations had a number

of employees on their payroll whose job it was to pass judgment on books, newspaper articles, films, etc., from an ideological perspective.

18.   In Japan and neighboring Korea, live narration became a cinematic institution, distinguishing itself from related practices around the world by its enduring and widespread popularity. According to J. L. Anderson, Japan's *benshi* or *katsuben* had three main functions: to narrate, comment, and mediate (1992, 284). He continues: "the *katsuben*'s presence denied film as a depersonalized, mass-produced object and made every show a unique, human-crafted experience" (ibid., 289).

19.   Hansen points out that the history of cinema has focused on the evolution of a "standardized" and "normative" approach, neglecting "configurations of film culture that are no longer" and discounting the "experiential perspective" (1991, 88). For more on Burch's elaboration of the "primitive mode of representation," see Burch 1990, 186-201.

20.   Uricaru recalls how impressed she was when a friend of her parents was able to procure a copy of Tengiz Abuladze's *Monanieba* (Repentance [1984]) just two months after it premiered at the Cannes Film Festival in 1987.

21.   A 2005 Universal Studios DVD warning "clip" advertises fines of up to US$60,500 per offense for individuals and US$302,500 per offense for corporations.

22.   In Japan, the term *anime* is used intermittently with "animation," from which it derives. Thus, in Japan the term refers to the animation genre as a whole irrespective of national origin. In non-Japanese language contexts, the term is used to refer specifically to animation produced by Japanese companies, mainly for the Japanese market.

23.   According to Analee Newitz, the line "Subtitled by fans for fans. Not for sale or rent" (or similar) is commonly edited into fansubbed anime. See also Hatcher 2005, appendix, image 6.

24.   This situation remains the case in many non-English speaking countries.

25.   In Japan, *otaku* is a derogatory term for "fanboy/girl" or "obsessive geek." Outside Japan, however, the term is proudly worn in anime subculture (Newitz 1994; Cubbison 2005, 45).

26.   Also known as "digital audio extraction," the term "ripping" refers to the process of copying audio or video data from one media form to another, such as from a DVD to a hard disk.

27.   Exceptions include those fans that actively advocate for dubbing over subtitling, sometimes producing their own "fandubs" (Cubbison 2005, 46, 49; Hatcher 2005, 528; Tyler 2007).

28.   Hatcher notes the fansubber's "incentive to be innovative" as a means of gaining prestige within the fan community (Hatcher 2005, 529).

29.   Hatcher provides some illustrated examples in his appendix. For instance, in *Bleach* (episode 4, Anime-Keep, TV Tokyo broadcast, created by Kubo Tite), an evil character called a "Hollow" speaks "in an appropriately spooky font for full effect" (Hatcher 2005, appendix, image 5).

30.   In another variation on "niche piracy." Uricaru recalls a person in Romania
      circa 1987 who held a huge collection of opera recordings in Hi8 format,
      which meant that he could not exchange any of them on the underground
      market. As somebody who chose to pirate media of a highly specialized
      nature in a format that put him above and beyond the regular circuit, he
      became a kind of mythical figure.

31.   There are many unspoken rules within national subtitling practices. In the
      UK, professionals are taught to never hold subtitles more than six seconds
      or less than one and a half seconds; and not to carry subtitles over an image
      cut (Minchinton 1987, 279-280). In Japan, the rule is: four characters per
      second or one line per foot (Nornes 2007, 162). Indeed, as any experienced
      subtitler will readily admit, in transforming spoken dialogue into written
      form, subtitles are entirely dependent upon the "art" of condensation. This
      reductive nature results in an unavoidable degree of mismatch or non-
      equivalence with the "original" as, according to America's first foreign film
      subtitler Herman Weinberg, "The whole point of subtitling is to have as few
      words on the screen as possible" (1985, 10).

32.   At his request, we refer to him by his online nickname Patronu in order to
      preserve confidentiality.

33.   According to Hu, "DivX is primarily used for shrinking large video files
      ripped from DVDs into sizes that can fit on CDs and that can easily be
      transferred on the Internet. As such, it is the preferred format for illegally
      transferring movie files online" (2006, 6).

34.   As Hu explains, it is possible to purchase region-free DVD players. However,
      embedded playback restrictions (as supported by Warner Home Video and
      Columbia Tristar, for instance) mean that DVDs are often not able to be
      played on region-free players (2006, 4). The more successful strategy, there-
      fore, has been the release of easily modifiable players (such as the Philips
      DVP642) whose regions can be easily altered with the aid of a "secret"
      region-switching password that is widely known among Internet communi-
      ties. In the case of the Philips DVP642, the password is even advertised on
      the product pages of retailers such as Amazon (ibid., 6).

35.   Lawrence Lessig presents four types of content that can be shared (presum-
      ably illegally) through peer-to-peer downloading networks: content that
      could be otherwise purchased in "hard" form; sampling before (or instead
      of) purchasing; copyrighted content that is no longer available legally; and
      obtaining noncopyrighted or free-for-all content. Only the first two types
      could, potentially, be harmful from an economic point of view – the last
      three could, presumably, lead to harmless or even beneficial piracy (Lessig
      2007, 68-69). In the case of 1980s Romania, the pirated videotapes that cir-
      culated across the country were, we suggest, of the first type – but the harm
      they were causing was not directed at an economic system but an ideologi-
      cal one. In other words, in bypassing government controls and providing

illegal content instead of official, censorship-sanctioned content, piracy
effectively undermined the ideological effectiveness of the system.

36.   Another text that examines the intersection of film theory and translation
is the anthology edited by filmmaker Atom Egoyan and Ian Balfour: *Subtitles: On the Foreignness of Film* (2004).

37.   Nornes writes: "Rather than smothering the film under the regulations of
the corrupt subtitle, rather than smoothing the rough edges of foreignness,
rather than converting everything into easily consumable meaning, the
abusive subtitles always direct spectators back to the original text" (2007,
185).

38.   Not wishing to underestimate the extremely nuanced arguments set forth
in *Cinema Babel: Translating Global Cinema*, Nornes may well argue that piracy as a response to censorship is "abusive" in a way that it is not when produced for commercial purposes alone. In a chapter called "Loving Dubbing"
he praises the abusive nature of some translations that do depart radically
from the "original text in order to serve pressing local needs" (Nornes 2007,
194). However, in such instances, the extreme "domestication" (ibid., 193) of
the translation is intentional and self-reflexive, whereas "bad" or careless
pirated translations tend not to be so on purpose, having more in common
perhaps with the mechanisms of global translation clearinghouses that
come under serious critique in Nornes's conclusion.

39.   Lawrence Venuti refers to this type of translation in terms of "fluent
discourse" or "invisibility." He writes, "'Invisibility' is the term I will use to
describe the translator's situation and activity in contemporary Anglo-
American culture," continuing, "The illusion of transparency is an effect of
fluent discourse, of the translator's effort to insure easy readability" (1995, 1).

40.   The basic feature of this type of filmic expression (also used by fiction
writers) was the constant referral to a subtext or rather, para-text – a reality
or discourse located outside the text that is never explicitly enunciated
but is implicitly necessary for fully understanding the text. Concretely, the
films would bear certain codes through their narrative structure, themes,
character development, visual style, or dialogue – and the viewers could
decode the (literally) hidden meanings. It was an example of finding pleasure in decoding meanings, in sharing a secret with the filmmaker and the
other informed viewers – a pleasure fostered mainly by the notion that by
decoding the meaning one managed to "beat the system," thus transforming
the apparently passive act of viewing into an active instance of subversion.
Such practices lend themselves to the interpretative model proposed by
Stuart Hall: in the process of filmmaking, the reality (with its contradictions, frustrations, needs, desires, and relationships) generates in the artistic
conscience of the filmmaker the "meaning structures 1" (a subversive take
on reality), which are encoded in a discourse (the film) and then offered to
the audience who, through decoding in the act of spectatorship, obtains the
"meaning structures 2" (a subversive take on reality and the consciousness

of sharing this meaning with the filmmaker), which will "satisfy a need" (of participating in some kind of resistance through culture) or be "put to a use" (shaping a different type of consciousness which would eventually mold the behavior, attitudes, and, ultimately, actions of the audience) (2001, 168-70). In this application of Hall, the symmetry between encoding and decoding does not generate misunderstanding in the communicative exchange. On the contrary, the whole scope of the communication is to achieve this symmetry, and both encoders and decoders are ready to go out of their way for it. This happens because the understanding in the communicative exchange is built around the need to ensure the misunderstanding of the third party – the censor, as representative of the government or the system. The communication is not about getting the message across, but about getting the message around (the censor).

41.   Remarkably, Lessig finds an analogy between contemporary Japan's lax attitude toward copyright infringement in the comic book industry (2007, 26-27) and the US media landscape at the beginning of the 20th century, when filmmakers threatened by Edison's patent monopoly escaped to the West Coast (ibid., 54-55). This comparison resembles the analogy we pose between Romanian spectatorship in the 1980s and early cinema spectatorship.

42.   Larkin's essay is reprinted in this volume.

Bibliography

Acasa TV. 2008. Various posts on the Acasa Forum discussion board, 11 January. http://forum.acasatv.ro.

Anderson, J. L. 1992. "Spoken Silents in the Japanese Cinema; or, Talking to Pictures: Essaying the Katsuben, Contexturalizing the Texts." In Arthur Nolletti Jr. and David Desser, eds., *Reframing Japanese Cinema: Authorship, Genre, History*. Bloomington and Indianapolis: Indiana University Press, 259-311.

Burch, Noël. 1990. *Life to Those Shadows*, ed. and trans. Ben Brewster. London: BFI.

Cubbison, Laurie. 2005. "Anime Fans, DVDs, and the Authentic Text." *The Velvet Light Trap* 56: 45-57.

Dries, Josephine. 1994-1995. "Breaking Language Barriers behind the Broken Wall (Voice-over, Dubbing or Sub-titling?" *Intermedia* 22.6: 35-37.

Egoyan, Atom, and Ian Balfour, eds. 2004. *Subtitles: On the Foreignness of Film*. Cambridge, MA: MIT Press and Alphabet City Media.

Gambier, Yves, and Henrik Gottlieb, eds. 2001. *(Multi)media Translation: Concepts, Practices, and Research*. Amsterdam and Philadelphia: John Benjamins.

Hall, Stuart. 2001. "Encoding/Decoding." In Meenakshi Gigi Durham and Douglas Kellner, eds., *Media and Cultural Studies: KeyWorks*. Oxford: Blackwell, 166-176.

Hansen, Miriam. 1991. *Babel and Babylon: Spectatorship in American Silent Film*. Cambridge, MA: Harvard University Press.

Hatcher, Jordan S. 2005. "Of Otakus and Fansubs: A Critical Look at Anime Online in Light of Current Issues in Copyright Law." *SCRIPTed – A Journal of Law, Technology & Society* 2.4: 514-542. http://www.law.ed.ac.uk/ahrc/script-ed/vol2-4/hatcher.asp

Heiss, Christine, and Rosa Maria Bollettieri Bosinelli, eds. 1996. *Traduzione multimediale per il Cinema, la Televisione e la Scena*. Bologna: Cooperativa Libraria Universitaria Editrice Bologna.

Hu, Brian. 2006. "Closed Borders and Open Secrets: Regional Lockout, the Film Industry, and Code-Free DVD Players." *Mediascape* 1.2: 1-9.

Jenkins, Henry. 2006. "When Piracy Becomes Promotion." *Reason.com*. 17 November. http://reason.com/archives/2006/11/17/when-piracy-becomes-promotion/print.

Larkin, Brian. 2004. "Degraded Images, Distorted Sounds: Nigerian Video and the Infrastructure of Piracy." *Public Culture* 16.2 (2004). Reprinted in this volume.

Lessig, Lawrence. 2004 *Free Culture: How Big Media Uses Technology and the Law to Lock Down Culture and Control Creativity*. New York: Penguin Press.

McNamara, Mary. 2005. "Dubbing Makes 'Shrek' Funny in Foreign Languages." *Los Angeles Times* 6 Feb. Rpt. in the *Boston Globe*. http://www.boston.com/ae/movies/articles/2005/02/06/dubbing_makes_shrek_funny_in_foreign_languages/.

Mihalcea, Miruna. 2006. "Intre Fuck you si Du-te naibii." *Jurnalul National*, 29 March. http://old.jurnalul.ro/articol.php?id=49442.

Minchinton, John. 1987. "Fitting Titles." *Sight and Sound* 56.4: 279-280.

Newitz, Annalee. 1994. "Anime Otaku: Japanese Animation Fans Outside Japan." *Bad Subjects* 13. http://eserver.org/bs/13/Newitz.html.

Nistor, Irina Margareta. 2008. "Re: Intrebari." E-mail to Ioana Uricaru. 2 February.

Nornes, Abé Mark. 2007. *Cinema Babel: Translating Global Cinema*. Minneapolis: University of Minnesota Press.

Patronu. 2008a. "Re: intrebari." E-mail to Ioana Uricaru. Trans. Ioana Uricaru. 6 January.

Patronu. 2008b. "Re: inca niste mici precizari." E-mail to Ioana Uricaru. Trans. Ioana Uricaru. 21 January.

Twitchfilm 2005. "Korean News in Brief: July 13 [Box Office, The Wig, Voice]." Twitchfilm, 14 July. http://twitchfilm.com/2005/07/korean-news-in-brief-july-13-box-office-the-wig-voice.html.

Tyler, L. 2007. "Anime Translation." Toonami Digital Arsenal: Rants Section (Ask Pepito). http://www.toonamiarsenal.com/rants/translation.html.

Venuti, Lawrence. 1995. *The Translator's Invisibility: A History of Translation*. London: Routledge.

Weinberg, Herman. 1985. "Herman Weinberg on Subtitling: Interview with Rick Rofihe." *Field of Vision* 13: 10.

Zabalbeascoa, Patrick, et al. 2001. "Disentangling Audiovisual Translation into Catalan from the Spanish Media Mesh." In Yves Gambier and Henrik Gottlieb, eds., *(Multi)media Translation: Concepts, Practices, and Research*. Amsterdam and Philadelphia: John Benjamins, 101-111.

Conclusion

11.   The Triumph of the Pirates

Books, Letters, Movies, and Vegan Candy – Not a Conclusion

Tilman Baumgärtel

After recently returning to Germany, the country of my birth after teaching media studies for seven years in Asia – first in the Philippines, then in Cambodia – I was slapped with two *Abmahnungen* in a month. An *Abmahnung* is a written warning in the German judicial system, similar to the "cease and desist" letter used in the Anglo-Saxon world: a formal request by one person, usually a lawyer, to another person to immediately stop a certain behavior. In my case, the undesirable behavior was the downloading and sharing of two movies: *Carnage* (2011) by Roman Polanski and *Merantau* (2009), a martial arts movie by Welsh director Gareth Evans set in Indonesia.

That this could happen to me – a media critic who has done research on piracy for a decade – is a major embarrassment. Of course, I was aware of the fact that film studios and distributors – in Germany as well as elsewhere – had started to hire law firms and specialized companies to track down Internet users who shared files thought to be the intellectual property of these companies. As part of my research I had read about these goings on in the West, even though I was in Cambodia, where none of this mattered to anyone: copyrighted DVDs were (and still are) widely available on the markets, new films could be bought shortly after (or even before) they were released in their respective home markets, and monitoring the downloading of music and movies by net surfers had not occurred to anyone.

There were two reasons, why I was caught: First, I always assumed that the films I typically downloaded and shared were so arcane that nobody would ever bother to look for offenders. Turned out that I had one (and only one) film on my hard disk that was "intellectual property" of, among others, a major Hollywood studio: Roman Polanski's *Carnage* (2011), coproduced by Wild Bunch from the US and Constantin from Germany, plus a number of other companies that shared the costs of making a film by a director who himself at this time was the subject of criminal prosecution because of his alleged affair with a minor. *Merantau* (2009) – most likely the first film shot in Indonesia that rose to international prominence since 1980s B-movie fare such as *Mystics in Bali* (1981) or *Lady Terminator* (1989) – had been purchased after successful screenings on international festivals by

German company Koch Media from Munich, wanted to prevent the film from being available in Germany before the local release date in July 2012.

The other reason was that I had simply forgotten that a little program on my computer called μTorrent still pumped bits and bytes of films I had downloaded on my computer back onto the Internet for the benefit of the international file-sharing public every time I turned the machine on. Well, I had been living in an environment where there were no lobby group, no "intellectual rights protection organization," no specialized police department, and no lawyers who had turned coming down hard on file sharers into a business model.

I quickly found out that combating the new German *Abmahnungsindustrie* (the law firms that served file sharers with threatening *Abmahnungen*) had brought a kind of anti-industry into existence. Just searching for the words "film" and "*Abmahnung*" on Google produced endless lists of law firms that were more than ready to help me in my fight against my prosecutors and that undercut themselves for the fee for their services. I felt like I had become a pawn in a version of the popular *Spy vs. Spy* cartoons in which some lawyers threatened to sue me while other lawyers reminded them that their demands were not actually legitimate according to German law.

To decide whether I had actually broken German law would have been the subject of a time-consuming and potentially very expensive confrontation before the German courts. I did not want to go down that route. So to make a long story short: I paid €150 each to the two law firms that helped me in this matter, and, after some short haggling over the phone between my lawyers and those of the movie companies, the penalties for my file-sharing activities went down to €700 for the Polanski movie (originally €2,500) and €500 for the Indonesian action flick (originally €5,000) – savor, if you will, the irony of the different sums for "pirating" a Western and an Asian film. The legality of all this is questionable – but that's the way I (and tens, if not hundreds of thousands of other accused of the same wrongdoing) chose to settle the business with the companies who felt that I had violated their intellectual property. Case closed – before it even began.

What is of importance for the purposes of this book are two things: First there was my sense of entitlement. I felt that as a temporary inhabitant of the Third World, I had the moral right to obtain whatever films, music, e-books, etc., I wanted from the net without charge. The countries of the Global South had been denied the possibility of availing themselves of most art house films or movie classics for decades, the reasoning goes among many intellectuals in these countries, so it was their right to get these films in the shadow economy of online sharing. I leave it up to the reader to decide how morally correct my stance was or is – after all, I was only a long-term guest first in the Philippines, then in Cambodia, where I had started to get interested in researching media piracy, which eventually resulted in the book you are currently reading.

However, the other thing of importance in this context is well beyond moral reasoning, but about the mere function of a technology – unchecked, in this case, because of my forgetfulness. I want to argue in this conclusion that piracy is a worthwhile subject for academic study, not just because of the economic, social, and political significance of this subject and the consequences that it has had for the way media are distributed and consumed. Working on piracy has also forced me to put schools of media theory in dialogue that typically do not have much to say to each other, but that I have found to be quite fruitful (as well as insightful) for the study of the subject of piracy: The "media materialist" approach of Friedrich Kittler I had grown up with and the insistence of scholars like John Fiske and Henry Jenkins that the audience had its own agency in the circulation of media "texts," the "Revaluation of All Values" of intellectual property and copyright that was undertaken both by the international hacker community and by thinkers such as Lawrence Lessig and Yochai Benkler, with the empiric studies that are still the bread and butter of Anglo-Saxon media studies.

I myself have grown up in the intellectual milieu of the poststructuralist German media studies that – inspired and shaped by the works of Friedrich Kittler – have put the autonomy of technology at the center of its discourse. Inspired by, among others, McLuhan (and his focus on "mediality"), Kittler developed a brand of media theory that has been labeled as "media materialism," a term he undoubtedly would have disagreed with. In this approach, he provoked the German film and media studies of the 1960s and 1970s – who often took their cue from the sociology of the Frankfurt School – by focusing exclusively on material networks and technologies used for the production, processing, transmission, and storage of information. Content became data, culture the effect of the workings of media technologies such as the typewriter, the record player, or, finally, the computer.

"There Is No Software," the title of one of his best-known essays, summarizes this approach (Kittler 1995), when he declares the Intel 4004 microprocessor to be the beginning of "our postmodern writing scene" or when – as in his book *Gramophone, Film, Typewriter* – he keeps reminding us of Nietzsche's insight that "our writing tools are also working on our thoughts," out of which he develops a whole genealogy of German literature at the turn of the century (Kittler 1999, 200-214). "Media determine our situation," as he wrote in the introduction to this book, "which deserves – in spite or because of it – a description" (Kittler 1999, xxxix). Kittler's works have been described as "techno-deterministic," which is an oversimplification, just as my reading of his works is here. Yet, he has clearly privileged the technological over the social in his media discourse analysis, and the tensions between users, communications technologies, and the socio-political systems that govern such technologies were of little interest to him. This approach seemed to provide a rich framework to analyze piracy with. After all, could there be a more radical proof of the all-encompassing power of a new technology, then the way digital recording media and the Internet wrecked and reconfigured the way we consume music and movies in the course of a decade?

On the one hand, there was this new technology, that ruthlessly – and with a cockiness that brought to mind Kittler's own personal style – imposed its rules on audio-visual culture: Whole cultural forms such as literature, music, film turned into digital data that could be copied and reproduced indefinitely without loss of quality. That could be sent around the globe via the Internet and be listened to or watched as a file downloaded onto a computer or received as a data stream. And that this data could be burned onto optical discs and sold for a dollar on the street corner in a city in any given Third World country. The grief and the economic upheaval that this caused to the media industry – an industry that was transformed beyond recognition in just a few years – seemed utmost proof of Kittler's claim that technology had become the new subject of history and that this technology neither possessed morals, nor experienced sociability.

But on the other hand, I could not help noticing that all this happened not just because of the inevitable power of technology that enabled the process, but also that human agency played a crucial role in what was happening. While technology made possible the piracy that I observed – both on the Internet and in the streets of Manila, Shanghai, Beijing, Jakarta, Kuala Lumpur, Ho Chi Min City, and Phnom Penh (and could have observed in Rio de Janeiro, Lagos, Bucharest, or Hanoi, as some of the essays in this book make clear) – it wasn't technology, that put these films and these records on the Internet or printed them on DVDs, even though technology enabled that process in a way inconceivable only a decade earlier.

Hence I had to look for theoretical models that would help me to understand the role of the facilitators of this process. I was about to talk about the audience of pirated media here, but the whole concept of the audience as a mass of consumers had been irretrievably pulverized by the very same digital media that facilitated the piracy I had become interested in. Every consumer of media content could potentially become a producer of digital media content, too – or at least upload the media content others had produced, on the net. The creativity of these new, technologically empowered "prosumers" could range from creating their own works from scratch to recombining songs and movies as digital collages/remixes/mash-ups to just ripping DVDs and putting them on the Internet.

If you find it frivolous to put both the creator of original works and the pirate who uploads movies on the net in the same category, keep in mind not only the fact that digitally enhanced creativity is reproductive by trend, but also that even Lawrence Lessig himself proudly described his organization of play lists of his MP3s as a creative act.[1] So how about the Chinese DVD pirate who chose movies for the ever-popular compilation disks (all the films of Bruce Lee or half a dozen movies with snakes, all on one DVD), designed the cover out of images he downloaded from the Internet, created Chinese-language subtitles, and found ways to have these film collections printed and distributed for a profit?

Of course, Lessig himself draws the line between unacceptable theft of intellectual property and creative use of digital raw material at what is referred to "transformative authorship" (2004, 203) – the use of other author's material that makes substantial changes to the original source. In one of the more problematic parts of his book *Free Culture* he constructs a brand of "Asian piracy" that precisely lacks this kind of authorship, as it adds no value and contributes nothing to the material it appropriates:

> All across the world, but especially in Asia and Eastern Europe, there are businesses that do nothing but take others people's copyrighted content, copy it, and sell it – all without the permission of a copyright owner. The recording industry estimates that it loses about $4.6 billion every year to physical piracy (that works out to one in three CDs sold worldwide). The MPAA estimates that it loses $3 billion annually worldwide to piracy. This is piracy plain and simple. Nothing in the argument of this book, nor in the argument that most people make when talking about the subject of this book, should draw into doubt this simple point: This piracy is wrong. (Lessig 2004, 63)

Apart from the fact that Lessig used the completely discredited numbers that the MPAA published as a fact, there is another reality that needs to be acknowledged here: in other parts of his book, Lessig went to considerable lengths to defend the users of file-sharing services such as Napster, a practice that at that time was – due to technical constraints and slow Internet connections outside of the "Global North" – more or less limited to the Western world. If North Americans use peer-to-peer services, it is acceptable, but if the people in countries "especially in Asia and Eastern Europe" sell or purchase DVDs with pirated content, it is wrong? These comments by a well-respected liberal scholar are but one reminder of how the discourse about the results of digital technology could wander into highly unpleasant territory once the ostensible neutrality of technology is left behind.

In any case, technology has social implications that I had to acknowledge if I wanted to understand the phenomenon of piracy better than the German media materialism matrix allowed me to – a fact that the judicial consequences of the unsupervised functioning of my little torrent program demonstrated to me with severe financial consequences. The Internet had brought into being a culture of fans and aficionados ready to share whatever cultural creation they have on their hard disk that would have a tremendous impact on the direction that the creation of art, music, and films would take. By cracking down on those who availed themselves of this possibility, the media industry also alienated some of their most loyal customers and criminalized those that experimented with new approaches to the distribution of media that the Internet seemed to suggest (Sinnreich 2013).

At the same time, musical newcomers from the Arctic Monkeys to Justin Bieber to OK Go to Psy to Foster the People were discovered because they took advantage of the mechanisms of free distribution that the Internet allowed. (These artists, of course, published their own songs on the net rather than just republishing material from other artists.) The much-praised new American television series from *The Sopranos* to *Lost*, from *Game of Thrones* to *Mad Men* might have never gotten so popular if it had not been for their most dedicated and Internet-savvy fans. The global success of these shows depended to no small degree on the websites, blogs entries, and postings on Facebook and Twitter where they were praised and dissected. Some of these fans enthusiastically put every new episode of these shows on the net for download minutes after they had been screened on US cable channels, often subtitling them in their own languages in the process (Bold 2011; Vandresen 2012). (Isn't that an example of the "transformative authorship" that Lawrence Lessig argued was the hallmark of original work?)

George R. R. Martin, the novelist on whose books and scripts *Game of Thrones* is based, director David Petrarca, and HBO programming president Michael Lombardo infuriate the American media industry by pointing out that piracy had not only not hurt the show financially, but the fact that the show was "the most pirated show in the world" was actually "a compliment" or even "better than a Grammy" (Dewey 2013). The pirated versions of the show, so their argument went, eventually led to HBO subscription going up, and added to the prestige of the cable company even among those who did not subscribe to the channel. Author Martin was particular verbal in pointing out that the old practice of releasing television shows in different markets according to marketing considerations was deemed obsolete by the new kind of Internet piracy that allowed right-here-right-now-access to them: If you wanted to stay ahead of the piracy game, you simply had to make your show available at every market at the same time.[2]

These developments made particular sense in the theoretical framework that media scholars like Henry Jenkins had developed. Influenced by the approach of the British cultural studies and particular by the writings of John Fiske, he focused on the active participation of the audience in the construction of meaning of culture – or even its (re)creation by that audience. When studying popular culture and Internet-enabled phenomena like fan fiction, he had come to the conclusion that the fans had played an important role in developing and canonizing shows such as *Star Trek* or *The Simpsons*. To Jenkins, the fans who turned media "texts" into playgrounds of their own imagination were "textual poachers," who heralded a new kind of participatory culture. The creative (and "ethical") appropriation of such media content is, according to Jenkins, one of the core media literacies of the 21st century (Jenkins 2012). He put this idea in relation to the concept of "Cultural Jamming," that Mark Dery developed in his influential 1993 essay "Culture Jamming: Hacking, Slashing, and Sniping in the Empire of Signs" (Dery 2014). I was sure to include this essay – which I had read when it first came out in 1993, but which now took on an entirely new meaning – as well as chapters from Jenkins's book *Textual Poachers* in the readings of the classes on piracy that I taught subsequently.

The materiality of information technology and their social foundation in very different cultures, however, had taken on an entirely new urgency in my research, and the best sources came from publications that looked at the phenomenon of piracy with the tool set of empirical research, often written from the perspective of intellectuals of the BRIC and Third World states. This book contains some essays that take this perspective, namely those on piracy in Vietnam, Brazil, Romania, and Nigeria. The writings on phenomena such as mod chips, digital rights management (DRM), and copy protection add to this rich discourse on piracy by looking at the plain facts on their respective subjects by employing the framework of cultural studies.

But there had been other examples of texts that took a more empirical stance toward piracy, some published before I had started my own research, namely William Alford's *To Steal a Book Is an Elegant Offence*

(1995), a groundbreaking book on the Chinese approach toward intellectual property. This book still stands out today, because it successfully integrated the discussion of piracy into a much larger cultural context (and in a way, preceded Laikwan Pang's two studies on the way contemporary China engages with the international copyright regime today, books written in a similar spirit [Pang 2007, 2012]).

An important publication that provided ample empirical material on the way how piracy operated differently in different countries was the pioneering "The CopySouth Dossier: Issues in the Economics, Politics, and Ideology of Copyright in the Global South" (Story, Darch, and Halbert 2006) that looked at intellectual property issues from the perspective of the Global South and took a decidedly political stance toward the issue. The well-funded and globally conducted study *Media Piracy in Emerging Economies* (Karaganis 2011) and Roman Lobato's *Shadow Economies of Cinema: Mapping Informal Film Distribution* (Lobato 2012) followed in the footsteps of this highly original work. My understanding of global piracy has also been improved by studies that looked at the culture of piracy in various countries (Mertha 2006; Liang 2009; Tolentino 2009; Sundaram 2010; Torres 2012) to which I myself added essays on the piracy in the Philippines (Baumgärtel 2006) and the impact of piracy on independent film production in Southeast Asia (Baumgärtel 2012).

Then there was, of course, Adrian Johns's far-reaching study *Piracy: The Intellectual Property Wars from Gutenberg to Gates* (2009). And no list of publications on piracy would be complete without mentioning some of the more popular studies on the subject (Lasica 2005), that also include relatively level-headed economic studies (Chaudhry and Zimmerman 2009), but also books that use the subject for spectacular accounts of international crime (Phillips 2005; Naím 2005), not to mention the by now legendary rant about how piracy supposedly funds terrorism from the RAND corporation (Treverton et al. 2009).[3]

This should by no means indicate that piracy has become (or even is on his way to become) a well-established subject of media studies or any other academic discipline. While intellectual property has been recognized as a highly relevant subject in the digital age (partly because of the insistence of the media industry) – "the oil of the 21st century" as Mark Getty, chairman of Getty Images, is often quoted as saying – piracy as its shady counterpart has received much less attention by scholars. This might be partly so, because piracy remains a moving target, both in terms of the discourse around the subject as well as a practice. Whatever you think piracy is, it stops being, it seems. Since the advent of the Internet, there has been a variety of brief "piracy periods" centered around scores of different technologies that appeared and disappeared in a kind of legal version of the popular Whac-A-Mole game – as soon as one technology and their providers were successfully sued and bullied out of existence a new way to share media online arrived.

Just to mention a few examples: The advent of the online distribution of copyrighted material by "warez groups" via early bulletin board systems and the Usenet beginning in the 1980s. Early – and painfully slow – download sites on the first iteration of the World Wide Web. The beginning of file sharing as a global phenomenon – almost a new youth subculture – with Napster, the development of more sophisticated and less easy-to-trace network protocols such as Kazaa, Gnutella, eMule, or LimeWire, and, finally, the triumph of BitTorrent technology, including the legal battles that brought some of these services to an early end. The cyberlockers, file-hosting services, cloud-storage services, and online file-storage providers, from MP3.com to Megaupload, that for a period made copyrighted content easily available, before the media industry again managed to squash the majority of these services with legal means. The rise of invitation-only "darknets," where the heavy-duty dealing with copyrighted material took place among warez groups that competed with each other to be the first to release much-anticipated films (see Lasica 2005, 47-67). The advent of the anonymous, heavily encrypted Tor network and its subsequent use for illegal purposes of all kinds, including the Silk Road, an anonymous online black market used for illegal transactions. The trend toward streaming sites such as movie4k.to. And – probably most relevant in the context of this book – the development of a whole political movement against the increasingly stifling effects of copyright that started with the founding of the Piratpartiet in Sweden, an example that was soon followed in other countries.

While the long-term perspectives of these political organizations are far from clear, it remains a fact that the Pirate parties in countries like Germany and Sweden were for a time able to channel a wide-ranging discontent – especially among young people – about their rights and freedoms in the digital age that resulted, for instance, in large mass protests against the Anti-Counterfeiting Trade Agreement (ACTA) treaty and articulated their concerns about numerous other Internet-related issues both on the Internet as well as with protests in public space. Hence, the rise of online piracy was accompanied by a new form of political activism.

That does not mean that the sharing of media has become a universally accepted practice, on the contrary. Of course, there have been initiatives such as Lawrence Lessig's Creative Commons that aims to give back the creators of culture some kind of control over the distribution and monetization of their works. And there is a growing political awareness that material from publicly funded institutions such as libraries or public radio and television stations should be available widely, which means online, and that the fruits of the intellectual labor that the government has supported at universities and other research institutions should be published in "open access" databases. However, as far as commercially distributed movies, music, and software is concerned, the battle between those who want to share this material online for free and those who want to make a profit out of it continues with no end in sight.

As I write this, the front page of the notorious torrent tracker The Pirate Bay asks for the support for their founders Gottfrid Svartholm and Peter Sunde, who are currently serving time in jail. Under pictures of the two young men, who at the height of the international controversy around the site served as the outspoken defenders of the right to share copyrighted material over the Internet, it says: "Show your support by sending them some encouraging mail! Gottfrid is only allowed to receive letters while Peter gladly received books, letter [sic] and vegan candy."

The pictures have an iconic quality to them; the two look the way we remember them from Simon Klose's film *TPB AFK: The Pirate Bay away from Keyboard* (2013), the documentary about their battle with the Swedish legal system. Despite international support, they were sentenced to two years in jail and also had to pay a joint fine of more than €3 million. According to a report by European MP Julia Reda, Sunde is now held in isolation in a prison populated by perpetrators of violent crimes in Sweden (Reda 2014). Svartholm, who has been accused of other crimes related to hacking, is in solitary confinement in Denmark.

However, The Pirate Bay that Svartholm and Sunde helped found in 2003 has seen an tremendous increase in the number of shared files in the last couple of years despite the conviction of the two and despite the efforts of the "content industry" to curb piracy. The Pirate Bay is still among the hundred most popular websites on the Internet, and the visitor numbers have doubled between 2011 and 2014 (Ernesto 2014); however, it is not known how the number of site visitors translates into downloaded content. At the same time, other statistics indicate that the net traffic generated by file sharing has gone down in relation to the total Internet traffic, while video-streaming sites such as YouTube or Netflix – that offer video content that you can watch in real time rather than waiting for them to download – are now responsible for more than 60% of network traffic. At the same time commercial digital services have helped boost the sales of video and music in the "Global North" according to figures released at the beginning of the year. In the UK, for instance, digital sales of video grew by 40% in 2013, helping to offset a 6.8% decline in sales of physical formats (Anon. 2014). In the same year, the German music companies recorded a rise by 11.7% of digital revenues, providing the industry with its first growth of income in 15 years (Anon., n.d.).

Even though nobody in the media industry will ever admit it, this development is paradoxically a triumph of the pirates. When millions around the globe started to share music, movies, software, and digital books via the Internet in the late 1990s, there was very little opportunity to get these media products in a legitimate way on the Internet. If piracy has accomplished nothing else, it has forced the international media companies to start thinking about how they can allow their customers ways to see films, listen to music, download software, or read books in a timely, easy-to-use and affordable fashion – at least in the affluent countries of the "Global North," Western Europe, North America, and the more developed countries in Asia.

This is a not the "triumph of the pirates" that is referred to in the title of this essay, though. This is about nothing more than about the convenience of the consumers. And even though the majority of people who pirate copyrighted content might have had nothing else in mind but just that – convenience – this is not the most important feat that the pirates accomplished. What they did, however, was taking a key property of digital media and turn it into the subject of a social, political, and economic debate. Piracy can be read in a multitude of ways: as a leveler of economic inequality; as an invitation to free speech, as an act of resistance or simply as an opportunity for new types of business. But in the end, piracy is about authorship and access, and often the only opportunity to participate in a global conversation and to make yourself heard. The global media pirates challenge the established way of how content is distributed, a model that had already been put into peril by the emergence of the Internet. In a way, they were doing what the Internet – as a medium that has turned distribution into the copying from one server computer to another – seemed to want.

Here, the digital machines that – according to Kittler – know no morals, have no subjectivity, possess no "content" seem to inscribe their value system (or rather its lack of a value system) onto the way large parts of the global population consume culture. But piracy also made it clear that we do not have to accept or even prop up what this new technological apparatus seems to suggest. As Evgeny Morozov has pointed out time and again in his critique of "Internet-centricism," ultimately it is up to the users of the net to shape it. What Morozov writes about the socio-political impact of the net also goes for the way we think about and handle online piracy: "Perhaps it was a mistake to treat the Internet as a deterministic one-directional force for either global liberation or oppression, for cosmopolitanism or xenophobia. The reality is that the Internet will enable all of these forces – as well as many others – simultaneously. But as far as laws of the Internet go, this is all we know. Which of the numerous forces unleashed by the web will prevail in a particular social and political context is impossible to tell without first getting a thorough theoretical understanding of that context" (Morozov 2011, 29). Simplistic and ultimately essentialist generalizations about an inherent logic of the net might even keep us from fully realizing its possibilities. As Steven Johnson has argued, what the Internet wants is "a lot of contradictory things" (Morozov and Johnson 2013), and it is up to us to figure out which of these contradictory things we actually want to happen and to become part of our lives.

The battle about piracy is one of the most prominent conflicts where the conflict between how these digital networks function and what they do with us, is played out, but it is by far not the only one, and most likely not even the most important one anymore. US whistleblower Edward Snowden made us realize through his disclosures about the global spying that the NSA and other secret service undertake that potentially a large part of our electronic communications can be intercepted and stored. Here we have another instance where the dialectic of the new digital technologies achieve crucial importance. As with piracy, in the phenomenon of global surveillance the distinct affordances and characteristics of digital media play out – not in a clean room of "cyberspace," but in a specific social context with its own set of norms, values, and practices, and that can be a messy process.

As with piracy, digital networks might have encouraged certain kinds of control and surveillance. Their existence and their practice are not laws of nature, however. Just as online piracy has been shaped and transformed by the resistance that it has encountered in the last decade and a half – a resistance of which the cease and desist letter I mentioned at the beginning of this essay were part of – so the global surveillance will be shaped by similar dialectics. Hence, the mass spying that Snowden exposed might encompass the conditions of its own downfall: While only digital networks made this kind of mass spying feasible, the net also facilitate the large-scale leaking of information that was supposed to stay secret. Piracy did its part in shaping the discourse about intellectual property in the age of digital media by posing as the most excessive Other to the far-reaching ownership demands of the MPAA, the Business Software Alliance. and all these other media industry lobby groups – without actually and outspokenly participating in that debate. Hence, online surveillance – which has been a result of the unique characteristics of an open network – could also be far from being technological determined and without alternative, but might contain the conditions for its own downfall.

Notes

1.   "I have begun a large process at home of ripping all of my and my wife's CDs, and storing them in one archive. Then, using Apple's iTunes, or a wonderful program called Andromeda, we can build different play lists of our music: Bach, Baroque, Love Songs, Love Songs of Significant Others – the potential is endless. And by reducing the costs of mixing play lists, these technologies help build a creativity with play lists that is itself independently valuable. Compilations of songs are creative and meaningful in their own right" (Lessig 2004, 203).
2.   This pattern – then using the uniquely Asian medium of VDCs – had been sharply observed in the context of North Asia already ten years earlier by Kelly Hu in an essay on the appropriation of Japanese television shows by highly specialized fan audiences in Hong Kong in 2004, long before this became an international and global phenomenon (Hu 2004).
3.   It speaks to the lucidity of global pop culture that America DJ Diplo and British singer M.I.A. debunked as early as 2004 these – often alleged, but never proven – connections between terrorism and piracy with the title of a mix tape called "Terrorism Funds Terrorism Vol. I." The compilation contained "mash-up" versions of original songs by M.I.A. from her debut album with samples from songs from artists such as the Bangles, Jay-Z, Salt-n-Pepa, Missy Elliott, Ciara, LL Cool J, and Cutty Ranks. In keeping with the motto of the compilation, it was never officially released because of irresolvable copyright issues.

Bibliography

Alford, William P. 1995. *To Steal a Book Is an Elegant Offence: Intellectual Property Law in Chinese Civilization*. Stanford, CA: Stanford University Press.
Anon. N.d. "Deutscher Musikmarkt wächst insgesamt um 1,2 Prozent." Bundesverband Musikindustrie. http://www.musikindustrie.de/statistik/.
Anon. 2014. "Digital Services Boost Sales of Video and Music Sales." BBC website, 1 January. http://www.bbc.com/news/entertainment-arts-25559821.

Baumgärtel, Tilman. 2006. "The Culture of Piracy in the Philippines." Presented at Asian Edition: A Conference on Media Piracy and Intellectual Property in South East Asia, University of the Philippines Film Institute, University of the Philippines Diliman, Quezon City, Philippines, 24 November. http://www.asian-edition.org/piracyinthephilippines.pdf.

Baumgärtel, Tilman. 2012. "The Piracy Generation: Media Piracy and Independent Film in Southeast Asia." In May Adadol Ingawanij and Benjamin McKay, eds., *Glimpses of Freedom: Independent Cinema in Southeast Asia*. Ithaca, NY: Cornell Southeast Asia Program Publications, 195-208.

Bold, Bianca. 2011. "The Power of Fan Communities: An Overview of Fansubbing In Brazil." *Tradução em Revista* 11.2: 1-19

Chaudhry, Peggy, and Alan Zimmerman. 2010. *The Economics of Counterfeit Trade: Governments, Consumers, Pirates, and Intellectual Property Rights*. Berlin: Springer.

Dery, Mark. 2014. "Culture Jamming: Hacking, Slashing, and Sniping in the Empire of Signs." Shovelware Blog. http://markdery.com/?page_id=154.

Dewey, Caitlin. 2013. "'Game of Thrones' Exec Says Piracy Is 'Better Than an Emmy.' He Has a Point." *Washington Post*, 9 August. http://www.washingtonpost.com/blogs/the-switch/wp/2013/08/09/game-of-thrones-exec-says-piracy-is-better-than-an-emmy-he-has-a-point/.

Ernesto. 2014. "Pirate Bay Traffic Doubles Despite ISP Blockades." *TorrentFreak*, 17 July. http://torrentfreak.com/pirate-bay-traffic-doubles-despite-isp-blockades-140717/.

Hu, Kelly. 2004. "Chinese Re-makings of Pirated VCDs of Japanese TV dramas." In Koichi Iwabuchi, ed., *Feeling Asian Modernities: Transnational Consumption of Japanese TV Dramas*. Hong Kong: Hong Kong University Press, 205-226.

Jenkins, Henry. 2006. *Fans, Bloggers, and Gamers: Media Consumers in a Digital Age*. New York: NYU Press.

Jenkins, Henry. 2012. "Digital Detournement: Jamming (with) the Simpsons-Banksy Intro, Jonnystyle." Confessions of an Aca-Fan: The Official Weblog of Henry Jenkins, 5 October. http://henryjenkins.org/2012/10/digital-detournement-jamming-with-the-simpsons-banksy-intro-jonnystyle.html.

Johns, Adrian. 2009. *Piracy: The Intellectual Property Wars from Gutenberg to Gates*. Chicago: University of Chicago Press.

Karaganis, Joe, ed. 2011. *Media Piracy in Emerging Economies*. New York: Social Science Research Council.

Kittler, Friedrich. 1995. "There Is No Software." *CTheory.net*, 18 October. http://www.ctheory.net/articles.aspx?id=74.

Kittler, Friedrich. 1999. *Gramophone, Film, Typewriter*. Stanford, CA: Stanford University Press.

Lasica, J. D. 2005. *Darknet: Hollywood's War against the Digital Generation*. Hoboken, NJ: John Wiley and Sons.

Liang, Lawrence. 2009. "Piracy, Creativity and Infrastructure: Rethinking Access to Culture." Social Science Research Network Working Papers, July. http://papers.ssrn.com/sol3/papers.cfm?abstract_id=1436229.

Lessig, Lawrence. 2004. *Free Culture: How Big Media Uses Technology and the Law to Lock Down Culture and Control Creativity*. New York: Penguin.

Lobato, Ramon. 2012. *Shadow Economies of Cinema: Mapping Informal Film Distribution*. London: British Film Institute.

Mertha, Andrew C. 2006. *The Politics of Piracy: Intellectual Property in Contemporary China*. Singapore: National University of Singapore Publishing

Morozov, Evgeny. 2011. *The Net Delusion: The Dark Side of Internet Freedom*. New York: Perseus Books

Morozov, Evgeny, and Steven Johnson. 2013. "Up for Debate: Can Social Media Solve Real-World Problems?" *New Republic*, 6 February. http://www.newrepublic.com/article/112336/future-perfects-steven-johnson-evgeny-morozov-debate-social-media.

Naím, Moisés. 2005. *Illicit: How Smugglers, Traffickers and Copycats are Hijacking the Global Economy*. New York: Doubleday.

Pang, Laikwan. 2005. "Global Modernity and Movie Piracy." Paper presented at "Contested Commons/Trespassing Publics: A Conference on Inequalities, Conflicts and Intellectual Property," New Delhi, India, January. (A summary of the talk has been published in Sarai Media Lab, *Contested Commons/Trespassing Publics: A Public Record*, Delhi: Sarai Media Lab, 2006, 40-50, http://archive.sarai.net/files/original/b6fe93e8dbe6d3cc655aa00f11d743f8.pdf.)

Pang, Laikwan. 2009. *Cultural Control and Globalization in Asia: Copyright, Piracy and Cinema*. New York: Routledge.

Pang, Laikwan. 2012. *Creativity and Its Discontents: China's Creative Industries and Intellectual Property Rights Offenses*. Durham, NC: Duke University Press.

Phillips, Tim. 2005. *Knock-Off: The Deadly Trade in Counterfeit Goods: The True Story of The World's Fastest Growing Crime Wave*. London: Kogan Page.

Reda, Julia. 2014. "'Prison Is a Bit Like Copyright,' Says Jailed Pirate Bay Founder." *Senficon*, 14 August. http://senficon.eu/2014/08/prison-is-a-bit-like-copyright-peter-sunde/.

Sarai Media Lab. 2006. *Contested Commons/Trespassing Publics: A Public Record*. Delhi: Sarai Media Lab. http://archive.sarai.net/files/original/b6fe93e8dbe6d3cc655aa00f11d743f8.pdf.

Sinnreich, Adam. 2013. *The Piracy Crusade: How the Music Industry's War on Sharing Destroys Markets and Erodes Civil Liberties*. Amherst: University of Massachusetts Press.

Story, Alan, Colin Darch, and Debora Halbert, eds. 2006. "The CopySouth Dossier: Issues in the Economics, Politics, and Ideology of Copyright in the Global South." The Copy/South Research Group. http://www.opensocietyfoundations.org/sites/default/files/csdossier_20060613.pdf.

Sundaram, Ravi. 2010. *Pirate Modernity: Delhi's Media Urbanism*. Oxford: Routledge.

Tolentino, Rolando B. 2009. "Piracy Regulation and the Filipino's Historical Response to Globalization." *Social Science Diliman* 5.1-2: 1-25. http://journals.upd.edu.ph/index.php/socialsciencediliman/article/view/2043/1953.

Torres, John. 2012. "Piracy Boom Boom." In May Adadol Ingawanij and Benjamin McKay, eds., *Glimpses of Freedom: Independent Cinema in Southeast Asia*. Ithaca, NY: Cornell Southeast Asia Program Publications, 63-72.

Treverton, Gregory F., et al. 2009. *Film Piracy, Organized Crime, and Terrorism*. Santa Monica, CA: RAND Corporation.

Vandresen, Monique. 2012. "Free Culture." *Lost in Translation: International Journal of Communication* 6: 626-642.

Contributors

Jonas Andersson Schwarz is a postdoc researcher of digital media culture affiliated to Södertörn University (Stockholm, Sweden). His book *Online File Sharing: Innovations in Media Consumption* (New York, 2013) is in circulation (both legitimate and illegitimate) and he has written extensively on the subject throughout the years.

Tilman Baumgärtel teaches media theory at the Hochschule Mainz after appointments at the University of the Philippines in Manila and the Royal University of Phnom Penh in Cambodia. His most recent publication is *Southeast Asian Independent Cinema* (Hong Kong University Press, 2012).

Tessa Dwyer teaches in screen studies at the University of Melbourne and at Monash University. Her latest publication is "B-Grade Subtitles" in *B Is for Bad Cinema: Aesthetics, Politics, and Cultural Value* (Albany, 2014). E-mail: trdwyer@unimelb.edu.au.

Brian Larkin is the Tow Associate Professor for Distinguished Scholars at Barnard College and the author of *Signal and Noise: Media, Infrastructure, and Urban Culture in Nigeria* (Durham, NC, 2008).

Jonathan Marshall is a failed musician, novelist, and dramatist who does research work at the Faculty of Arts and Social Sciences at the University of Technology, Sydney. His publications include *Living on Cybermind: Categories Communication and Control* (Berne, 2001) and edited collections such as *Depth Psychology, Disorder and Climate Change* (Sydney, 2009), and *Crisis, Movement, Management* (with James Goodman, New York, 2013). Homepage: https://uts.academia.edu/jonmarshall/.

Stefan Meretz is a computer scientist, commons theorist, and columnist for the Vienna Magazine *Streifzüge*. He is blogging on keimform.de.

Yonatan Reinberg holds a doctorate in interdisciplinary anthropology, technology, and intellectual property from the City University of New York. His main interests include avenues of technology in the Global South and intimate connections among diasporic groups. Outside of academic pursuits, Yonatan is the lead developer at Social Ink, a web development firm he started in 2007 to work with civic institutions, NGOs, and social justice activists.

Francesca da Rimini is an associate at the School of Software at the University of Technology, Sydney, where she completed a dissertation on concepts of activism in current informational capitalism. She has been a member of the cyberfeminist art collective VNS Matrix (1991-1997) and of identity_runners (1998-present).

Jens Schröter is professor for the theory and practice of multimedial systems at the University of Siegen, Germany. He was director of the graduate school "Locating Media" and is currently codirector of the research project "TV Series as Reflection and Projection of Change." Recent publications: *3D: History, Theory and Aesthetics of the Transplane Image* (New York/London/ New Delhi/Sydney, 2014); *Handbuch Medienwissenschaft* (Stuttgart, 2014).

Mirko Tobias Schaefer is assistant professor for new media and digital culture at the University of Utrecht, the Netherlands, and director of the Utrecht Data School. He is coeditor and coauthor of the volume *Digital Material: Tracing New Media in Everyday Life and Technology* (Amsterdam University Press, 2009) and author of *Bastard Culture! How User Participation Transforms Cultural Production* (Amsterdam University Press, 2011). He blogs at www.mtschaefer.net and is @mirkoschaefer on Twitter.

Tony Tran is a PhD dissertator in media and cultural studies in the Department of Communication Arts at the University of Wisconsin-Madison, where he researches various topics surrounding cultural identity and global media. His specific interests include the circulation of media among Vietnamese diaspora and its intersection with discourses of cultural authenticity and education.

Ioana Uricaru is a Romanian filmmaker and film scholar. She is an assistant professor of film and media culture at Middlebury College. She is currently developing her first feature film, *Lemonade*.

Index

MediaMatters

Maaike Bleeker
Anatomy Live. Performance and the Operating Theatre, 2008
ISBN 978 90 5356 516 2

Marianne van den Boomen, Sybille Lammes, Ann-Sophie Lehmann, Joost Raessens, Mirko Tobias Schäfer (eds.)
Digital Material. Tracing New Media in Everyday Life and Technology, 2009
ISBN 978 90 8964 068 0

Maaike Lauwaert
The Place of Play. Toys and Digital Cultures, 2009
ISBN 978 90 8964 080 2

Sarah Bay-Cheng, Chiel Kattenbelt, Andy Lavender, Robin Nelson (eds.)
Mapping Intermediality in Performance, 2010
ISBN 978 90 8964 255 4

Tanja Sihvonen
Players Unleashed! Modding The Sims *and the Culture of Gaming*, 2011
ISBN 978 90 8964 201 1

Mirko Tobias Schäfer
Bastard Culture! How User Participation Transforms Cultural Production, 2011
ISBN 978 90 8964 256 1

Imar O. de Vries
Tantalisingly Close. An Archaeology of Communication Desires in Discourses of Mobile Wireless Media, 2012
ISBN 978 90 8964 354 4

Nanna Verhoeff
Mobile Screens. The Visual Regime of Navigation, 2012
ISBN 978 90 8964 379 7

René Glas
Battlefields of Negotiation. Control, Agency, and Ownership in World of Warcraft, 2013
ISBN 978 90 8964 500 5

Valerie Frissen, Sybille Lammes, Michiel de Lange, Jos de Mul, Joost Raessens (eds.)
Playful Idenities. The Ludification of Digital Media Cultures, 2015
ISBN 978 90 8964 639 2

Koen Leurs
Digital Passages: Migrant Youth 2.0. Diaspora, Gender and Youth Cultural Intersections, 2015
ISBN 978 90 8964 640 8